From Behind the Veil

From Behind the Veil

A STUDY OF

AFRO-AMERICAN

NARRATIVE

ROBERT B. STEPTO

University of Illinois Press

Urbana Chicago London

©1979 by the Board of Trustees of the University of Illinois
Manufactured in the United States of America

Library of Congress Cataloging in Publication Data

Stepto, Robert B.
   From behind the veil.

   Bibliography: p.
   Includes index.
   1. American prose literature—Afro-American authors
—History and criticism. 2. Narration (Rhetoric)
3. Autobiography. 4. Afro-Americans in literature.
PS366.A35S7   813'.009'352   79-11283
ISBN 0-252-00752-2

FOR MILDRED AND OCIE BURNS
—AND COUSIN COLEMAN

I sit with Shakespeare and he winces not.
Across the color line I move arm in arm
with Balzac and Dumas, where smiling men
and welcoming women glide in gilded halls.
From out the caves of evening that swing
between the strong-limbed earth and the
tracery of the stars, I summon Aristotle
and Aurelius and what soul I will, and they
come all graciously with no scorn or
condescension. So, wed with Truth, I dwell
above the Veil. Is this the life you grudge us,
O knightly America? Is this the life you
long to change into the dull red hideousness
of Georgia? Are you so afraid lest peering
from this high Pisgah, between Philistine
and Amalekite, we sight the Promised Land?
—W. E. B. Du Bois,
The Souls of Black Folk

"Didn't Lenin read bourgeois books?"
I asked.

"But you're not Lenin," he shot at me.

"Are there some books reserved for some
people to read, while others cannot read
them?" I asked.

"Comrade, you do not understand,"
he said.
—Richard Wright,
American Hunger

Preface

This book is quite intentionally a study far more critical, historical, and textual than biographical, chronological, and atextual. Throughout, I have worked from three underlying assumptions. The first is that Afro-American culture, like all cultures, has its store of what Northrop Frye has called "canonical stories" or what I call "pregeneric myths"—shared stories or myths that not only exist prior to literary form, but eventually shape the forms that comprise a given culture's literary canon. The primary pregeneric myth for Afro-America is the quest for freedom and literacy. The second is that once the pregeneric myth is set in motion in search of its literary forms, the historian of Afro-American literature must attempt to define and discuss how the myth both assumes and does not assume the properties of genre—notably, in this context, the properties of autobiography, fiction, and, to a lesser degree, historiography. The final assumption is that if an Afro-American literary tradition exists, it does so not because there is a sizeable chronology of authors and texts, but because those authors and texts collectively seek their own literary forms—their own admixtures of genre—bound historically and linguistically to a shared pre-generic myth. With these assumptions in mind, I have attempted to avoid writing yet another survey of Afro-American literature that systematically moves from texts to non-literary structures and passively allows those structures to become the literature's collective "history," and to write instead what might best be called a history or fiction of the historical consciousness of an Afro-American art form—namely, the Afro-American written narrative.

The book is divided into two sections, "The Call" and "The Response." Each section describes a fairly discrete period in the history of the Afro-American narrative as a literary form. "The Call" begins with a discussion of four types of slave narratives—which I term the eclectic narrative, the integrated narrative, the generic narrative, and the authenticating narrative—and completes itself by describing how Booker T. Washington's *Up from Slavery* and W. E. B. Du Bois's *The Souls of Black Folk* revise and revoice the latter two slave narrative types. The section ends with the Du Bois discussion not because his narrative is the most recent of those discussed there, but because *The Souls* is the first substantial immersion narrative in the tradition; with its publication, all of the prefiguring forms and tropes that will develop another literary period are finally on display. Proof of this comes in the following section, "The Response," where I demonstrate how certain major Afro-American narratives written in what is unhelpfully termed the "modern era" answer the call of certain prefiguring texts. To put the matter as simply as possible, my argument is that James Weldon Johnson's *The Autobiography of an Ex-Coloured Man* is an intentionally aborted immersion narrative that revoices both *Up from Slavery* and *The Souls*—but especially *The Souls;* that Richard Wright's *Black Boy* is a narrative of ascent that revoices Frederick Douglass's *Narrative* of 1845; and that Ralph Ellison's *Invisible Man* is a narrative of hibernation that answers the calls of both *The Souls* and the Douglass *Narrative,* while en route to discovering a new narrative form that bursts beyond those of ascent and immersion. (What I don't say in the Ellison discussion but might say here is that the next period in the literary history of the Afro-American narrative will be formed in substantial part by narrative expressions that advance the historical consciousness of the form beyond the posture of hibernation.)

As I hope my remarks thus far make clear, I am interested far more in the contrapuntal and dialectical aspects of the relationship between these two period formations—that is, in how they speak to one another and also speak as one—than in how they may be discrete units. Furthermore, I especially hope that the names I've given these periods imply that, while I see the narrative form developing from one period to the other, I do *not* see that development as an absolute progression, especially in any strict qualitative sense. In song, responses are not inherently "better" than calls, and I believe that the same is true in literature. Anyone who wants to argue, for example, that Wright's "response" to Douglass's "call" is a "better" narrative, or that it is an improvement upon Douglass's text, is barking (rather incoherently) up the wrong critical tree. A response is fundamentally an artistic act of closure performed upon a formal unit that already possesses substantial coherence. There can be no one response, no one and final closure; there can only be appropriate and inappropriate responses, and what is appropriate is defined by the prefiguring call that has come before. In accord with the terms afforded here, the two periods of literary history with which this book is concerned are constructions in which appropriate responses to prefiguring calls accumulate to a point where a new prefiguring call—a prologue to the epilogue of a prologue—is inevitable.

The individual chapters may be described in the following way. In the first, "I Rose and Found My Voice: Narration, Authentication, and Authorial Control in Four Slave Narratives," I examine the formal characteristics and narrative strategies of Henry Bibb's *Narrative of the Life and Adventures of Henry Bibb, an American Slave* (1849); Solomon Northrup's *Twelve Years a Slave* (1854); Frederick Douglass's *Narrative of the Life of Frederick Douglass, an American Slave, Written by Himself* (1845); and William Wells Brown's *Narrative of the Life and Escape of William Wells Brown* (1852)—by way of making the point that "slave narrative" is really an umbrella term for many types of narratives, and that while all slave narratives are personal histories of one sort or another, personal histories are not always autobiographies. In this way, I inaugurate a distinction between personal history and autobiography that leads to an additional and almost correlative distinction between autobiography and authentication as narrative impulses and forms. These distinctions, along with that which I also make between a narrative's tale and the narrative as a whole, inform the rest of the book. The second chapter, "Lost in a Cause: Booker T. Washington's *Up from Slavery*," picks up where the discussion of the Brown narrative leaves off in examining the authenticating narrative as a strategy and a form. At the heart of my remarks lies the point that Washington's narrative is more sophisticated than Brown's chiefly because it is as much written as edited; this development raises the question of whether self-authentication may be as sophisticated a narrative mode as autobiography. The third chapter, "The Quest of the Weary Traveler: W. E. B. Du Bois's *The Souls of Black Folk*," is divided into three parts. The first begins with a discussion of how *The Souls* results in part from Du Bois's efforts to revise and gain a measure of authorial control over certain previously published "fugitive essays," and ends with a brief comparative study of Douglass and Du Bois as autobiographers. The second describes a theory and system of symbolic geography occasioned by the journey of Du Bois's persona into the Black Belt. Part Three studies Du Bois's response to the "literary offenses" of Booker T. Washington.

Chapter Four, "Lost in a Quest: James Weldon Johnson's *The Autobiography of an Ex-Coloured Man*," begins the second half of the book with a brief explanation of why I prefer to use terms such as "epiloging text" and "narrative" instead of "modern text" and "novel." The main activity of the chapter's first section is, however, a study of how *The Autobiography* fuses aspects of authenticating rhetoric with aspects of generic narrative form, and in that way revoices *Up from Slavery* and *The Souls of Black Folk*. In the second section I examine the Ex-Coloured Man's Club as a fresh expression of an Afro-American ritual ground. In the subsequent chapter, "Literacy and Ascent: Richard Wright's *Black Boy*," my attention shifts away from how a text may answer the prefiguring call of *Up from Slavery* and *The Souls*, and toward a study of how one may answer that of *Up from Slavery* and the Douglass *Narrative* of 1845. In the chapter's final two sections, I study two strategies through which Wright attempts to position his text and self-fiction in literary history. The sixth and final chapter, "Literacy and Hibernation: Ralph Ellison's *Invisible Man*," clarifies how the narratives of ascent and immersion issue a call for the response that is *Invisible Man*.

In his preface to *The Fate of Reading and Other Essays* (1975),

Geoffrey Hartman offers the following advice to the literary historian: "That literary history may be a *fable convenue* makes it all the more important for the historian to be conscious of his debt to fiction and rhetorical configuration." While writing this book, I have attempted to be conscious of my debt to fiction and rhetorical configuration, especially in the texts I study, and to write a complementary (if not comparable) fiction and rhetorical configuration. I was not attempting to write a scholarly book or a meditation (although this book does have certain scholarly and meditative qualities), but I did want to write a *fable convenue*. All this pertains to how I have pursued documentation and reference in the text. I have from the start tried to write a narrative whose movement by allusion and reference is uninterrupted with numbers and the competing, authenticating fictions that we commonly refer to as notes. For this reason, the writers and scholars who have been unsually helpful are simply named in the study, and full notation of their works and those of others is made elsewhere, in the bibliography. The allusions and references that guide the narrative's movement are, however, my true notes, and in a sense my best notes; I hope they provide a resonance and historical depth through language that is usually unattainable in annotations. The phrase "epiloging text"—however awkward—is, in the context of this fable, a necessary and concise reference to the aesthetic principles put forth in the epilogue of *Invisible Man*. My repeated mention of "protean narrators" and "protean narratives" is, I hope, a *literary* way of acknowledging my debt to Ellison's famous language in "Brave Words for a Startling Occasion" (in *Shadow and Act* [1964]). Similarly, my repeated use of "protection"—Frederick Douglass's term for a pass *usually* written by a slave's master that allows him, almost paradoxically, to travel while in bondage—is a literary way of encouraging readers to see the continuity as well as the dialectic between the historical periods I've constructed and the texts I discuss. If the historian's voice here partakes of that of Du Bois's "weary traveler" and Jay Wright's "dutiful dyeli" or archivist, then I have succeeded in writing into my narrative a substantial acknowledgment of these great writers. If the vision of history advanced here is finally far more modal ("both/and") than Cartesian ("either/or"), then the book is in some figurative sense an acknowledgment of the poetic canon of Michael S. Harper. In short, I have attempted throughout not only to place but to write my references in the *primary* text of my narrative, and thereby to minimize the presence of ancillary texts or fictions.

From Behind the Veil began in some measure as a Ph.D. dissertation written for the Department of English at Stanford University. To be specific, the chapters on *Up from Slavery, The Souls of Black Folk,* and *The Autobiography of an Ex-Coloured Man* draw on the research, if not the language, in my dissertation chapters on those same texts. They also draw on the invaluable advice generously given by my principal professors at Stanford: William Chace, Albert Gelpi, the late Claude Simpson, and, especially, David Levin. The remaining three chapters on four slave narratives, *Black Boy,* and *Invisible Man* result directly from my teaching the course on the Afro-American literary tradition at Yale from 1974 to 1976. I thank the following students for seeing where I was going and encouraging me to get there: Sharon Ciccarelli, Patrick Lalley, Bisa Williams, and James Woodruff.

Most of the book was written during 1977–78 while I was on leave from Yale with a Morse Fellowship. I thank the fellowship committee, as well as those colleagues in English and Afro-American Studies who supported my nomination, for their faith and generosity. Portions of the first chapter appear in my contributions to Dexter Fisher and Robert Stepto, eds., *Afro-American Literature: The Reconstruction of Instruction* (New York: Modern Language Association, 1979). I am grateful to the publisher for allowing me to return those discussions to their original context, and grateful as well to Dexter Fisher for improving them while they were en route, as it were, back to this book.

While the book was in progress, I was sustained by the advice and encouragement of many friends: Kimberly W. Benston, John W. Blassingame, John F. Callahan, Melvin Dixon, Henry-Louis Gates, Jr., Geoffrey Hartman, Robert Hayden, Keneth Kinnamon, Arnold Rampersad, Robert Farris Thompson, and Jay Wright. Once I had a draft of the manuscript in hand, Henry-Louis Gates, Robert Hemenway, Keneth Kinnamon, and David Levin selflessly aided me in improving both the ideas and the prose. Charles T. Davis has been a guide in this and other endeavors; like the other Afro-Americanists at Yale, I am indebted to him for fostering a supportive context in which to work. I must especially thank Gwen Williams for typing the initial manuscript, and Sue Hart for typing the additions and revisions.

My most profound thanks are due to Michele Stepto and Michael Harper, who took time from their own important work to read the entire manuscript at every juncture and offer invaluable advice and assistance. I will acknowledge finally Gabriel and Rafael Stepto, and only for this reason: they were continually impressed by the fact that Robert was writing a book, even when Robert most certainly was not. For that I forgive their equally continual theft of my paper and pencils.

The book is dedicated to my maternal grandparents and to my grandfather's first cousin, Coleman Hawkins, whom I never met but know through family stories and his marvelous music. Generally, however, it is for all my kin: without their love and example, I could not begin, in Jay Wright's words, "to understand the claims the living/owe the dead."

—Robert Burns Stepto

New Haven

Contents

PART ONE

The
Call

I Rose and Found My Voice: Narration, Authentication, and Authorial Control in Four Slave Narratives

The strident, moral voice of the former slave recounting, exposing, appealing, apostrophizing, and above all *remembering* his ordeal in bondage is the single most impressive feature of a slave narrative. This voice is striking because of what it relates, but even more so because the slave's acquisition of that voice is quite possibly his only permanent achievement once he escapes and casts himself upon a new and larger landscape. In their most elementary form, slave narratives are full of other voices which are frequently just as responsible for articulating a narrative's tale and strategy. These other voices may belong to various "characters" in the "story," but mainly they appear in the appended documents written by slaveholders and abolitionists alike. These documents—and voices —may not always be smoothly integrated with the former slave's tale, but they are nevertheless parts of the narrative. Their primary function is, of course, to authenticate the former slave's account; in doing so, they are at least partially responsible for the narrative's acceptance as historical evidence. However, in literary terms, the documents collectively create something close to a dialogue—of forms as well as voices—which suggests that, in its primal state or first phase, the slave narrative is an *eclectic narrative* form. A "first phase" slave narrative that illustrates these points rather well is Henry Bibb's *Narrative of the Life and Adventures of Henry Bibb, an American Slave* (1849).

When the various forms (letters, prefaces, guarantees, tales) and their accompanying voices become integrated in the slave narrative text, we are presented with another type of basic narrative which I call an *integrated narrative*. This type of narrative represents the second phase of slave narrative narration; it usually yields a more sophisticated text, wherein most of the literary and rhetorical functions previously performed by several texts and voices (the appended prefaces, letters, and documents as well as the tale) are now rendered by a loosely unified single text and voice. In this second phase, the authenticating documents "come alive" in the former slave's tale as speech and even action; and the former slave—often while assuming a deferential posture toward his white friends, editors, and guarantors—carries much of the burden of introducing and authenticating his own tale. In short, as my remarks on Solomon Northup's *Twelve Years a Slave* (1854) will suggest, a "second phase" narrative is a more sophisticated narrative because the former slave's voice is responsible for much more than recounting the tale.

Because an integrated or second-phase narrative is less a collection of texts and more a unified narrative, we may say that, in terms of narration, the integrated narrative is in the process of becoming—irrespective of authorial intent—a generic narrative, by which I mean a narrative of discernible genre such as history, fiction, essay, or autobiography. This process is no simple "gourd vine" activity: an integrated narrative does not become a generic narrative overnight, and indeed, there are no assurances that in becoming a new type of narrative it is transformed automatically into a distinctive generic text. What we discover, then, is a third phase to slave narration wherein two developments may occur: the integrated narrative (phase II) may be dominated either by its tale or by its authenticating strategies. In the first instance, as we see in Frederick Douglass's *Narrative of the Life of Frederick Douglass, an American Slave, Written by Himself* (1845), the narrative and moral energies of the former slave's voice and tale so resolutely dominate the narrative's authenticating machinery (voices, documents, rhetorical strategies) that the narrative becomes, in thrust and purpose, far more metaphorical than rhetorical. When the integrated narrative becomes, in this way, a figurative account of action, landscape, and heroic self-tranformation, it is so close generally to history, fiction, and autobiography that I term it a *generic narrative*.

In the second instance, as we see in William Wells Brown's *Narrative of the Life and Escape of William Wells Brown* (1852; appended to his novel, *Clotel, or The President's Daughter*), the authenticating machinery either remains as important as the tale or actually becomes, usually for some purpose residing outside the text, the dominant and motivating feature of the narrative. Since this is also a sophisticated narrative phase, figurative presentations of action, landscape, and self may also occur; however, such developments are rare and always ancillary to the central thrust of the text. When the authenticating machinery dominates in this fashion, the integrated narrative becomes an *authenticating narrative*.

As these remarks suggest, one reason for investigating the phases of slave narrative narration is to gain a clearer view of how some slave narrative types become generic narratives, and how, in turn, generic narratives—once formed, shaped, and set in motion by certain distinctly Afro-American cultural imperatives—have roots

The Three Phases of Narration

PHASE I: Basic Narrative (a): "Eclectic Narrative"—authenticating
documents and strategies (sometimes including one
by the author of the tale) are *appended* to the tale

PHASE II: Basic Narrative (b): "Integrated Narrative"—authenticating
documents and strategies are *integrated* into the tale and
formally become voices and/or characters in the tale

PHASE III:

(a) "Generic Narrative"—authenticating documents and strategies are totally *subsumed by the tale;* the slave narrative becomes an identifiable generic text, e.g., autobiography

(b) "Authenticating Narrative"—the tale is *subsumed by the authenticating strategy;* the slave narrative becomes an authenticating document for other, usually generic, texts, e.g., novels, histories

in the slave narratives. All this is, of course, central to our discussion of Washington's *Up from Slavery,* Du Bois's *The Souls of Black Folk,* Johnson's *The Autobiography of an Ex-Coloured Man,* Wright's *Black Boy,* and Ellison's *Invisible Man.* Moreover, it bears on our ability to distinguish between narrative modes and forms, and to describe what we see. When a historian or literary critic calls a slave narrative an autobiography, for example, what he or she sees most likely is a first-person narrative that possesses literary features to distinguish it from ordinary documents providing historical and sociological data. But a slave narrative is *not* necessarily an autobiography. We need to observe the finer shades between the more easily discernible categories of narration, and we must discover whether these stops arrange themselves in progressive, contrapuntal, or dialectic fashion—or if they possess any arrangement at all. As the scheme described above and diagrammed above suggests, I believe there are at least four identifiable modes of narration within the slave narratives, and that all four have a direct bearing on the development of subsequent Afro-American narrative forms.

PHASE I: ECLECTIC NARRATIVE

Henry Bibb's *Narrative of the Life and Adventures of Henry Bibb, an American Slave,* begins with several introductory documents offering, collectively, what may be the most elaborate guarantee of authenticity found in the slave narrative canon. What is most revealing—in terms of eclectic narrative form, authenticating strategy, and race rituals along the color line—is the segregation of Bibb's own "Author's Preface" from the white-authored texts of the "Introduction." Bibb's "Author's Preface" is further removed from the preceding introductory texts by the fact that he does not address or acknowledge what has gone before. There is no exchange, no verbal bond, between the two major units of introductory material; this reflects not only the quality of Bibb's relations with his benefactors, but also his relatively modest degree of control over the text and event of the narrative itself.

The "Introduction" is basically a frame created by Bibb's publisher, Lucius Matlack, for the presentation of guarantees composed mostly by abolitionists in Detroit (where, in freedom, Bibb chose to reside). Yet Matlack, as the publisher, also has his own authenticating duties to perform. He assures the reader that while he did indeed "examine" and "prepare" Bibb's manuscript, "The work of preparation . . . was that of orthography and punctuation merely, an arrangement of the chapters, and a table of contents—little more than falls to the lot of publishers generally." When Matlack tackles the issue of the tale's veracity, he mutes his own voice and offers instead those of various "authentic" documents gathered by the abolitionists. These gentlemen, all members of the Detroit Liberty Association, appear most sympathetic to Bibb, especially since he has spoken before their assemblies and lived an exemplary Christian life in their midst. To aid him—and their cause—they have interrogated Bibb (to which he submitted with "praiseworthy spirit") and have solicited letters from slaveholders, jailors, and Bibb's acquaintances, so that the truth of his tale might be established. No fewer than six of these letters plus the conclusion of the Association's report, all substantiating Bibb's story, appear in the "Introduction"; and, as if to "guarantee the guarantee," a note certifying the "friendly recommendation" of the abolitionists and verifying Bibb's "correct deportment" (composed, quite significantly, by a Detroit *judge*) is appended as well.

The elaborate authenticating strategy contained in Matlack's "Introduction" is typical of those found in the first-phase or eclectic narrative. The publisher or editor, far more than the former slave, assembles and manipulates the authenticating machinery, and seems to act on the premise that there is a direct correlation between the quantity of documents or texts assembled and the readership's acceptance of the narrative as a whole. I would like to suggest that Matlack's "Introduction" also constitutes a literary presentation of race rituals and cultural conditions, and that, as such, it functions as a kind of metaphor in the narrative.

To be sure, Matlack displays typical nineteenth-century American enthusiasm and superficiality when he writes of the literary merits of slave narratives: "Gushing fountains of poetic thought have started from beneath the rod of violence, that will long continue to slake the feverish thirst of humanity outraged, until swelling to a flood it shall rush with wasting violence over the ill-gotten heritage of the oppressor." However, the thrust of his "Introduction" is to guarantee the truth of a tale and, by extension, the *existence* of a man calling himself Henry Bibb. In his own aforementioned remarks regarding the preparation of Bibb's text for publication, Matlack appears to address the issue of the author's—Bibb's—credibility. However, the issue is really the audience's—white America's—credulity: their acceptance not so much of the former slave's escape and newfound freedom, but of his literacy. Many race rituals are enacted here, not the least of which is Matlack's "conversation" with white America across the text and figurative body of a silent former slave. The point we may glean from them all is that, insofar as Bibb must depend on his publisher to be an intermediary between his text and his audience, he relinquishes control of the narrative—which is, after all, the vehicle for the account of how he obtained his voice in freedom.

While we are impressed by the efforts of the Detroit Liberty Association's members to conduct an investigation of Bibb's tale, issue a report, and lend their names to the guarantee, we are still far more overwhelmed by the examples of the cultural disease with which they wrestle than by their desire to find a cure. That disease is, of course, cultural myopia, the badge and sore bestowed upon every nation mindlessly heedful of race ritual instead of morality: Henry Bibb is alive and well in Detroit, but by what miraculous stroke will he, as a man, be able to cast his shadow on this soil? The effort in the narrative's "Introduction" to prove that Bibb exists, and hence has a tale, goes far to explain why a prevailing metaphor in Afro-American letters is, in varying configurations, one of invisibility and translucence. Indirectly, and undoubtedly on a subconscious level, Matlack and the abolitionists confront the issue of Bibb's inability "to cast his shadow." But even in their case we may ask: Are they bolstering a cause, comforting a former slave, or recognizing a man?

The letters from the slaveholders and jailors Bibb knew while in bondage must not be overlooked here, for they help illuminate the history of the disease we are diagnosing. The letter from Silas Gatewood, whose father once owned Bibb, is designed solely to portray Bibb as "a notorious liar . . . and a rogue." Placed within the compendium of documents assembled by the abolitionists, the letter completes, through its nearly hysterical denunciation of Bibb, the "Introduction's" portrait of America at war with itself. The debate over Bibb's character, and, by extension, his right to a personal history bound to that of white Americans, is really nothing less than a literary omen of the Civil War. In this regard, the segregation of Bibb's "Author's Preface" from the introductory compendium of documents is, even more than his silence within the compendium, indicative of how the former slave's voice was kept muted and distant while the nation debated questions of slavery and the Negro's humanity.

Bibb's "Preface" reveals two features to his thinking, each of which helps us see how the former slave approached the task of composing a narrative. In answer to his own rhetorical question as to why he wrote the narrative, he replies, "in no place have I given orally the detail of my narrative; and some of the most interesting events of my life have never reached the public ear." This is not extraordinary except in that it reminds us of the oral techniques and traditions that lay behind most of the written narratives. The former slave's accomplishment of a written narrative should by no means be minimized, but we must also recognize the extent to which the abolitionist lecture circuit, whether in Michigan, Maine, or New York, gave former slaves an opportunity to structure, to embellish, and above all to polish an oral version of their tale—and to do so before the very audiences who would soon purchase hundreds, if not thousands, of copies of the written account. The former slave, not altogether unlike the semi-literate black preacher whose sermons were (and are) masterpieces of oral composition and rhetorical strategy, often had a fairly well developed version of his or her tale either memorized or (more likely) sufficiently *patterned* for effective presentation, even before the question of written composition was entertained. Certainly such was the case for Bibb, and this reminds us not to be too narrow when we call the basic slave narrative an eclectic narrative form. Oral as well as written forms are part of the eclectic whole.

The second revealing feature of Bibb's "Preface" returns us to a point on which his publisher, Matlack, began. Bibb appears extremely aware of the issue of his authorship when he writes:

> The reader will remember that I make no pretension to literature; for I can truly say, that I have been educated in the school of adversity, whips, and chains. Experience and observation have been my principal teachers, with the exception of three weeks schooling which I have had the good fortune to receive since my escape from the "grave yard of the mind," or the dark prison of human bondage.

That Bibb had only three weeks of formal schooling is astonishing; however, I am intrigued even more by the two metaphors for slavery with which he concludes. While both obviously suggest confinement—one of the mind, the other of his body—it seems significant that Bibb did not choose between the two (for reasons of style, if no other). Both images are offered *after* the act of writing his tale, possibly because Bibb is so terribly aware of both. His body is now free, his mind limber, his voice resonant; together they and his tale, if not his narrative, are his own.

On a certain level, we must study Matlack's "Introduction," with all its documents and guarantees, and Bibb's "Author's Preface" as a medley of voices, rather than as a loose conglomerate of discrete and even segregated texts. Together, both in what they do and do not say, these statements reflect the passions, politics, interpersonal relations, race rituals, and uses of language of a cross-section of America in the 1840's. But on another level, we must hold fast to what we have discovered regarding how Bibb's removal from the primary authenticating documents and strategy (that is, from the "Introduction") weakens his control of the narrative and, in my view, relegates him to a posture of partial literacy. Bibb's tale proves that he has acquired a voice, but his narrative shows that his voice does not yet control the imaginative forms which his personal history assumes in print.

In the Bibb narrative, the various texts within the "Introduction" guarantee Bibb and his tale; Bibb sustains this strategy of guarantee late in his tale by quoting letters and proclamations by many of the same figures who provided documents for the "Introduction." As we will discover in Solomon Northup's narrative, this use of authenticating documents within the text of the tale indicates the direction of more sophisticated slave narrative texts. Indeed, the question of whether the authenticating documents and strategies have been integrated into the central text (usually the tale) of the slave narrative is a major criterion by which we may judge author and narrative alike. The inclusion and manipulation of peripheral documents and voices suggests a remarkable level of literacy and self-assurance on the part of the former slave, and the reduction of many texts and strategies into one reflects a search, irrespective of authorial intent, for a more sophisticated written narrative form. Here, then, is a point of departure from which we may study the

development of pregeneric narratives into generic and other sophisticated narrative types.

PHASE II: INTEGRATED NARRATIVE

While I am not prepared to classify Solomon Northup's *Twelve
Years a Slave* (1854) as an autobiography, it is certainly a more
sophisticated text than Henry Bibb's, principally because its most
important authenticating document is integrated into the tale as a
voice and character. *Twelve Years a Slave* is, however, an integrated
narrative unsure of itself. Ultimately, its authenticating strategy depends as much upon an appended set of authenticating texts as upon
integrated documents and voices.

In comparison to the Bibb "Introduction," the Northup introductory materials appear purposely short and undeveloped. Northup's
editor and amanuensis, a Mr. David Wilson, offers a one-page "Preface," not a full-blown "Introduction," and Northup's own introductory words are placed in the first chapter of his tale, rather than in
a discrete entry written expressly for that purpose. Wilson's "Preface"
is, predictably, an authenticating document, formulaically acknowledging whatever "faults of style and of expression" the narrative
may contain while assuring the reader that he, the editor and a white
man, is convinced of Northup's strict adherence to the truth. Northup's own contributions, like Bibb's, are not so much anthenticating
as they are reflective of what a slave may have been forced to consider while committing his tale to print.

Northup's first entry is simply and profoundly his signature—
his proof of literacy writ large, with a bold, clear hand. It appears
beneath a pen-and-ink frontispiece portrait entitled "Solomon in
His Plantation Suit." His subsequent entries quite self-consciously
place his narrative amid the antislavery literature of the era, in particular, with Harriet Beecher Stowe's *Uncle Tom's Cabin* (1852) and
Key to Uncle Tom's Cabin (1853). If one wonders why Northup
neither establishes his experience among those of other kidnapped
and enslaved blacks nor positions his narrative with other narratives,
the answer is provided in part by his dedicatory page. There, after
quoting a passage from *Key to Uncle Tom's Cabin* which, in effect,
verifies his account of slavery because it is said to "form a striking
parallel" to Uncle Tom's, Northup respectfully dedicates his narrative to Miss Stowe, remarking that his tale affords "another *Key to
Uncle Tom's Cabin*."

This is no conventional dedication; it tells us much about the requisite act of authentication. While the Bibb narrative is authenticated by documents provided by the Detroit Liberty Association, the Northup narrative begins the process of authentication by assuming kinship with a popular antislavery novel. Audience, and the former slave's relationship to that audience, are the key issues here: authentication is, apparently, a rhetorical strategy designed not only for verification purposes, but also for the task of initiating and insuring a readership. No matter how efficacious it undoubtedly was for Northup (or his editor) to ride Miss Stowe's coattails and share in her immense notoriety, one cannot help wondering about the profound implications involved in authenticating personal history by binding it to historical fiction. In its way, this strategy says as much about a former slave's inability to confirm his existence and "cast his shadow" as does the more conventional strategy observed in the Bibb narrative. Apparently, a novel may authenticate a personal history, especially when the personal history is that of a former slave.

While not expressing the issue in these terms, Northup seems to have thought about the dilemma of authentication and that of slave narratives competing with fictions of both the pro- and anti-slavery variety. He writes:

> Since my return to liberty, I have not failed to perceive the increasing interest throughout the Northern states, in regard to the subject of Slavery. Works of fiction, professing to portray its features in their more pleasing as well as more repugnant aspects, have been circulated to an extent unprecedented, and, as I understand, have created a fruitful topic of comment and discussion.
>
> I can speak of Slavery only so far as it came under my own observation—only so far as I have known and experienced it in my own person. My object is, to give a candid and truthful statement of facts: to repeat the story of my life, without exaggeration, leaving it for others to determine, whether even the pages of fiction present a picture of more cruel wrong or a severer bondage.

Clearly, Northup felt that the authenticity of his tale would not be taken for granted, and that, on a certain peculiar but familiar level enforced by rituals along the color line, his narrative would be viewed as a fiction competing with other fictions. However, in this passage Northup also inaugurates a counter-strategy. His reference to his own observation of slavery may be a just and subtle dig at the "armchair sociologists" of North and South alike, who wrote of the slavery question amid the comforts of their libraries and verandas. But more important, in terms of plot as well as point of view, the remark establishes Northup's authorial posture as a "participant-observer" in the truest and (given his bondage) most regrettable sense of the phrase. In these terms, then, Northup contributes personally to the authentication of *Twelve Years a Slave*: he challenges the authenticity of the popular slavery fictions and their power of authenticating his own personal history by first exploiting the bond between them and his tale and then assuming the posture of an authenticator. One needn't delve far into the annals of American race relations for proof that Northup's rhetorical strategy is but a paradigm for the classic manipulation of the master by the slave.

As the first chapter of *Twelve Years a Slave* unfolds, Northup tells of his family's history and circumstances. His father, Mintus Northup, was a slave in Rhode Island and in Rensselaer County, New York, before gaining his freedom in 1803 upon the death of his master. Mintus quickly amassed property and gained suffrage; he came to expect the freedoms that accompany self-willed mobility and self-initiated employment, and gave his son, Solomon, the extraordinary advantage of being born a free man. As a result, Solomon writes of gaining "an education surpassing that ordinarily bestowed upon children in our condition," and he recollects leisure hours "employed over my books, or playing the violin." Solomon describes employment (such as lumber-rafting on Lake Champlain) that was not only profitable but also, in a way associated with the romance of the frontier, adventurous and even manly. When Solomon Northup married Anne Hampton on Christmas Day of 1829, they did not jump over a broomstick, as was the (reported) lot of most enslaved black Americans; rather, the two were married by a magistrate of the neighborhood, Timothy Eddy, Esq. Furthermore, their first home was neither a hovel nor a hut but the "Fort House," a residence "lately occupied by Captain Lathrop" and used in 1777 by General Burgoyne.

This saga of Solomon's heritage is full of interest, and it has its rhetorical and strategical properties as well. Northup has begun to establish his authorial posture removed from the condition of the black masses in slavery—a move which, as we have indicated, is as integral to the authenticating strategy as to the plot of his tale. In addition to portraying circumstances far more pleasant and fulfilling than those which he suffers in slavery, Northup's family history also yields some indication of his relations with whites in the district, especially the white Northups. Of course, these indications also advance both the plot and the authenticating strategy. One notes, for example, that while Mintus Northup did indeed migrate from the site of his enslavement once he was free, he retained the Northup surname and labored for a relative of his former master. Amid his new prosperity and mobility, Mintus maintained fairly amicable ties with his past; apparently this set the tone for relations between Northups, black and white. One should be wary of depicting New York north of Albany as an ideal or integrated area in the early 1800's, but the black Northups had bonds with whites—perhaps blood ties. To the end Solomon depends on these bonds for his escape from slavery and for the implicit verification of his tale.

In the first chapter of *Twelve Years a Slave*, Henry B. Northup, Esq., is mentioned only briefly as a relative of Mintus Northup's former master; in the context of Solomon's family history, he is but a looming branch of the (white) Northup family tree. However, as the tale concludes, Henry Northup becomes a voice and character in the narrative. He requests various legal documents essential to nullifying Solomon's sale into bondage; he inquires into Solomon's whereabouts in Bayou Boeuf, Louisiana; he presents the facts before lawyers, sheriffs, and Solomon's master, Edwin Epps; he pleads Solomon's case against his abductors before a District of Columbia court of law; and, most important, after the twelve years of assault on Solomon's sense of identity, Henry Northup utters, to Solomon's profound thanksgiving, Solomon's given name—not his slave name. In this way Henry Northup enters the narrative, and whatever linguistic authentication of the tale Solomon inaugurated by assuming the rather objective posture of the participant-observer-authenticator is concluded and confirmed, not by appended letter, but by Henry Northup's presence.

This strategy of authentication functions hand in hand with the narrative's strategy of reform. Like the carpenter, Bass, who jeopardizes his own safety by personally mailing Solomon's appeals for help to New York, Henry Northup embodies the spirit of reform in the narrative. In terms of reform strategy, Henry Northup and Bass—who, as a Canadian, represents a variation on the archetype of deliverance in Canada—are not only saviors but also models whose example might enlist other whites in the reform cause. Certainly abolitionists near and far could identify with these men, and that was important. Slave narratives were often most successful when they were as subtly pro-abolition as they were overtly anti-slavery—a consideration which could only have exacerbated the former slave's already sizeable problems with telling his tale in such a way that he, and not his editors or guarantors, controlled it.

But Henry Northup is a different kind of savior from Bass: he is an American descended from slaveowners, and he shares his surname with the kidnapped Solomon. Furthermore, his posture as a family friend is inextricably bound to his position in the tale as a lawyer. At the end of *Twelve Years a Slave,* Henry Northup appears in Louisiana as an embodiment of the law, as well as of Solomon Northup's past (in all its racial complexity) come to reclaim him. In this way, Solomon's *tale* assumes the properties of an integrated narrative—the authenticating texts (here, the words and actions of Henry Northup) are integrated into the former slave's tale. But in what follows after the tale, we see that Solomon's *narrative* ultimately retrogresses to the old strategies of a phase-one eclectic narrative. Whereas the Bibb narrative begins with a discrete set of authenticating texts, the Northup narrative ends with such a set—an "Appendix."

The Northup Appendix contains three types of documents. First comes the New York state law, passed May 14, 1840, employed by Henry Northup and others to reclaim Solomon Northup from bondage in Louisiana. There follows a petition to the Governor of New York from Solomon's wife, Ann Northup, replete with legal language that persists in terming her a "memorialist." The remaining documents are letters, mostly from the black Northups' white neighbors, authenticating Solomon's claim that he is a free Negro. Despite our initial disappointment upon finding such an orthodox authenticating strategy appended to what had heretofore been a refreshingly sophisticated slave narrative (the narrative does not need the Appendix to fulfill its form), the Appendix does have its points of interest. Taken as a whole, it portrays the unfolding of a law; the New York law with which it begins precipitates the texts that follow, notably, in chronological order. On one level, then, Northup's Appendix is, far more than Bibb's Introduction, a story in epistolary form that authenticates not only his tale but also those voices within the tale, such as Henry Northup's. On another level, however, the Appendix becomes a further dimension to the reform strategy subsumed within the narrative. Just as Bass and Henry Northup posture as model reformers, the narrative's Appendix functions as a primer, complete with illustrative documents, on how to use the law to retrieve kidnapped free Negroes. Thus, the Appendix, as much as the tale itself, can be seen (quite correctly) as an elaborate rhetorical strategy against the Fugitive Slave Law of 1850.

In the end, the Northup narrative reverts to primitive authenticating techniques, but that does not diminish the sophistication and achievement of the tale within the narrative. We must now ask: To what end does the immersion of authenticating documents and strategies within the texture of Northup's tale occur? Furthermore, is this goal literary or extraliterary? In answering these questions we come a little closer, I think, to an opinion on whether narratives like Northup's may be autobiographies.

Northup's conscious or unconscious integration and subsequent manipulation of authenticating voices advances his tale's plot and most certainly advances his narrative's validation and reform strategies. However, it does little to develop what Albert Stone has called a literary strategy of self-presentation. The narrative renders an extraordinary experience, but not a remarkable self. The two need not be exclusive, as Frederick Douglass's 1845 *Narrative* illustrates, but in the Northup book they appear to be distinct entities, principally because of the eye or "I" shaping and controlling the narration. Northup's eye and "I" are not so much introspective as they are inquisitive; even while in the pit of slavery in Louisiana, Northup takes time to inform us of various farming methods and of how they differ from practices in the North. Of course, this remarkable objective posture results directly from Northup assuming the role of a participant-observer for authentication purposes. But it all has a terrible price. Northup's tale is neither the history nor a metaphor for the history of his life; and because this is so, his tale cannot be called autobiographical.

PHASE IIIa: GENERIC NARRATIVE

In the first two phases of slave narrative narration we observe the former slave's ultimate lack of control over his own narrative, occasioned primarily by the demands of audience and authentication. This dilemma is not unique to the authors of these narratives; indeed, many modern black writers still do not control their personal history once it assumes literary form. For this reason, Frederick Douglass's *Narrative of the Life of Frederick Douglass, an American Slave, Written by Himself* (1845) seems all the more a remarkable literary achievement. Because it contains several segregated narrative texts—a preface, a prefatory letter, the tale, an appendix—it appears to be, in terms of the narrative phases, a rather primitive slave narrative. But each ancillary text is drawn to the tale by some sort of extraordinary gravitational pull or magnetic attraction. There is, in short, a dynamic energy between the tale and each supporting text that we do not discover in the Bibb or Northup narratives, save perhaps in the relationship between Solomon Northup and his guarantor-become-character, Henry Northup. The Douglass narrative is an integrated narrative of a very special order. The integrating process does, in a small way, pursue the conventional path found in Northup's narrative, creating characters out of authenticating texts (William Lloyd Garrison silently enters Douglass's tale at the very end); however, its new and major thrust is the creation of that aforementioned energy which binds the supporting texts to the tale, while at the same time removing them from participation in the narrative's rhetorical and authenticating strategies. Douglass's tale dominates the narrative because it alone authenticates the narrative.

The introductory texts to the tale are two in number: a "Preface" by William Lloyd Garrison, the famous abolitionist and editor of *The Liberator;* and a "Letter from Wendell Phillips, Esq.," who was equally well known as an abolitionist, crusading lawyer, and judge. In theory, each of these introductory documents should be classic guarantees written almost exclusively for a white reading public, concerned primarily and ritualistically with the white validation of a newfound black voice, and removed from the tale in such ways that the guarantee and tale vie silently and surreptitiously for control of the narrative as a whole. But these entries are not fashioned that way. To be sure, Garrison offers a conventional guarantee when he writes, "Mr. DOUGLASS has very properly chosen to write his own Narrative, in his own style, and according to the best of his ability, rather than to employ some one else. It is, therefore, entirely his own production; and ... it is, in my judgment, highly creditable to his head and heart."

And Phillips, while addressing Douglass, most certainly offers a guarantee to "another" audience as well:

> Every one who has heard you speak has felt, and, I am confident, every one who read your book will feel, persuaded that you give them a fair specimen of the whole truth. No one-sided portrait,—no wholesale complaints,—but strict justice done, whenever individual kindliness has neutralized, for a moment, the deadly system with which it was strangely allied.

But these passages dominate neither the tone nor the substance of their respective texts.

Garrison is far more interested in writing history (specifically, that of the 1841 Nantucket Anti-Slavery Convention, and the launching of Douglass's career as a lecture agent for various antislavery societies) and recording his own place in it. His declaration, "I shall never forget his [Douglass's] first speech at the convention," is followed within a paragraph by, "*I rose,* and declared that PATRICK HENRY, of revolutionary fame, never made a speech more eloquent in the cause of liberty . . . *I reminded* the audience of the peril which surrounded this self-emancipated young man . . . *I appealed* to them, whether they would ever allow him to be carried back into slavery,—law or no law, constitution or no constitution" (italics added). His "Preface" ends, not with a reference to Douglass or his tale, but with an apostrophe very much like one he would use to exhort and arouse an antislavery assembly. With the following cry Garrison hardly guarantees Douglass's tale, but enters and reenacts his own abolitionist career instead:

> Reader! are you with the man-stealers in sympathy and purpose, or on the side of their down-trodden victims? If with the former, then you are the foe of God and man. If with the latter, what are you prepared to do and dare in their behalf? Be faithful, be vigilant, be untiring in your efforts to break every yoke, and let the oppressed go free. Come what may—cost what may—inscribe on the banner which you unfurl to the breeze, as your religious and political motto —"NO COMPROMISE WITH SLAVERY! NO UNION WITH SLAVE-HOLDERS!"

In the light of this closure, and (no matter how hard we try to ignore it) the friction that developed between Garrison and Douglass in later years, we might be tempted to see Garrison's "Preface" at war with Douglass's tale for authorial control of the narrative as a whole. Certainly there is a tension, but that tension is stunted by

Garrison's enthusiasm for Douglass's tale. Garrison writes:

> This *Narrative* contains many affecting incidents, many *passages* of
> great eloquence and power; but I think the most thrilling one of
> them all is the *description* DOUGLASS gives of his feelings, as he
> stood soliloquizing respecting his fate, and the chances of his one
> day being a free man. . . . Who can read that *passage,* and be in-
> sensible to its pathos and sublimity? [Italics added.]

Here Garrison does, probably subconsciously, an unusual and extraordinary thing—he becomes the first guarantor we have seen in this
study who not only directs the reader to the tale, but also acknowledges the tale's singular rhetorical power. Garrison enters the tale
by being at the Nantucket convention with Douglass in 1841 (the
same year Solomon Northup was kidnapped) and by, in effect, authenticating the impact, rather than the facts, of the tale. He fashions
his own apostrophe, but finally he remains a member of Douglass's
audience far more than he assumes the posture of a competing or
superior voice. In this way Garrison's "Preface" stands outside Douglass's tale but is steadfastly bound to it.

Such is the case for Wendell Phillips's "Letter" as well. As
I have indicated, it contains passages which seem addressed to credu-
lous readers in need of a "visible" authority's guarantee, but by and
large the "Letter" is directed to Frederick Douglass alone. It opens
with "My Dear Friend," and there are many extraliterary reasons
for wondering initially if the friend is actually Frederick. Shortly
thereafter, however, Phillips declares, "I am glad the time has come
when the 'lions write history,' " and it becomes clear that he both
addresses Douglass and writes in response to the tale. These features,
plus Phillips's specific references to how Douglass acquired his "A B
C" and learned "where the 'white sails' of the Chesapeake were
bound," serve to integrate Phillips's "Letter" into Douglass's tale.

Above all, we must understand in what terms the "Letter" is a
cultural and linguistic event. Like the Garrison document, it presents
its author as a member of Douglass's audience; but the act of letter-
writing, of correspondence, implies a moral and linguistic parity between a white guarantor and black author which we haven't seen
before—and which we do not always see in American literary history
after 1845. The tone and posture initiated in Garrison's "Preface"
are completed and confirmed in Phillips's "Letter"; while these docu-

ments are integrated into Douglass's tale, they remain segregated outside the tale in the all-important sense that they yield Douglass sufficient narrative and rhetorical space in which to render personal
history in—and as—a literary form.

What marks Douglass's narration and control of his tale is his
extraordinary ability to pursue several types of writing with ease and
with a degree of simultaneity. The principal types of writing we discover in the tale are: syncretic phrasing, introspective analysis, internalized documentation, and participant observation. Of course, each
of these types has its accompanying authorial posture, the result being
that even the telling of the tale (as distinct from the content of the
tale) yields a portrait of a complex individual marvelously facile
with the tones, shapes, and dimensions of his voice.

Douglass's syncretic phrasing is often discussed; the passage
most widely quoted is probably, "My feet have been so cracked with
the frost, that the pen with which I am writing might be laid in the
gashes." The remarkable clarity of this language needs no commentary, but what one admires as well is Douglass's ability to conjoin
past and present, and to do so with images that not only stand for
different periods in his personal history but also, in their fusion,
speak of his evolution from slavery to freedom. The pen, symbolizing
the quest for literacy fulfilled, actually measures the wounds of the
past, and this measuring process becomes a metaphor in and of itself
for the artful composition of travail transcended. While I admire
this passage, I find even more intriguing the syncretic phrases that
pursue a kind of acrid punning upon the names of Douglass's op-
pressors. A minor example appears early in the tale, when Douglass
deftly sums up an overseer's character by writing, "Mr. Severe was
rightly named: he was a cruel man." Here Douglass is content with
"glossing" the name; but late in the tale, just before attempting to
escape in 1835, he takes another oppressor's name and does not so
much gloss it or play with it as *work upon* it—to such an extent that,
riddled with irony, it is devoid of its original meaning: "At the close
of the year 1834, Mr. Freeland again hired me of my master, for the
year 1835. But, by this time, I began to want to live *upon free land*
as well as *with Freeland;* and I was no longer content, therefore, to
live with him or any other slaveholder." Of course, this is effective
writing—far more effective than what is found in the average slave
narrative. But my point is that Douglass seems to fashion these passages for both his readership and himself. Each example of his

increasing facility and wit with language charts his ever-shortening path to literacy; thus, in their way, Douglass's syncretic phrases reveal his emerging comprehension of freedom and literacy, and are another introspective tool by which he may mark the progress of his personal history.

But the celebrated passages of introspective analysis are even more pithy and direct. In these, Douglass fashions language as finely honed and balanced as an aphorism or Popean couplet, and thereby orders his personal history with neat, distinct, and credible moments of transition. When Mr. Auld forbids Mrs. Auld from teaching Douglass the alphabet, for example, Douglass relates, "From that moment, I understood the pathway from slavery to freedom. . . . Whilst I was saddened by the thought of losing the aid of my kind mistress, I was gladdened by the invaluable instruction which, by the merest accident, I gained from my master." The clarity of Douglass's revelation is as unmistakable as it was remarkable. As rhetoric, the passage is successful because its nearly extravagant beginning is finally rendered quite acceptable by the masterly balance and internal rhyming of "saddened" and "gladdened," which is persuasive because it is pleasant and because it offers the illusion of a reasoned conclusion.

Balance is an important feature to two other equally celebrated passages which open and close Douglass's telling of his relations with Mr. Covey, an odd (because he *worked* in the fields alongside the slaves) but vicious overseer. At the beginning of the episode, in which Douglass finally fights back and draws Covey's blood, he writes: "You have seen how a man was made a slave; you shall see how a slave was made a man." And at the end of the episode, to bring matters linguistically as well as narratively full circle, Douglass declares: "I now resolved that, however long I might remain a slave in form, the day has passed forever when I could be a slave in fact. I did not hesitate to let it be known of me, that the white man who expected to succeed in whipping, must also succeed in killing me."

The sheer poetry of these statements is not lost on us, nor is the reason why the poetry was created in the first place. One might suppose that in another age Douglass's determination and rage would take a more effusive expression, but I cannot imagine that to be the case. In the first place, his linguistic model is obviously scriptural; and in the second, his goal, as Albert Stone has argued, is the presentation of a "*historical* self," not the record of temporary hysteria.

This latter point, to refer back to the Northup narrative, is one of the prime distinctions between Solomon Northup and Frederick Douglass—one which ultimately persuades me that Douglass is about the business of discovering how personal history may be transformed into autobiography, while Northup is not. Both narratives contain episodes in which the author finally stands up to and soundly beats his overseer, but while Douglass performs this task and reflects upon its place in his history, Northup resorts to effusion:

> As I stood there, feelings of unutterable agony overwhelmed me. I was conscious that I had subjected myself to unimaginable punishment. The reaction that followed my extreme ebullition of anger produced the most painful sensations of regret. An unfriended, helpless slave—what could I *do,* what could I *say,* to justify, in the remotest manner, the heinous act I had committed . . . I tried to pray . . . but emotion choked my utterance, and I could only bow my head upon my hands and weep.

Passages such as these may finally link certain slave narratives with the popular sentimental literary forms of the nineteenth century, but Douglass's passages of introspective analysis create fresh space for themselves in the American literary canon.

Internal documentation in Douglass's tale is unusual in that, instead of reproducing letters and other documents written by white guarantors within the tale or transforming guarantees into characters, Douglass internalizes documents which, like the syncretic and introspective passages, order his personal history. Again a comparison of Douglass and Northup is useful, because while both authors present documents having only a secondary function in the authenticating process, their goals (and, perhaps one might say, their ambitions) seem quite different.

Northup, for example, documents slave songs in two major passages: first in the text of the tale, and then in a segregated text serving as a musical interlude between the tale and the Appendix. His discussion of the songs within the tale is one dimensional, by which I mean it merely reflects his limited comprehension and appreciation of the songs at a given moment in his life. Rather than establishing Northup within the slave community, remarks like "those unmeaning songs, composed rather for [their] adaptation to a certain tune or measure, than for the purpose of expressing any distinct idea" or "equally nonsensical, but full of melody" serve only to reinforce his displacement as a participant-observer. One might have assumed that

Northup (who was, after all, kidnapped into slavery partly because of his musicianship) found music a bond between him and his enslaved brethren, and in passages such as these would relinquish or soften his objective posture. But apparently the demands of audience and authentication precluded such a shift.

In contrast, Douglass's discussion of slave songs begins with phrases such as "wild songs" and "unmeaning jargon" but concludes, quite typically for him, with a study of how he grew to "hear" the songs and how that hearing affords yet another illumination of his path from slavery to freedom:

> I did not, when a slave, understand the deep meaning of those rude and apparently incoherent songs. I was myself within the circle; so that I neither saw nor heard as those without might see and hear. They told a tale of woe which was then altogether beyond my feeble comprehension. . . . Every tone was a testimony against slavery, and a prayer to God for deliverance from chains. The hearing of those wild notes always depressed my spirit, and filled me with ineffable sadness. I have frequently found myself in tears while hearing them. The mere recurrence to those songs, even now, afflicts me; and while I am writing these lines, an expression of feeling has already found its way down my cheek.

The tears of the past and present interflow. Douglass not only documents his saga of enslavement but also, with typical recourse to syncretic phrasing and introspective analysis, advances his presentation of self.

Douglass's other internalized documents are employed with comparable efficiency, as we see in the episode where he attempts an escape in 1835. There the document reproduced is the pass or "protection" Douglass wrote for himself and his compatriots in the escape plan:

> This is to certify that I, the undersigned, have given the bearer, my servant, full liberty to go to Baltimore, and spend the Easter holidays. Written with mine own hand, &c., 1835.
>   WILLIAM HAMILTON,
>   Near St. Michael's, in Talbot county, Maryland.

The protection exhibits Douglass's increasingly refined sense of how to manipulate language—he has indeed come a long way from that day when Mr. Auld halted his A B C lessons. But even more impressive, I believe, is the act of reproducing the document itself. We know from the tale that each slave managed to destroy his pass when the scheme was thwarted; Douglass is reproducing his language from memory, and there is no reason to doubt a single jot of his recollection. He can draw so easily from the wellsprings of memory because the protection is not a mere scrap of memorabilia, but a veritable roadsign on his path to freedom and literacy. In this sense, his protection assumes a place in Afro-American letters as an antedating trope for such documents as "The Voodoo of Hell's Half Acre" in Richard Wright's *Black Boy,* and the tale framed by the prologue and epilogue in Ralph Ellison's *Invisible Man.*

All of the types of narrative discourse discussed thus far reveal features of Douglass's particular posture as a participant-observer narrator, a posture that is as introspective as Solomon Northup's is inquisitive. But the syncretic phrases, introspective studies, and internalized documents only exhibit Douglass as a teller and doer, and part of the great effect of his tale depends upon what he does *not* tell, what he refuses to reenact in print. Late in the tale, at the beginning of the eleventh chapter, Douglass writes:

> I now come to that part of my life during which I planned, and finally succeeded in making, my escape from slavery. But before narrating any of the peculiar circumstances, I deem it proper to make known my intention not to state all the facts connected with the transaction . . . I deeply regret the necessity that impels me to suppress any thing of importance connected with my experience in slavery. It would afford me great pleasure indeed, as well as materially add to the interest of my narrative, were I at liberty to gratify a curiosity, which I know exists. . . . But I must deprive myself of this pleasure, and the curious gratification which such a statement would afford. I would allow myself to suffer under the greatest imputations which evil-minded men might suggest, rather than exculpate myself, and thereby run the hazard of closing the slightest avenue by which a brother slave might clear himself of the chains and fetters of slavery.

John Blassingame has argued, in *The Slave Community* (1972), that one way to test a slave narrative's authenticity is by gauging how much space the narrator gives to relating his escape, as opposed to describing the conditions of his captivity. If the adventure, excitement, and perils of the escape seem to be the *raison d'être* for the narrative's composition, then the narrative is quite possibly an exceedingly adulterated slave's tale or a bald fiction. The theory does not always work perfectly: Henry "Box" Brown's narrative and that

of William and Ellen Craft are predominantly recollections of extraordinary escapes; yet, as far as we can tell, these are authentic tales.
But Blassingame's theory nevertheless has great merit, and I have
often wondered to what extent it derives from the example of Douglass's tale and from his fulminations against those authors who unwittingly excavate the Underground Railroad and expose it to the
morally thin mid-nineteenth-century American air. Douglass's tale is
spectacularly free from suspicion because he never divulges a detail
of his escape to New York. (That information is given ten years
later, in *My Bondage and My Freedom* and other statements.) This
marvelously rhetorical omission or silence both sophisticates and authenticates his posture as a participant-observer narrator. When a
narrator wrests this kind of preeminent authorial control from the
ancillary voices in the narrative, we may say that he controls the
presentation of his personal history, and that his tale is becoming
autobiographical. In this light, then, Douglass's last few sentences of
the tale take on special meaning:

> But, while attending an anti-slavery convention at Nantucket, on the
> 11th of August, 1841, I felt strongly moved to speak. . . . It was a
> severe cross, and I took it up reluctantly. The truth was, I felt my-
> self a slave, and the idea of speaking to white people weighed me
> down. I spoke but a few moments, when I felt a degree of freedom,
> and said what I desired with considerable ease. From that time
> until now, I have been engaged in pleading the case of my brethren
> —with what success, and what devotion, I leave those acquainted
> with my labors to decide.

With these words, the *narrative,* as Albert Stone has remarked, comes
full circle. We are returned not to the beginning of the *tale,* but to
Garrison's prefatory remarks on the convention and Douglass's first
public address. This return may be pleasing in terms of the sense of
symmetry it affords, but it is also a remarkable feat of rhetorical
strategy: having traveled with Douglass through his account of his
life, we arrive in Nantucket in 1841 to hear him speak. We become,
along with Mr. Garrison, his audience. The final effect is that Douglass reinforces his posture as an articulate hero, while supplanting
Garrison as the definitive historian of his past.

Even more important, I think, is Douglass's final image of a
slave shedding his last fetter and becoming a man by first finding
his voice and then, as surely as light follows dawn, speaking "with

considerable ease." In one brilliant stroke, the quest for freedom and literacy, implied from the start even by the narrative's title, is resolutely consummated.

The final text of the narrative, the Appendix, differs from the one attached to the Northup narrative. It is not a series of letters and legal documents, but a discourse by Douglass on *his* view of Christianity and Christian practice, as opposed to what he exposed in his tale to be the bankrupt, immoral faith of slaveholders. As rhetorical strategy, the discourse is effective because it lends weight and substance to what passes for a conventional complaint of slave narrators, and because Douglass's exhibition of faith can only enhance his already considerable posture as an articulate hero. But more specifically, the discourse is most efficacious because at its heart lies a vitriolic poem written by a northern Methodist minister that Douglass introduces by writing: "I conclude these remarks by copying the following portrait of the religion of the south, (which is, by communion and fellowship, the religion of the north,) which I soberly affirm is 'true to life,' and without caricature or the slightest exaggeration." The poem is strong and imbued with considerable irony, but what we must appreciate here is the effect of the white Northerner's poem conjoined with Douglass's *authentication* of the poem. The tables are clearly reversed: Douglass has not only controlled his personal history, but also fulfilled the prophecy suggested by his implicit authentication of Garrison's "Preface" by explicitly authenticating what is conventionally a white Northerner's validating text. Douglass's narrative thus offers what is unquestionably our best portrait in Afro-American letters of the requisite act of assuming authorial control. An author can go no further than Douglass did without himself writing all the texts constituting the narrative.

PHASE IIIb: AUTHENTICATING NARRATIVE

In an authenticating narrative, represented here by William Wells Brown's *Narrative of the Life and Escape of William Wells Brown* (not to be confused with Brown's 1847 volume, *Narrative of William Wells Brown, a Fugitive Slave, Written by Himself*), the narrator exhibits considerable control of his narrative by becoming an editor of disparate texts for authentication purposes, far more than for the goal of recounting personal history. The texts Brown displays include passages from his speeches and other writings, but for the most part they are testimonials from antislavery groups in both America and England, excerpts from reviews of his travel book, *Three Years in Europe* (1852), selections from antislavery verse, and, quite significantly, letters to Brown's benefactors from his last master in slavery, Mr. Enoch Price of St. Louis. Brown's control of his narrative is comparable to Douglass's, but while Douglass gains control by improving upon the narrative failures of authors like Henry Bibb, Brown's control represents a refinement of the authenticating strategies used by publishers like Bibb's Lucius Matlack, who edited and deployed authenticating documents very much like those gathered by Brown. In this way, Brown's narrative is not so much a tale of personal history as it is a conceit upon the authorial mode of the white guarantor. Control and authentication are achieved, but at the enormous price of abandoning the quest to present personal history in and as literary form.

Brown's "Preface," written notably by himself and not by a white guarantor, is peculiar in that it introduces both his narrative and the text authenticated by the narrative, *Clotel; or, The President's Daughter*. By and large, the tone of the "Preface" is sophisticated and generally that of a self-assured writer. Unlike Bibb or Northup, Brown does not skirmish with other authenticators for authorial control of the text, nor is he anxious about competition from other literary quarters of the antislavery ranks. He scans briefly the history of slavery in North America and reasons, with the British (with whom he resides after passage of the 1850 Fugitive Slave Law), that they who controlled the American colonies when slavery was introduced should feel "a lively interest in its abolition." All this is done without resort to conventional apologia or the confession of verbal deficiencies; Brown is humble not so much in his rhetoric as in his goal: "If the incidents set forth in the following pages should add anything new to the information already given to the public through similar publications, and should thereby aid in bringing British influence to bear upon American slavery, the main object for which this work was written will have been accomplished." That Brown introduces a personal narrative and a somewhat fictive narrative (*Clotel*) with language and intentions commonly reserved for works of history and journalism constitutes his first admission of being motivated by extraliterary concerns. His second admission emerges from his persistent use of the term "memoir." In contrast to a confession or autobiography, a memoir refers specifically to an author's recollections of his public life, far more than to his rendering of personal history as literary form or metaphor. This former kind of portrait is, of course, exactly what Brown gives us in his narrative.

The narrative is, as I have indicated, bereft of authorship. Brown rarely renders in fresh language those incidents of which he has written elsewhere; he simply quotes himself. His posture as the editor and not the author of his tale disallows any true expression of intimacy with his personal past. This feature is reinforced by certain objectifying and distancing qualities created by third-person narration. Brown's 1847 narrative begins, "I was born in Lexington, Ky. The man who stole me as soon as I was born, recorded the births of all the infants which he claimed to be born his property, in a book which he kept for that purpose. . . . " Thus, it inaugurates the kind of personal voice and hardboiled prose which is Brown's contribution to early Afro-American letters. In contrast, the opening of the 1852 narrative is flat, without pith or strength: "William Wells Brown, the subject of this narrative, was born a slave in Lexington, Kentucky, not far from the residence of the late Hon. Henry Clay." These words do not constitute effective writing, but that is not Brown's goal. The goal is, rather, authentication, and the seemingly superfluous aside about Henry Clay—which in another narrative might very well generate the first ironic thrust against America's moral blindness—appears for the exclusive purpose of validation. In this way Brown commences an authentication strategy which he will pursue throughout the tale.

The tale or memoir is eclectic in its collection of disparate texts; however, very few of the collected texts merit discussion. I will simply list their types to suggest both their variety and their usefulness to Brown:

1. The scrap of verse, usually effusive, always saccharine, culled from antislavery poets known and unknown. The verse expresses high sentiment and deep emotion when the text requires it, engages the popular reading public, and suggests erudition and sensitivity.

2. Quotations from Brown's speeches at famous institutions like Exeter Hall and from "addresses" bestowed on him after such speeches. These advance the memoir, embellish Brown's

résumé, and authenticate his claim that he was where he said he was.

3. Quotations from Brown's travel book, *Three Years in Europe*, and from the book's reviews. The passages of personal history advance the memoir and validate "The energy of the man," as well as call attention to the book. The reviews call further attention to the book, and authenticate Brown's literacy and good character.

4. Testimonies and testimonials from various abolitionist groups in the United States and England, white and colored. These texts profess the success of Brown's labors as a lecturing agent, "commend him to the hospitality and encouragement of all true friends of humanity," and, upon his departure for England, provide him with what Douglass would have termed a "protection" for his travels. These are, in short, recommending letters attached to Brown's résumé validating his character and the fact that he is a fugitive slave.

5. Two letters from a former master, Enoch Price of St. Louis, dated before and after the Fugitive Slave Law was passed in 1850.

The Enoch Price letters are undoubtedly the most interesting documents in Brown's compendium, and he makes good narrative use of them. While the other assembled documents merely serve the authenticating strategy, Price's letters, in their portrait of a slaveholder ironically invoking the dictates of fair play while vainly attempting to exact a bargain price for Brown from his benefactors, actually tell us something about Brown's circumstances. Despite the lionizing illustrated by the other documents, Brown is still not a free man. He is most aware of this, and for this reason the narrative concludes, not with another encomium, but with the second of Price's letters once again requesting payment—payment for lost property, payment for papers that will set Brown free. All Brown can do under the circumstances is refuse to acknowledge Price's supposed right to payment, and order his present condition by controlling not so much his tale, which is his past, as the authentication of himself, which is his present and possibly his future. As the editor of his résumé—his present circumstance—Brown must acknowledge slavery's looming presence in his life, but he can also attempt to bury it beneath a mountain of antislavery rhetoric and self-authenticating documentation. Through the act of self-authentication Brown may contextualize slavery and thereby control it. In these terms, then, the heroic proportions to Brown's editorial act of including and manipulating Enoch Price's letters become manifest.

Brown's personal narrative most certainly authenticates himself, but how does it also authenticate *Clotel?* The answer takes us back to Brown's "Preface," where he outlines the extraliterary goals of both narratives, and forward to the concluding chapter of *Clotel,* where he writes:

> My narrative has now come to a close. I may be asked, and no doubt shall, Are the various incidents and scenes related founded in truth? I answer, Yes. I have personally participated in many of those scenes. Some of the narratives I have derived from other sources; many from the lips of those who, like myself, have run away from the land of bondage. . . . To Mrs. Child, of New York, I am indebted for part of a short story. American Abolitionist journals are another source from whence some of the characters appearing in my narrative are taken. All these combined have made up my story.

Brown's personal narrative functions, then, as a successful rhetorical device, authenticating his *access* to the incidents, characters, scenes, and tales which collectively make up *Clotel.* In the end, we witness a dynamic interplay between the two narratives, established by the need of each for resolution and authentication within the other. Since *Clotel* is not fully formed as either a fiction or a slave narrative, it requires completion of some sort, and finds this when it is transformed into a fairly effective antislavery device through linkage with its prefatory authenticating text. Since Brown's personal narrative is not fully formed as either an autobiography or a slave narrative, it requires fulfillment as a literary form through intimacy with a larger, more developed but related text. *Clotel* is no more a novel than Brown's preceding personal narrative is autobiography, but together they represent a roughly hewn literary tool which is, despite its defects, a sophisticated departure from the primary phases of slave narration and authentication.

Brown's personal narrative is hardly an aesthetic work, but that is because Brown had other goals in mind. He is willing to forsake the goal of presenting personal history in literary form in order to promote his books and projects like the Manual Labor School for fugitive slaves in Canada, to authenticate *Clotel,* and to authenticate himself while on British soil. He is willing to abandon the goals of true authorship and to assume instead the duties of an editor in order to gain some measure of control over the present, as opposed to illuminating the past. Brown's narrative is present and future oriented: most of his anecdotes from the past are offered as testimony to the energy and character he will bring to bear on future tasks. In short, just as Douglass inaugurates the autobiographical mode in Afro-American letters, Brown establishes what curiously turns out to be the equally common mode of the authenticating narrative. To see the popularity and great effect of the Afro-American authenticating narrative—once it assumes a more sophisticated form —one need look no further than Booker T. Washington's *Up from Slavery.*

CHAPTER 2

Lost in a Cause:
Booker T. Washington's
Up from Slavery

Tuskeegee Institute is sho' a fine place, bes' thing
de 'Niggers' got anywha' in de worl'. Ya git
up dere in som'er dem fine buildin's, ya jes
think ya right up in Hebben. Co'se som'er
dem up dere in dem buildin's jest'ta 'bout ne'er
Hebben as dey gwin get. . . . Booker Washington,
he wuz de daddy uv'em all. . . . He sho' wuz
a good man. . . . He wuz a wise man too,
he al'ays let de white man shine, so he could
live an' wurk he'er.
> —Sarah Fitzpatrick (1938)
> in John W. Blassingame,
> ed., *Slave Testimony*, p. 654.

Like W. E. B. Du Bois's *The Souls of Black Folk* (1903) and
James Weldon Johnson's *The Autobiography of an Ex-Coloured Man*
(1912), Booker T. Washington's second and most famous "autobiography," *Up from Slavery* (1901), is universally touted as a turn-
of-the-century black classic. What readers have meant by the term
"classic" has varied through the years. Some simply wish to com-
municate that these texts are "famous" or in some vague sense "seminal"; others allude to more sophisticated judgments such as the
argument that these works, in their treatment of history, sociology,
and literary conventions, as well as by their position in literary
chronology, inaugurate modern Afro-American letters. What interests me about these texts are those features which affect literary
form, and thereby make it extremely difficult for the literary scholar
to relegate the works to ordinary generic categories—even for the
sake of convenience. My reasons for terming them "classics" would
therefore include some expression of how they create generic and,
by extension, historical space for themselves, usually by manipulat-

ing and invariably by sophisticating the modes of narration, authentication, and authorial control found in early Afro-American texts
such as slave narratives. Interestingly enough, the effort to discover
what is classic about *Up from Slavery* helps to clarify why the text is
not, in any exclusive sense, what we most often describe it to be: a
slave narrative or, more commonly, an autobiography. I suggest
that *Up from Slavery* is an Afro-American classic precisely because
it fits neatly in neither formal category, and probably does not even
aspire to generic form.

When I argue that *Up from Slavery* is a major Afro-American
text partly because it does not assume a distinct generic or nearly
generic form, I am only too aware that I have rejected certain common assumptions about and approaches to Afro-American literature
and its history. There is really nothing wrong with asking: Is this
work a slave narrative or an autobiography? But there is something
wrong with how the question has been pursued. On one level, a problem in definition has prevailed: what are good working definitions of
"slave narrative" and "autobiography"? Usually both terms, but
especially the former, are defined by features of content far more
than by those of form, or of content and form envisioned as some
sort of whole. As a result, some discussions say little more than that
Up from Slavery is a slave narrative because Washington was born
a slave, or that it is an autobiography because it is the story of his life.

On another level, there has been a comparable problem in recognizing the assumptions about Afro-American literary history that
lie behind the question. All of those assumptions have had a fairly
disastrous effect upon Afro-American criticism and historiography,
largely because they have gone more or less unquestioned. One such
premise argues that, once certain literary forms are set in motion in
literary and historical time, they "express" from one major "station"
to another without making any intermediate stops. This premise—
which is, at least in origin, more of a pedagogical than a critical concept—sustains the unfortunate idea that, in literature, a historical
event occurs only when literary materials assume generic form. As
I have indicated earlier in my discussion of slave narratives, several
types of slave narratives spawn other types of narratives which may
or may not aspire to traditional generic form. Rigid adherence to this
premise therefore places many Afro-American texts either "outside"
literary history (Ralph Ellison might say it renders them invisible)

or "inside" literary history after some manipulation or obscuration of textual features.

Another premise contends that literary history may be cogently organized by associating—and perhaps defining—literary forms in chronological (as opposed to historical) terms. By this argument, descriptions of slave narratives and autobiographies as nineteenth-century and twentieth-century forms respectively are useful, meaningful, and historiographical. Adherence to this premise encourages the impulse to assign formal or generic appellations for reasons having more to do with chronological "facts" than with features and strategies.

A third premise argues that Afro-American literary history chronicles the incorporation—but not necessarily the integration—of an aberrant literature into the literature of "mainstream" American (or, more broadly, Western) culture. Among the implications of this premise is the idea that, once a literature shifts its point of reference from the environs of a subculture (Afro-American) to that of a dominant culture (American), the literature itself develops in sophistication from pre-form (slave narrative, for example) to form (autobiography, etc.). Such a view of Afro-American literary history often occasions abandonment of Afro-American literary historiography in favor of what may turn out to be a rather peculiar and essentially synchronic view of American letters as an unwieldy whole.

We need better working definitions of the critical terms essential to Afro-American literary historiography, and we need to question and probably abandon implicit literary historiographical premises such as those outlined above. The study of Afro-American literature —especially of its "classic" texts, such as *Up from Slavery*—requires an approach which employs critical terms expressive of the indivisibility of form and content. Such study places entire texts (not "parts," such as a single archetype) in literary history because of what they *are,* not what they might be; it liberates text and reader alike from both chronology and what Geoffrey Hartman calls a text's site in history; and it avoids placing certain works in literary histories contiguous to the Afro-American construction in order for them to be "seen" or discussed at all.

In studying *Up from Slavery,* all these requirements are met when we investigate the ways in which the text pursues those modes of narration, authentication, and authorial control initiated in that type of slave narrative which I have termed an "authenticating narrative." The effort here is not to categorize the work as a slave narrative, but to identify its point of departure for rhetorical, formal, and even historical destinations which are perhaps unknown. In this way, we discover that *Up from Slavery* is, despite the "public" rhetoric of its hero-narrator, a rather extraordinary portrait of a single life within what Du Bois called the deeper recesses beyond the Veil. Indeed, the fact that *Up from Slavery* does not ultimately become an autobiography is a formal clue that the text is preoccupied with subtler intentions.

As I have argued before, an authenticating narrative is an integrated narrative in which the various authenticating texts are controlled and manipulated by the author, and very few of the texts appear outside the author's tale. *Up from Slavery* follows this pattern to the letter. For example, the few authenticating texts outside the tale are a short "Preface" and a dedication written by Washington, not by an editor, publisher, or white guarantor sympathetic to Washington's plight or cause. These texts are not merely written but controlled by Washington, by which I mean that he fashions them as vehicles for the introduction of certain goals, rhetorical strategies, and authorial postures which he will pursue throughout the central text of *Up from Slavery*. The dedication is as follows:

> *This volume is dedicated to my Wife*
> MRS. MARGARET JAMES WASHINGTON
> *And to my Brother*
> MR. JOHN H. WASHINGTON
> *Whose patience, fidelity, and hard work have gone far*
> *to make the work at Tuskegee successful*

What we witness here is a deliberate skewing of customary dedicatory language for the sake of establishing what are, in effect, the narrative line and authorial intentions of Washington's tale. *Up from Slavery* is generally the story of the rise of Tuskegee, the institution. But more specifically, it is the story of a former slave's immersion in a grander construction which we may refer to as Tuskegee, the myth of uplift. The last two lines of Washington's dedication may express his gratitude for his wife's and brother's support of *his* work at Tuskegee, but their central purpose is really to laud two of his closest fellow travelers in the quest for uplift. Kinship, the dedication tells

us, will be explored in Washington's tale of personal history as a
bond of shared precepts, values, and energies, not as a web of
lineage or of intimate personal relations. *Up from Slavery* pursues,
even in its dedication, what we have observed before to be the
authenticating narrative's peculiar thrust to control the past by cen-
tering its tale and tropes in a highly orchestrated present. In the
dedication, as in Washington's tale, history is by and large defined
in both substance and span as "the work at Tuskegee." What the
tale does (and what the dedication cannot do, chiefly because of its
brevity) is to define history in far subtler terms by charting Tuskegee's
transformation from a mere school located in an enclosed geo-
historical space into a controlling vehicle, literal and figurative and
pervading all kinds of spaces, for the myth of uplift. Nevertheless, the
tale only consummates what the dedication begins.

When written by former slaves, prefaces in slave narratives often
tell us much about how the tale was written or transcribed and how
the former slave feels about committing his story to print. Washington's "Preface" recalls the slave narratives by performing these same
tasks and by providing a conventional apology for his narrative
talents as well: "I have tried to tell a simple, straightforward story,
with no attempt at embellishment. My regret is that what I have
attempted to do has been done so imperfectly." There are, however,
some subtle features that not only distinguish Washington's "Preface"
from those in the slave narrative canon, but also join the "Preface"
to the dedication in the task of initiating Washington's narrative goals
and strategies. The first such feature is advanced in the first paragraph: "This volume is the outgrowth of a series of articles, dealing
with incidents in my life, which were published consecutively in the
Outlook. While they were appearing in that magazine I was con-
stantly surprised at the number of requests which came to me from
all parts of the country, asking that the articles be permanently preserved in book form." Above and beyond such matters as the level
of literacy quite deliberately implied, are the suggestions here of
Washington's *national* posture and of the extent of his authorial control. In Frederick Douglass's *Narrative* of 1845, Wendell Phillips's
prefatory "Letter" appears as a historical and linguistic event: the
parity of forthright communication has been extended to a former
slave and, in turn, that former slave's tale has been prefaced by a
text addressed far more to himself than to an anonymous and skep-

tical readership. In Washington's "Preface," it is as if Washington saw this trope of epistolary exchange as a requisite prefatory convention and transformed it into yet another expression of authorial control—inevitably masked, of course, by veils of gracious propriety. *Up from Slavery* is hardly authenticated by these "outside" letters; on the contrary, it is a response to them, and therefore in some baroque sense—matched only in the extraliterary realm by Washington's surreptitious political machinations—an authentication of *them* which yields its author the pleasure of having the power to fulfill a "national" need.

In the second and final paragraph of the "Preface," Washington is more concerned with advancing the myth of uplift than with establishing authorial control. After beginning with the aforementioned apology for narrative deficiencies, he writes:

> The greater part of my time and strength is required for the executive work connected with the Tuskegee Normal and Industrial Institute, and in securing the money necessary for the support of the institution. Much of what I have said has been written on board trains, or at hotels or railroad stations while I have been waiting for trains, or during the moments that I could spare from my work while at Tuskegee.

The statement is so self-servingly calculating that one is almost tempted to chide Washington. But really, he deserves better treatment. It is far more productive, I think, to admire how Washington has embraced one of his favorite homilies—"In order to be successful in any kind of undertaking. . . . The main thing is for one . . . to lose himself in a great cause"—and indeed has "lost" himself in Tuskegee, the school, the philosophy, the myth. All of these aspects of Tuskegee surface in the cited passage. While deftly issuing the first of many veiled calls for funds, Washington portrays himself with great indirection and care as a practical man imbued with the very American philosophy of which his particular myth of uplift is an extension. Above all, the sense of motion and intense activity generated by the passage has great narrative importance, not only because it presents Washington as a man of action but also because it enforces the narrative's nearly excessive focus, as an authenticating narrative, on the here and now. The "Preface," especially when seen in conjunction with the dedication, establishes most of the pivotal ideas and narrative strategies found in *Up from Slavery*'s tale. What is left for the tale to present is Washington's personal story of how he achieved authorial control of the myth that made him.

As an authenticating narrative, *Up from Slavery* is a more sophisticated text than William Wells Brown's 1852 *Narrative,* primarily because it is both a written and an edited text. Indeed, one might say that *Up from Slavery* is almost as "written" or "authored" as Douglass's 1845 *Narrative,* at the same time that it is as "edited" as Brown's narrative. In pursuing his activities as a writer, Washington's chief goal seems to be the creation of certain rhetorical and narrative devices that minimize immersion in the past and reinforce his authorial posture as an authenticator. One need look no further than the tale's first paragraph to see these strategies at work:

> I WAS BORN a slave on a plantation in Franklin County, Virginia. I am not quite sure of the exact date of my birth, but at any rate I suspect I must have been born somewhere and at some time. As nearly as I have been able to learn, I was born near a cross-roads post-office called Hale's Ford, and the year was 1858 or 1859. I do not know the month or the day. The earliest impressions I can now recall are of the plantation and the slave quarters—the latter being the part of the plantation where the slaves had their cabins.

The passage begins in a conventional way with language that quite intentionally echoes the beginnings of many slave narratives. However, instead of waxing vitriolic and launching his first broadside against slavery (recall William Wells Brown's memorable second sentence in his 1847 narrative: "The man who stole me as soon as I was born"), Washington modulates his potentially bitter tone by offering one of his patented jokes: "I must have been born somewhere and at some time." This is a calculated rhetorical move; undoubtedly Washington knew (since his brother John knew) that his birthdate was April 5, 1856. But that kind of accuracy is not the goal of his remarks. What he wishes to establish here is not so much a date as an authorial posture that breaks with slave narrative traditions, and thus creates fresh space in which he can pursue his own narrative strategies as an author of the present far more than of the past. Much of this is accomplished in the paragraph's final sentence, which appears at first glance to be unremarkable and matter of fact.

The heart of the sentence is Washington's gracious effort to decode "the slave quarters" for his readership: "the part of the plantation where the slaves had their cabins." Just as the aforementioned "toastmaster" joke confirms what some turn-of-the-century figures called Washington's proper spirit toward slavery and its aftermath, this passage transforms that spirit into a distinct authorial posture which is grounded in the present, directed to a particular contemporary and uninformed audience, and therefore as removed from the immediate event or object being described as is the posture fashioned for authentication purposes by Solomon Northup. In *Up from Slavery,* this stress on observation in Washington's authorial posture occasions a dominance of the past by the present—a dominance which is probably its primary distinction from the equally controlled Douglass narrative, in which a stress on participation conjoins past and present as a continuous event or even a sustained sensation. Of course, all of this has much larger ramifications: if we may say that "participant-observation" is a central mode in Afro-American narration, then we may venture also that different Afro-American narrative types are generated by shifts in narrative balance from participation to observation, or the reverse.

All in all, the earliest passages and texts of *Up from Slavery* demonstrate two fundamental aspects of Washington's writing that recur throughout his tale. One, which I call "modulation," derives primarily from his authorial posture; the other, Washington's particular type of syncretic phrasing (which is, I think, ultimately inferior to Douglass's), is a product of continued efforts to dominate the past by recontextualizing it in the present. Examples of modulation abound, but the most interesting are some of those passages in which Washington carefully reinforces the notion that he is a Negro of proper spirit. In Chapter I, for instance, Washington slyly appeals to the counter-Reconstruction and, to a lesser degree, to the nostalgic sentiments of his readers by describing his "most trying ordeal" of slavery as "the wearing of a flax shirt." Chapter V begins with Washington carefully modulating what might be construed as assertive or intellectual in his authorial posture by writing, "THE YEARS FROM 1867 to 1878 I think may be called the period of Reconstruction." Finally, late in the text, Washington demonstrates remarkable restraint of feeling when he cautiously inveighs against the "evil habit of lynching."

The syncretic passages are more interesting for their range in purpose than for felicity of expression. In Chapter III, for example,

Washington's remarks on a reception held in his honor by the "coloured citizens" of Richmond include the following: "This reception was held not far from the spot where I slept the first night I spent in that city, and I must confess that my mind was more upon the sidewalk that first gave me shelter than upon the reception, agreeable and cordial as it was." Here Washington seemingly allows the past to dominate the present; but in fact the reverse is true, because the passage is ultimately a testimonial to the myth and practice of uplift. This is one of the more calculated syncretic passages in that it foreshadows the tale's conclusion ("As I write the closing words of this autobiography I find myself—not by design—in the city of Richmond, Virginia: The city which only a few decades ago was the capital of the Southern Confederacy, and where, about twenty-five years ago, because of my poverty I slept night after night under a sidewalk") and thereby affords some measure of symmetry to an otherwise chronolinear tale.

Other passages, such as the one in which Washington describes his daily Bible reading, portray the teachings of Hampton's devoted instructors as part of his daily life, and thus as being "alive" or "of the present." Still others allow Washington a modest expression of revenge against the past—which is as far as he will go toward assuming the strident tone of Douglass: "I determined to learn the business of waiting, and did so within a few weeks and was restored to my former position. I have had the satisfaction of being a guest in this hotel several times since I was a waiter there." One imagines, however, that Washington received the greatest pleasure from fashioning those passages which are not only syncretic but also useful for his tale's more practical purposes:

> I reached Hampton . . . with a surplus of exactly fifty cents with which to begin my education. To me it had been a long, eventful journey; but the first sight of the large, three-story, brick school building seemed to have rewarded me for all that I had undergone in order to reach the place. If the people who gave the money to provide that building could appreciate the influence the sight of it had upon me, as well as upon thousands of other youths, they would feel all the more encouraged to make such gifts.

Here, the shift from the past to the present involves a shift from private memory to public appeal. In the process, Washington's self is indeed "lost" in a cause, and the public which in a sense constructed the past is reminded that the present and future, of Hampton but especially of Tuskegee, are subject to its control as well. In sum, the passage is a rather elegant and ingenious appeal for gifts—much more so, in fact, than that which is assumed to be the typical appeal of a fund-raiser.

As an editor, Washington has some interest in carefully orchestrating texts written by himself so that they authenticate his tale at least as much as the various "outside" texts do. In this regard, his anecdote about the slaves on his plantation mourning the death of "Mars' Billy" is an authenticating document for his future remarks on the fidelity of blacks to whites during the War—which is, of course, the linchpin to his argument for the South to "Cast down your bucket where you are." Similarly, as I will discuss later on, "The Atlanta Exposition Address," which is reproduced in its entirety in Chapter XIV, is an authenticating text of a very special kind. But generally, like William Wells Brown in composing his 1852 narrative, Washington is concerned with assembling a patchwork of texts for which the documents appended by white guarantors to "primitive" slave narratives are prototypes. Once assembled, these documents not only authenticate Washington's tale, but also, because they have been edited and contextualized within the tale, enhance Washington's authorial control.

Like those documents found in the Brown narrative, few of the texts in *Up from Slavery* are worthy of discussion. However, as the following catalog suggests, they are interesting in their variety of type and usefulness to Washington:

1. Letters to Washington *from* benefactors, as well as letters *to* benefactors from Washington. The former confirm his success as a fund-raiser and thus, in a sense, authenticate Tuskegee as well as himself. The latter offer Washington's theories about fund-raising "in action" and, most important, present his rhetorical and authorial posture *vis-à-vis* his chief audience. In one notable instance, an exchange of authenticating letters between Andrew Carnegie and Washington is printed, thereby establishing in *Up from Slavery* a rhetorically useful parity between author and benefactor similar to that observed earlier in the implied exchange between Wendell Phillips and Frederick Douglass. This parity augments

Washington's authenticating strategy far more than it advances his tale's preeminence or narrative line, thus confirming all the more the supposition that *Up from Slavery* is an authenticating narrative.

2. Speeches and excerpts from speeches (the Atlanta Exposition Address is the only one published *in toto*) and newspaper accounts of the occasions where these addresses were given. Both types of documents allow Washington to authenticate certain events and his successful participation in them, without recourse to personal or subjective (and hence questionable) commentary. In the passages orchestrating these documents, résumé becomes narration and a calculated substitute for personal history. At the same time, however, the speeches and accounts of them constitute another kind of exchange inaugurating, in turn, another type of linguistic and rhetorical parity between documents in the narrative. While personal history is forsaken, a hidden voice is achieved through Washington's posture as an editor. With an eye to balance and to reaching all segments of his audience, Washington includes accounts from newspapers north and south, such as the Atlanta *Constitution,* the Chicago *Times-Herald,* and the New York *World.* In this way he also advances his posture as a national figure.

3. Documents from statesmen including an "autograph reply" from Grover Cleveland to a forwarded copy of the Atlanta address, excerpts from speeches at Tuskegee on December 16, 1897, by President McKinley and members of his cabinet, and a letter to Washington from McKinley's secretary, John Addison Porter, authenticating the visit to Tuskegee by the McKinley entourage and confirming Washington's ability to both organize such an occasion and behave properly amid such luminaries. ("I cannot close without assuring you that the modesty shown by yourself . . . was most favourably commented upon by all the members of our party.") These documents bolster Washington's already burgeoning résumé and recommend Tuskegee to benefactors, present and future.

4. Letters requesting Washington's participation in or presence at ceremonial functions such as the Atlanta Exposition, pub-

lic receptions in his honor, and the Harvard commencement
at which he received an honorary degree. Once again, these
documents fatten Washington's résumé; but more important,
they join the letters alluded to in the "Preface" in sustaining
the essential illusion that Washington is a modest Negro
whose mobility on the American landscape is, in effect, by
invitation and not by acts of aggression.

5. Two time schedules or itineraries which are, quite notably,
the final two documents in Washington's tale. The first is the
daily schedule at Tuskegee which regulates each student's
waking hours; the second is a newspaper clipping describing
the pell-mell pace of a typical evening when Washington is
out speaking, meeting, receiving, and generally pursuing his
lifework. Both documents confirm what many have described
to be *Up from Slavery*'s Franklinesque quality. More important, however, in terms of narrative strategies, they sustain Washington's effort to center his account steadfastly in
the present, up from slavery and out of the past. In sum,
they are of a piece with Washington's description, in his
"Preface," of how he found time to compose *Up from Slavery,* and thus they afford the narrative an additional measure
of symmetry in its opening and closure.

As different as these authenticating documents are, they share
two essential features. While they become voices in the tale, they do
not become characters in the tale, principally because they are en-
listed more for authenticating than for narrative purposes. Second,
while the documents validate Tuskegee as both idea and institution,
they also authenticate Washington himself—for him they are authenticating and self-authenticating texts. I am especially interested
in this latter feature not only because self-authentication may be as
sophisticated a narrative mode as autobiography, but also because,
in *Up from Slavery,* self-authentication is achieved at what seems to
be, morally and perhaps aesthetically, a very high price.

For example, while "the noted war correspondent" James
Creelman's New York *World* account of Washington's Atlanta address undoubtedly authenticates both speech and event, it does so
while perpetuating certain popular stereotypes of blacks—and indeed
resorts to clichés in describing Washington. The most offensive pas-

sage occurs when Creelman attempts to add a little sentiment and
"color" to his story: "A ragged ebony giant, squatted on the floor
in one of the aisles, watched the orator with burning eyes and tremulous face until the supreme burst of applause came, and then the
tears ran down his face. Most of the Negroes in the audience were
crying, perhaps without knowing just why." We needn't labor over
Creelman's opinion of the Negroes in the audience, or strain to
mine his attitude toward (or anxiety over) the responses of the white
women: "The fairest women of Georgia stood up and cheered. . . .
It was as if the orator [Washington] had bewitched them." Of Washington, Creelman writes that he is a "Negro Moses," a "tall tawny
Negro" with "heavy jaws, and strong, determined mouth, with big
white teeth, piercing eyes . . . bronzed neck . . . muscular right arm
. . . clenched brown fist . . . big feet . . . and dusky hand." The point
here is not so much that this language is cliché ridden or racist,
or even that it is, in its obvious similarities with the cant of popular
novelists such as Thomas Dixon, Jr., unquestionably of the culture of
the American 1890's. Rather, it is that Washington is willing to
display Creelman's account prominently, and thus to forsake any
notions of accurate or autobiographical portraiture in order to
achieve other rhetorical and narrative ends.

Obviously Washington wishes to authenticate his great triumph
in Atlanta, but is he pursuing other goals as well? What is more
important to him than autobiographical history? Or, to put it another
way, what *kind* of personal history may he most suitably render and
control by composing an authenticating text? Quintessentially, as I
have suggested before, an authenticating text not only edits and
manipulates ancillary texts, such as letters and newspaper accounts,
but also seeks to authenticate or at the very least complete—through
fulfilling itself—another text of grander scale and intention. This
idea goes far in illuminating the relationship between William Wells
Brown's "London" slave narrative of 1852 and his pseudo-novel,
Clotel, or between Richard Wright's "How Bigger Was Born" and
Native Son, and it tells us something about *Up from Slavery* as well.
To be sure, *Up from Slavery* is not directly appended to another
grander text, but historically and linguistically it bears an authenticating relationship to not one text, but two: Washington's own Atlanta Exposition address, and what I will term the text of the myth
of uplift. *Up from Slavery* authenticates Washington's greatest public

statement by contextualizing it not so much in cultural or autobiographical history as in the history of his increasingly personal control of the myth of uplift, for which his consummate authorial control in *Up from Slavery* is the supreme metaphor.

Authorial control of a narrative need not always result from an author's defeat of competing voices or usurpation of archetypes or pregeneric myths, but it is usually occasioned by such acts. What may distinguish one literary history or tradition from another is not the issue of whether such battles occur, but that of who is competing with whom and over what. In Afro-American letters, for example, while there are notable exceptions, the battle for authorial control has been more of a race ritual than a case of patricide. Author has been pitted against author, primarily to reenact the eighteenth- and nineteenth-century struggles between author and guarantor. The competition has rarely been between artist and artist for control of an image, line, or trope; rather, it has been between artist and authenticator (editor, publisher, guarantor, patron) for control of a fiction—usually, an idea of history or of the artist's personal history—that exists outside the artist's text and functions primarily as an antagonistic force with regard to that text's imaginative properties.

All this implies that there have been (until recently) few covering cherubs in the literary world with whom the Afro-American writer has had to do battle, and many who have impeded, in some extraliterary way, his or her achievement of text and voice. But this premise is not strictly true. The conflict is not a simple matter of author versus authenticator or literary compulsions versus extraliterary governors, since authenticating statements are almost always texts in their own right. The battle remains text versus text, and hence a literary conflict, even though the literary feature conjoining the texts is sometimes little more than a minimally shared content. The confusion inherent in this pattern of influence has probably been the chief obstacle before the Afro-American writer, and this fact has been recognized by the more astute writers and *littérateurs*. When Du Bois, for example, urges that a true self-consciousness must replace the Afro-American's seemingly innate double-consciousness, and when Ralph Ellison implies in *Invisible Man* that an artist must step outside the boundaries of what others call reality (an imposed fiction of history) in order to create, each is, I believe, championing an authorial posture beyond that which mistakenly attempts to control *two* texts—the author's and the one imposed. The author must also transcend those aspects of the influence pattern which separates form from content. The trap before the Afro-American writer—which develops inevitably from the predominant influence pattern in his literary tradition—is that his texts will never do more than challenge the *content* of the exterior authenticating texts surrounding them.

In creating *Up from Slavery,* Washington avoids all of the pitfalls just described; for this reason, if for no other, his book deserves a prominent position in Afro-American letters. But this is not to say that Washington deftly sidestepped the wars of influence altogether. On the contrary, his control of his text was indeed won from others, principally Frederick Douglass and Samuel Chapman Armstrong. In doing battle with the former, his struggle was more or less conventional in that it was primarily textual: Douglass's *Life and Times* (1882), the third of his autobiographical narratives, stands as a precursor text for *Up from Slavery,* as Washington himself acknowledges implicitly in *My Larger Education* (1911). In confronting the latter, Washington's struggle took a new turn: while Armstrong never wrote a text that is in any definitive way a precursor for *Up from Slavery,* he was, as an architect and custodian of the myth of uplift, founder of Hampton Institute (the prototype for Tuskegee), and, in Louis Harlan's phrase, Washington's "Great White Father," a model and force that Washington had to conquer in order to control his own personal history. While all this may suggest that the conflict with Douglass was textual while that with Armstrong was atextual, unfortunately the situation cannot be tidied up in this way. For Washington, Douglass is both an author of texts and a public idea to be supplanted; and Armstrong's myth of uplift *does* assume textual properties when one follows Roland Barthes's persuasive argument that a myth is not "an object, a concept, or an idea," but "a system of communication . . . a message . . . a mode of signification, a form." This latter point is hardly new or of my own devising: when Du Bois writes in *The Souls of Black Folk* of his concern over Washington's adoption of "the speech and thought of triumphant commercialism," he is acknowledging, I believe, the formal and linguistic properties of the uplift myth that Washington came to control in *Up from Slavery.*

As I have indicated, the conflict between Douglass and Washington is illuminated very well in one of Washington's last publications, *My Larger Education.* In a section entitled "The Intellectuals and the Boston Mob," Washington devotes several pages to what is, in effect, a retelling of his life story in response to Douglass the author, leader, and obstacle to his ultimate control of his lifework. Quite notably, the first references position Douglass as a force in Washington's personal quest for literacy and acknowledge the influence of a particular text:

> Even before I had learned to read books or newspapers, I remember hearing my mother and other coloured people in our part of the country speak about Frederick Douglass's wonderful life and achievements. I heard so much about Douglass when I was a boy that one of the reasons why I wanted to go to school and learn to read was that I might read for myself what he had written and said. In fact, one of the first books that I remember reading was his own story of his life, which Mr. Douglass published under the title of "My Life and Times." This book made a deep impression upon me, and I read it many times.

As his story continues, Washington unveils a fairly elaborate strategy for diminishing Douglass's influence—one which is in some sense both historiographic and linguistic. The immediate thrust of the strategy, to associate Douglass (and others) in public history with an unruly and unnamed pack of twentieth-century black figures intermittently calling themselves "The Intellectuals" or "The Talented Tenth," takes us far afield from *Up from Slavery* and into the subterranean workings of *My Larger Education.* But those phases of the strategy reported as aspects of Washington's life story have a direct bearing on how he wrote his greatest work.

One such phase is Washington's challenge to Douglass's posture as a reputed rare individual and leader. That challenge is implied by the assertion that he was one of many "prominent coloured men" whom Washington heard of when young, such as John M. Langston, Blanche K. Bruce, P. B. S. Pinchback, and John R. Lynch —in other words, another card in a small, unshuffled deck. (How Washington mentally engineers a leap from this "pack" to the Boston "Mob" should be all too obvious.) Another phase develops when Washington casually mentions his inherited methods of contextualizing, and hence controlling, the influence of the venom and vigor of these spokesmen's pronouncements: "learning something" about these men while under General Armstrong's tutelage at Hampton and, in the years shortly thereafter, inviting them all "to come to

Tuskegee and speak to our students and to the coloured people in our community." Still another phase—the one which led first to the Atlanta Exposition Address and then, a scant six years later, to an authenticating narrative for that address, *Up from Slavery*—comes about when Washington describes that point in his life when he decided to assume the mantle of spokesman by fashioning ahistorical and apolitical images of the present, grounded in the language and forms of the myth of uplift:

> As a matter of course, the speeches (as well as the writings) of most of these men were concerned for the most part with the past history, or with the present and future political problems, of the Negro race. Mr. Douglass's great life-work had been in the political agitation that led to the destruction of slavery. He had been the great defender of the race, and in the struggle to win from Congress and from the country at large the recognition of the Negro's rights as a man and a citizen he had played an important part. But the long and bitter political struggle in which he had engaged against slavery had not prepared Mr. Douglass to take up the equally difficult task of fitting the Negro for the opportunities and responsibilities of freedom. The same was true to a large extent of other Negro leaders. At the time when I met these men and heard them speak I was invariably impressed, though young and inexperienced, that there was something lacking in their public utterances. I felt that the millions of Negroes needed something more than to be reminded of their sufferings and of their political rights; that they needed to do something more than merely to defend themselves.

Washington's ambitions for his Atlanta address and, indeed, his own comprehension of the extent to which these ambitions were fulfilled, are tersely summarized in the paragraph appearing directly thereafter: "Frederick Douglass died in February, 1895. In September of the same year I delivered an address in Atlanta at the Cotton States Exposition."

Above and beyond whatever the Atlanta address meant to Washington personally, in the public eye it unquestionably thrust him into the leadership position created by Douglass's death—a posture in which Washington's desire (and, indeed, need) to assert his particular forms of history and language could only have intensified. Washington confides later in *My Larger Education* that "I was not a little embarrassed, when I first began to appear in public, to find myself continually referred to as 'The successor of Frederick Douglass,' " and adds, "Wherever I spoke—whether in the North or in the South—I found, thanks to the advertising I had received, that large audiences turned out to hear me." What he describes here is really a dilemma of influence brought on by the Atlanta address. This dilemma could only be resolved by writing an authenticating text that articulated the address's site in what was, for Washington, a public and yet secretly private history. In this way *Up from Slavery* was called into being. Most certainly, as Washington's definitive biographer, Louis R. Harlan, has suggested, it completes "the work of the Atlanta Compromise speech."

While there is little doubt that *Up from Slavery* fulfilled Washington's requirements, it is interesting to note that he also wrote a biography of Douglass for "The American Crisis Biographies" series, published in 1907. He almost lost the commission for the book to Du Bois—partly because he was tardy in replying to the publishing firm's invitation, and partly because at least one editor, Ellis Oberholtzer, felt that Washington should be assigned "some character" and period "that calls for less historical learning." Washington's biography is not seminal (Du Bois unquestionably would have produced a more scholarly study), but it did allow him one great personal triumph: the opportunity to impose a controlling fiction upon Douglass's entire life. In this way the biography, together with the Atlanta address and its authenticating text, *Up from Slavery,* represents the collective arsenal that Washington deployed in his quest for authorial control of his myth and life.

Although his outward reverence for Samuel Chapman Armstrong never would have allowed such language, Washington could easily have echoed his epitaphic remarks on Douglass and captured his response to Armstrong's death by writing: "Samuel Armstrong died in May, 1893. In September of 1895 I delivered an address in Atlanta at the Cotton States Exposition." Harlan has described the death of "the Fatherly Armstrong" as being "a liberation" for Washington, in the sense that he was now free to pursue new goals, new philanthropic sources, and to become "more of a 'race man.' " In terms of Washington's quest for control of the uplift myth, Armstrong's death was a liberation as well; however, the public *expression* of this liberation and quest for control was two full years away. Above and beyond whatever strategies the Atlanta address fulfilled against the Douglassonian school of race spokesmen obsessed with the past, it also aided Washington in his literal and figurative take-over of the uplift myth from Armstrong. After Atlanta, the myth was his not so much because he had succeeded Armstrong in the public's eye—indeed, the public declared that he had succeeded Douglass—but because Washington's Tuskegee, as an institution, idea, and perhaps even a metaphor, was now to dominate Armstrong's Hampton.

Harlan also remarks on how Washington emulated Armstrong's philosophy, demeanor, and mode of dress, but the parallels between Tuskegee and Hampton—which are, of course, physical and structural embodiments of the ideas these men held in common—are even more striking. The most interesting parallels are those which do not merely indicate mutual attention to education of the "hand and heart," but which show how both schools are in some sense rhetorical constructions and hence prefigurements of acts of language. One such parallel involves the naming of major buildings and, indeed, of the institutions themselves: Virginia Hall, Hampton Institute, Hampton, Virginia; Alabama Hall, Tuskegee Institute, Tuskegee, Alabama. In each case, the names are coded references to spatial relationships in the process of becoming rhetorical relationships and, hence, instruments of power. They reflect a shared philosophy and strategy of subtle yet binding commitments between school, town, state, and nation (and thus between the races) which Armstrong and Washington both carefully cultivated and eagerly exploited.

All this finally points to the fact that Tuskegee and Hampton are not merely parallel institutions, but nearly identical systems of signification. They are myths in the Barthesian sense of the term—which means in part (to paraphrase Barthes) that they are objects that have become a type of speech chosen by history. In this way, Tuskegee and Hampton are texts, most certainly of a cultural and quite probably of a literary variety; more specifically still, they are *names* for the *same* text, which, like the text itself, must be chosen by history in order for the one to dominate the other. When we speak of a Tuskegee philosophy of Negro uplift, or of a certain prominent black American being a Tuskegean, our language most specifically and radically bears witness to the extent to which Washington's control of the myth of uplift as a type of speech or text—occasioned, as I have argued, by his completion and hence control of the "work" (task and text) begun by the Atlanta address—is pervasive, even today. This is so because both the man and the myth, the author and what came to be *his* text, continue to authenticate each other.

Finally, what is extraordinary about *Up from Slavery* as an authenticating narrative is not that it established itself as the ascendant prototype for post-Reconstruction expressions of black life-stories (thus superseding and dominating similar texts, including, most notably for Washington, Douglass's *Life and My Times*), or that it helped establish Tuskegee in the public mind as the site, source, and name for the myth of uplift (thus liberating Washington from both Alma Mater and Great White Father). Rather, it forged in Afro-American letters a new idea of textual historicity. Part of this idea reflects Fernand Braudel's notion that historiography must study both discrete and sustained events (in his terms, *courtes durées* and *longues durées*) and express, thereby, what Claudio Guillén has called "the interplay of a number of durations." Tuskegee in particular develops, in *Up from Slavery,* as a historical event of multiple durations, once it becomes an act of language as well as a geo-cultural site in public history. Indeed, Tuskegee is of its historical time (as that is conventionally conceived), and transient *vis-à-vis* its time, in such a way that all future examinations of its varying postures as school, town, myth, coded cultural reference, and obsession for its most visible architect and custodian should necessarily be diachronic in conception and execution.

The other part of this new idea of textual historicity involves a fresh conception of how to compose personal history. Whereas the Frederick Douglass *Narrative* of 1845 shows how personal history is fashioned through the self becoming metaphor, Washington's narrative instructs that personal history may be created as well through immersing the self in an elaborately authenticated historical event. Washington's task is ultimately the harder one: how, indeed, does one illuminate a historical event so that it may be the equivalent of a metaphor in resonance, endurance, and other trans-temporal properties? The answer lies in what we have already discovered about Washington's positioning of Tuskegee in history: a historical event may be equivalent to a metaphor in rhetorical usefulness once it becomes, for author and audience alike, an act of language.

CHAPTER 3

The Quest of the Weary Traveler: W. E. B. Du Bois's *The Souls of Black Folk*

The Souls AS A GENERIC NARRATIVE

As I have suggested in earlier chapters, the study of how pregeneric and extrageneric Afro-American narratives are assembled, and of how Afro-American authors assume control of these assemblages, is unquestionably one of the most compelling tasks before the contemporary literary scholar. The importance of this activity lies very simply in the fact that it yields much of what we want to know about specific texts, as well as about the broad construction of Afro-American literary history. It is a scholarly endeavor that speaks directly to the major issues confronting anyone who seeks an integrated vision of literary tradition and transition, bound as one to the sweeping chronicle of cultural circumstance impinging upon art forms.

W. E. B. Du Bois's most inventive turn-of-the-century work, *The Souls of Black Folk,* provides a rich field of study in this regard. First, it is not merely an assembled text, but also an orchestrated one; second, the orchestrated materials are far more written, metaphorical, and archetypal than they are edited, prosaic, or documentary. Du Bois clarifies, in his own remarkable way, the distinction between a document (usually, an ancillary text brought into the central text) and documentation in process (most often, requisite documentation pursued through the transformation of data into metaphor). Indeed, as this chapter will suggest, Du Bois's effort to pursue documentation in process as a narrative goal is an abiding feature of *The Souls* that identifies it as a generic narrative.

The place to begin is with the text that never was. In 1900, when the Chicago publishing firm of A. C. McClurg & Co. invited Du Bois to submit a manuscript that collected his recent essays for *Atlantic Monthly* and other journals, he had already published three essays that would become, after varying degrees of revision, chapters of *The Souls*. By 1901 the number of chapters in progress had increased to eight. As Du Bois makes clear in one of his autobiographies, *Dusk of Dawn* (1940), he did not share A. C. McClurg's enthusiasm for the eight-essay volume "because books of essays almost always fall so flat." Nevertheless, he proceeded with the volume; it is essential for us to observe how he not only revised individual essays into chapters, but also transformed a collection of texts into an integrated narrative. Indeed, his mode of revision precipitates what is finally both a rhetorical posture and a strategy for greater authorial control of what is, in effect, not simply a single volume but a major portion of his canon up to that time.

Du Bois's revision of the "preliminary" text took three basic forms: the inclusion of prefatory quotations and, especially, of bars of song (which I will discuss later); the more completely realized development of a proudly self-conscious (as opposed to "double-conscienced") racial voice; and, most important, the addition of six new chapters—that is to say, five new pieces plus the chapter resulting from the substantial revision of an earlier essay, "The Negro As He Really Is" (1901), into two chapters. Although a catalog of all the textual revisions that collectively create the racial (and, indeed, heroic) voice in *The Souls* would be tedious and out of place here, a modest examination of the first chapter, "Of Our Spiritual Strivings," yields examples of the sort of revisions Du Bois carried out throughout the preliminary text.

To begin with, Du Bois's change of title from the original, more detached "Strivings of the Negro People" to the more personal and strident "Of Our Spiritual Strivings," in which the author's racial self-identification is not only more pronounced but also offered as a "given"—as something simply and profoundly understood by author and audience alike—is indicative of the new tone Du Bois sought while forging a book out of what he termed his earlier "fugitive essays." Other revisions of titles pursue a similar goal—"The Religion of the American Negro," for example, becomes, in *The Souls,* "Of the Faith of the Fathers"—while others still function more as agents for the historical overlay of the volume's narrative line ("The Freedmen's Bureau" becoming "Of the Dawn of Freedom"). But "Of Our Spiritual Strivings" is the single most important title revision, because it establishes the tone for the volume as a whole.

Within the first chapter, similar refashionings of old language into new, self-conscious, and more strident expressions are encountered again and again. Du Bois's interest in and longing for the harmonious posture beyond the discord of double-consciousness is underscored when, in his very first textual revision, he seemingly italicizes the phrase "self-consciousness" by expanding it to "true self-consciousness." Shortly thereafter he moves more quickly to his point—and desired tone—when he transforms "for he [the Negro] believes—foolishly, perhaps, but fervently—that Negro blood has yet a message for the world" to read, "for he knows that Negro blood has a message for the world." Another revision occasions an altogether new and, quite typically for Du Bois, romanticized expression of cultural and racial heritage. The original language reads,

> These powers of body and mind have in the past been so wasted and dispersed as to lose all effectiveness, and to seem like absence of all power, like weakness.

The new phrasing in *The Souls* is,

> These powers of body and mind have in the past been strangely wasted, dispersed, or forgotten. The shadow of a mighty Negro past flits through the tale of Ethiopia the Shadowy and of Egypt the Sphinx. Throughout history, the powers of single black men flash here and there like falling stars, and die sometimes before the world has rightly gauged their brightness. Here in America, in the few days since Emancipation, the black man's turning hither and thither in hesitant and doubtful striving has often made his very strength to lose effectiveness to seem like absence of power, like weakness.

In each case, Du Bois goes on to explain that "it is not weakness,

—it is the contradiction of double aims." But clearly in the second instance, far more than in the first, what precedes this explanation is a historical, cultural, and rhetorical contextualization of a racial dilemma which is, to a degree, a discrete model for Du Bois's extraordinary and nearly outrageous ambition to fashion a book that situates the soul of a race in space and time.

Other revisions of phrasing abound—by my count, more than twenty—but of these I will cite only two. The first involves a completely rewritten paragraph in which the most significant fresh language is the concluding sentence: "Nevertheless, out of the evil [of prejudice, slavery] came something good,—the more careful adjustment of education to real life, the clearer perception of the Negroes' social responsibilities, and the sobering realization of the meaning of progress." Besides providing the language for the new title of the fourth chapter ("Of the Meaning of Progress" appeared before as "The Negro Schoolmaster in the New South"), this passage sharpens Du Bois's focus not only on the trials and tribulations of his people, but also on their own responsibilities in the making of a better world. In this way Du Bois initiates the hortatory quality of *The Souls,* a quality which is unquestionably either absent or unfulfilled in the original essays and which is, in theory if not so much in practice, the feature of the volume which renders it as practical or useful a text as Washington's *Up from Slavery.*

The other revision is a simple yet well-calculated addendum that captures in a phrase the new spiritual thrust of the revised piece. Appearing as part of the triumphant, almost Wagnerian finale of the essay, the original sentence reads: "Freedom, too, the long-sought, we still seek,—the freedom of life and limb, the freedom to work and think." In *The Souls* Du Bois extends the final clause in an effort to express the inspirational and even ethereal heights for which his book is a rhetorical and narrative vehicle: "—the freedom of life and limb, the freedom to work and think, the freedom to love and aspire." What we see here is nothing less than the full blossoming of Du Bois's own rhetoric of Negro uplift, occasioned in large part by the publication of Washington's *Up from Slavery* in the period just before he revised his 1897 language for publication in *The Souls.* The original sentence is admirable but finally, one imagines, too much of an echo of Washington's rhetoric for Du Bois to abide. With the added phrase, "the freedom to love and aspire,"

Du Bois creates a more inspirational declaration while he clarifies how he wishes to revise and move beyond the rhetorical models
and implicit social policies of his most immediate precursor. In short,
Du Bois's revisions of his original language suggest the full-blown
strategy against Washington that emerges in *The Souls* as a whole.

As I have already suggested, not all of Du Bois's revisions
of what I am calling the preliminary text or "the text that would
have been" were textual or limited to the boundaries of the original
essays becoming chapters. He was also quite critical of the total
scheme and statement of the preliminary text, and he added to *The
Souls* almost as many chapters as he devised from earlier materials.
The revisions, intended to portray "the spiritual world" of a race,
were macrocosmic as well as microcosmic; we must note what Du
Bois felt was missing from his preliminary statement. It is apparent
that, drawing on his remarks in "The Forethought" to *The Souls,*
he saw most of his earlier essays as depictions of "the world of the
white man," by which he meant more specifically the travels and
travails of blacks in a white world, as well as the dialectics of race
ritual between a black and white world. The "white world" of *The
Souls*—in Du Bois's estimation, the first nine chapters—includes
the chapters on the Freedmen's Bureau, Booker T. Washington, the
geo-cultural symbolism of Atlanta, the Black Belt of Georgia, the
post-Reconstruction relations between "Master and Man," and the
autobiographical statements covering the years from his birth through
most of the 1890s. In turn, most of what Du Bois appends to the
preliminary text consists of those final five chapters which limn
the "deeper recesses" of a black world "within the Veil." The "black
world" of *The Souls* includes Du Bois's three portraits of "weary
travelers"—his son "torn away" in infancy, Alexander Crummell,
and an archetypal figure, John Jones—placed quite suggestively between vivid portraits of Afro-American church life and the abiding
presence of the Sorrow Songs.

Like his textual revisions of the original essays, Du Bois's
alterations of the preliminary text taken as a whole involve, in the
simplistic terms he encourages, a conjoining of a black spirit and
world to a white one. But this activity does not represent the whole
of his elaborate revision. A more appropriately detailed and layered
portrait of his strategies is afforded when we also examine what is
"old" within the "new" or "Veil" section of *The Souls* and, especially,
what is "new" within the "old" or "white world" section.

In the first instance, "Of the Faith of the Fathers" is the only previously published essay in the "Veil" section. It is central to the unit in that its study of "the Preacher, the Music, and the Frenzy" establishes the two dominant subjects of the four remaining chapters: the issue of Negro leadership as it derives from the singular prototype of the black preacher (cf. especially "Of Alexander Crummell" and "Of the Coming of John"), and the various modes of black spiritual expression (particularly Du Bois's prose elegy for his son, "Of the Passing of the First-Born," and "The Sorrow Songs"). Viewed in this way, the "new" section turns out to be not so new after all, primarily because it may be seen as a remarkable embellishment full of various narrative modes, voicing subjects and concerns which Du Bois first expressed in a Unitarian journal (*The New World*) in 1900. A compelling question here is why, of all his previous essays, Du Bois chose "The Religion of the American Negro" to be the catalyst for the "Veil" section of his book. Obviously a discussion of religious principles and practices directly impels further explorations of a race's spiritual world, but Du Bois has other intentions as well. The issue of leadership, especially as it had been implanted in Du Bois's mind by the example of Booker T. Washington, is the key here, I think—because the "Faith" initiates an implicit attack on Washington's brand of leadership and rhetoric that sustains Du Bois's explicit remarks in the "white world" chapters. In this sense, Du Bois's embellishment (which is a kind of revision) of "The Religion of the American Negro" provides not only the corpus of the "Veil" section, but also an enduring link between the major sections of his book. "Faith of the Fathers" is thus an encouraging phrase, suggesting beliefs and expectations in both a spiritual and a secular realm.

Given these discoveries in the "Veil" section of *The Souls,* there is every reason to suspect that what Du Bois added to the preliminary version of the "white world" section—which was, after all, the "book" he had in hand when A. C. McClurg wrote him in 1900—would be designed to embellish what was already there concerning the twin issues of race leadership and race spiritual expression. For the most part, this is precisely the case. Three chapters— "Of Mr. Booker T. Washington and Others" and the tandem pieces on the Black Belt, "Of The Black Belt" and "Of the Quest of the Golden Fleece"—represent essays so substantially rewritten that they might very well be described as new. Based upon a short yet pungent essay-review of *Up from Slavery* that Du Bois placed in the *Dial* in 1901, "Booker T. Washington" is six times the length of the original statement, which was significantly entitled "The Evolution of Negro Leadership." The tandem chapters on the Black Belt have less to do with issues of leadership and more with the inner spirit of the race, but this theme is pursued on a different note from that struck in the "Veil" section. Based upon a single essay, "The Negro As He Really Is," which is, as I will discuss later, Du Bois's un-intended contribution to turn-of-the century photojournalism, these chapters portray the inner spirit of a people as it is expressed by their physical lives and material well-being. Houses, land, crops, economic entanglements, the weight of the past, fleeting glimpses of the future—these are the texts Du Bois reads while attempting to gauge the psychic condition of black people in a white world. In sum, these radically rewritten essays revise what would have been the "white world" section (and, indeed, the original book) in that they transform Du Bois's previous critique of Washingtonian-ism into something far greater than a review of *Up from Slavery* (Washington's book is not even mentioned or alluded to in *The Souls*). They portray, more fully than ever before in Du Bois's writings, the creation and conditions of the Black Belt, for him a distinctly Afro-American development that is almost as extraordinary as the evolution of the black preacher. Du Bois is able to shape the "white world" section so that it offers the true variegated con-text or landscape in which the weary travelers of the "Veil" section, including finally Du Bois himself, will wander in search of a spiri-tual wholeness that is, in part, racially based.

There is one new essay in the "white world" section—new in the sense of not having been published in any form before. Bound rather tediously to the ancient myth of Atalanta, Hippomenes, and the golden apples, "Of the Wings of Atalanta" expresses Du Bois's fear that the Mammonism of the new South, as symbolized by the postwar prosperity of Atlanta, will soon engulf and corrupt the black race. The issue is not whether or not Du Bois's fear is justified, but why he chose to alter the "white world" section by placing this new essay within it. On one level, the answer is apparent: Atlanta, as an urban mecca in the new South pumped up with Yankee dol-lars and riddled with the contradictions of modernism, capitalism, and racism, *is* the *fin de siècle* American "white world"—or at least one of its most representative expressions. On another level, the answer is less apparent but involves, once again, Du Bois's intentions in revising *vis-à-vis* the issues of leadership, education, and Booker T. Washington. What "Atalanta" adds to the "white world" section is a depiction on various levels of a white cultural circle or ritual ground (Atlanta) that is, in Du Bois's geo-cultural vision of America, the defined space antithetical to the black ritual ground or Black Belt. Between these spatial antipodes lies the architectonic motif of the book. But of course, what develops here as well is an implicit juxtaposition of Du Bois's Atlanta with Washington's. Du Bois lived and worked in Atlanta at the turn of the century, and the western hill whereupon his classroom and study at Atlanta University were situated was, in some sense, his personal space; Washington never lived in Atlanta, but he came to possess a fair portion of its demi-myth, if not precisely its territory, through his 1895 Exposition Address. In sum, Atlanta serves in *The Souls* as both a sphere of cultural reference in opposition to that of the Black Belt, and as a battleground wherein Du Bois can struggle with the language and influence of a predecessor.

Thus far I have concentrated on the primary ways in which Du Bois revised the language, form, content, and tone of the "preliminary" text of *The Souls,* but I do not mean to suggest that he was exclusively about the business of strengthening and shaping the myriad parts of a literary work. Other concerns emerge, for example, when one examines the original text and context of "The Negro As He Really Is" (a 1901 essay that appeared in the journal *World's Work*), which, as mentioned, blossomed into two chapters upon revision for *The Souls*. The text provides fruitful information; one learns, for example, that the first sentence of "Of the Black Belt" and the last sentence of "Of the Quest for the Golden Fleece" are indeed the initial and concluding sentences of the original statement, and that Du Bois's extraordinary meditation at the Swamp and his rousing declaration, "If you wish to ride with me you must come into the 'Jim Crow Car,' " do not appear in the 1901 essay. But the context is of greater interest, chiefly because Du Bois apparently had so little authorial control of the environment in which his words saw print.

The heart of the matter is the series of photographs, or more precisely the captions, that accompany Du Bois's prose. Taken by one A. Radclyffe Dugmore, they are of a documentary sort, hardly the stuff of a Walker Evans or of the best work by Lewis Hine or James Van Der Zee, but serviceable and occasionally memorable, much like Jacob Riis's earliest portraits of New York's Lower East Side. Their subjects include women in the fields and behind the plow; men working at various crafts such as cobbling and broom-making; buildings, including the "big house" and, in the language of the captions, "Negro quarters," "Negro cottages," "a Negro school," "huts," "a typical Negro store," and a "log cabin home"; and scenes from a Saturday afternoon "in town." The offending photographs—"offending" in the sense that they, together, with their captions, wrestle with Du Bois's prose for authorial control of the text—are three in number. Two are portraits of frolicking children (none of whom look older than, say, nine or ten), and the other captures for posterity the remarkable face of an older black man whose hat and coat suggest that he has donned his best for the occasion.

What offends, and indeed assaults, is the fact that the photographs of the children at play are encaptioned "Learning to Shuffle Early" and "A Pickanninny Cake Walk," and the portrait of the man is paired with the following language:

A FRIEND OF GEORGE WASHINGTON
He believes that he was with Washington when the cherry tree was cut down and allowed his photograph to be taken only on condition that a copy would be sent to his old friend

One wonders who wrote these "light-hearted" epigrams. Dugmore? An editor at *World's Work?* Most certainly they are not from the pen of Du Bois. The issue here is not simply that the photographs (and, more particularly, their captions) do not "fit" the content of Du Bois's article, but more profoundly that they inaugurate a rhetoric, authorial posture, and mode of documentation at war (and, especially in American letters, an ancient war) with those fashioned by Du Bois. As a result, complete control of his own text is unavailable to Du Bois; indeed, insofar as there is always a considerable audience that "reads" the photographs and skims or ignores the text, a far different and essentially "white" interpretation of "The Negro As He Really Is" is the dominant impression of the article.

We should not be surprised, then, that in preparing a revision of "The Negro As He Really Is" for *The Souls,* Du Bois wrote and rewrote to the point that the piece became two chapters of the book. All of the new information, whether scientific or personal, is germane and often fascinating; one could argue persuasively that the article expanded simply because Du Bois wished to weave new data, anecdotes, and reminiscences in with the old. But there is also a distinct element of contextual purgation: in some sense, "The Negro As He Really Is" required purification, and that was to be achieved by Du Bois's revising it until it was once again his own expression. His revisions of the "preliminary" text involved textual reworkings, a near doubling of essays to be orchestrated into chapters, and the inculcation of a system of symbolic geography as well as of a new race-conscious and self-conscious tone; furthermore, they necessitated an immersion in private rituals for the reclamation of former texts and, in that sense, aspects of a former self. All these activities are integral parts of the story of how *The Souls* came to be.

Given all the parts and strands of *The Souls,* how may we describe the resulting narrative? What signals are being broadcast when, in "The Forethought," Du Bois quite purposefully terms his units "chapters" and not "essays"? To begin with, *The Souls* is an eclectic narrative of fourteen major texts, raised to the level of an integrated narrative because of Du Bois's authorial control of those texts. While Du Bois brings into his narrative a number of ancillary texts (notably, the phrases from the Sorrow Songs prefacing each chapter), none of these are composed by potentially competing voices such as those of most editors, publishers, and guarantors in slave narratives, and none are major texts to the degree assumed by each of the fourteen chapters. Like most integrated slave narratives, *The Souls* exhibits a narrative impulse toward yet another phase of narrative sophistication—a phase in which, as I have already mentioned, either the authenticating strategies dominate the tale, or the tale, which is generally the narrative manifestation of the author's personal history, dominates the authenticating strategies. The former development yields an authenticating narrative, and the latter a generic narrative; in the case of *The Souls,* Du Bois's impulse is unquestionably toward the creation of a generic narrative text. The ancillary texts employed within *The Souls,* together with the passages of explicit personal history, fashion the narrator as one of the narrative's archetypal "weary travelers" and, finally, as a black man of vision and voice. In this way *The Souls* strives energetically toward autobiography and yet, in a sense, bursts beyond it. The supreme fiction of a life generated by Du Bois's soaring model of uplift is most likely beyond his world—and ours.

A most fascinating aspect of Du Bois's construction is how authentication is pursued, achieved, and yet dominated by his tale. At the heart of his approach is a new way of thinking about documentary writing and about what constitutes authenticating evidence that we haven't encountered before. What Du Bois collects and weaves into the tapestry of *The Souls* are not so much documents (letters, testimonials, speech texts) as varying modes of formal writing, including historiography, autobiography, eulogy, and, in the instance of his "twice-told tale," fiction. Insofar as these various modes of writing may be distinguished—and the difficulty of the task testifies to the success of Du Bois's efforts at textual fusion and orchestration—they initiate discrete authenticating passages in *The Souls.* What is interesting here is not only the modes of writing that function in place of self-written or wholly "exterior" documentary texts, but also the types of evidence generated by the writings, to be subsumed within the single voice and rhetoric of the hero-narrator. Beyond the matter of voice, the bond between these various types of evidence is that they all are in some sense scholarly or authoritative. My use of the term "scholarly" is admittedly broad, for I refer here to both the investigative processes that confirm Du Bois's assertions and to something approximating a "scholarly" narrative mode or radical of presentation. Two brief comparisons will, I think, clarify this point.

In the slave narratives abundant with "exterior" texts usually written by white guarantors, and in *Up from Slavery,* the power of authentication attributed to these exterior texts often lies in the race and personage of the authenticator, rather than in the quality or quantity of firsthand experience, systematic thought, or empirical investigation that may exist behind his pronouncements. Even when the Detroit Liberty Association submits their brief for the veracity of Henry Bibb's account of his life, and has its authentication in turn verified by a local judge, one senses that within the rhetorical strategies of the narrative the success of their venture is as dependent on the amassing of white guarantors as upon whatever evidence they have assembled. The situation in *Up from Slavery* is more clear-cut: Creelman's effusive account of Washington's Exposition Address, complete with its discussion of the principal's physiognomy and feet and of "ragged ebony giants" crouching in the audience, is hardly an incisive, objective, or thoughtful appraisal. But that is not the issue: what matters in the narrative's scheme of authentication is that Mr. Creelman is a credentialed white reporter for a famous New York newspaper.

In the Afro-American narratives antedating *The Souls,* there is a sustained history of authentication based at least as much on race as on fact. When distilled, the goal of such authentications is usually the verification of the black author's existence, including, as a simple variation on a race ritual generated by slavery, the confirmation that "he was where he said he was." In *The Souls* Du Bois not only assumes the responsibilities for authenticating his voice and tale, but also advances a new scientific standard for what constitutes authenticating evidence. He seeks nothing less than a new narrative mode and form in which empirical evidence, scientifically gathered in a literal and figurative field (e.g., the Black Belt), performs the authenticating chores previously completed by white opinion.

The scholarly narrative posture or radical of presentation found in *The Souls* may be seen not merely as the appropriate posture accompanying Du Bois's standard for authenticating evidence, but as a direct response to the implicit (and most certainly public) deferential authorial posture necessitated, in previous narratives, by deferences of whatever intention to the real or mythic power of white authenticating voices. When Washington defines the period of Reconstruction or the phrase, "the black belt," and for strategical purposes inserts the words "I think," as if to suggest uncertainty or unfamiliarity, he makes room in his narrative for other authenticating voices in a way that is anathema to Du Bois. Du Bois wants that space for his own voice, his own array of narrative modes, his own arsenal of authenticating evidence whether it be empirical in scientific terms, or "twice-told" or archetypal in literary terms. He seeks to create an eclectic mode of self-initiated authentication in which exterior documents to be pieced into a tale are largely forsaken in favor of a scheme of documentation that reinforces the tale by becoming an integral part of the narration.

Du Bois's desire to fill *The Souls* with his own tremulous voice is one more indication that the volume is envisioned as a generic narrative. In terms I've used before, the narrator of *The Souls* is, like Frederick Douglass's narrator, both the primary participant and chief observer; thus any modulation between these two narrative postures or points of view is but another expression of the configured personal history that is the tale and of the full-ranging voice that is the narrator as articulate hero. Curiously enough, the kind of remarkable syncretic phrases binding past and present that heighten Douglass's authorial posture as both a participant and observer are strangely absent from *The Souls,* or at least are pursued in a different way. Du Bois's binding language is, temporally speaking, more horizontal than vertical. As we observe in the revision of the first chapter's title ("Of Our Spiritual Strivings") and in the famous Jim Crow car passage wherein the narrator remarks, "Of course this car is not so good as the other, but it is fairly clean and comfortable. The discomfort lies chiefly in the hearts of those four black men yonder —and in mine," Du Bois's efforts at binding or combining create expressions of a special unity between "we" and "I," "our" and "my," "theirs" and "mine," that is unquestionably central to the rhetorical and narrative strategies of *The Souls* and, quite likely, essential to Du Bois's personal sense of self. Only in writing of the Sorrow Songs does Du Bois pursue a syncretism of vertical and horizontal dimensions: "Even so is the hope that sang in the songs of my fathers well sung. . . . My children, my little children, are singing up to the sunshine. . . . " And of course this is most appropriate. The "I" of the Sorrow Songs is, as Du Bois knows, the quintessential, atemporal, Afro-American "we." The narrative voice that becomes one with that "we" has indeed achieved an affirmative posture against the nightmare and travels, weary but not forlorn, above the Veil. For this reason, and most likely this reason alone, Du Bois is quite comfortable with his device of deploying bars from the Sorrow Songs, which are the only "exterior" authenticating texts of any stature, throughout his text. Any sense we have of them competing with his prose for control of *The Souls* is defused in the final chapter, when Du Bois claims union with their eternal "we" by weaving them within his personal history.

However, syncretic language is hardly the only evidence of a narrator's posture as a participant-observer. Another and probably truer criterion is whether, in the course of the narrative, the distinction between modes of narration initiated by participation (ranging from pregeneric subjective accounts to generic autobiography) and those initiated by observation (ranging from pregeneric objective accounts to generic historiography) is, for all intents and purposes, obliterated. Such blurrings of the distinction transport us to unique narrative spaces such as those discovered in Douglass's *Narrative* and Du Bois's *The Souls,* and they also go far in determining the new generic constructions that underpin the literary tradition of which these texts are seminal expressions. In the case of these particular works, the blurring of participant and observer narrative modes creates, for narrative and rhetorical purposes, a narrator of a protean narrative which is an appropriate vehicle for portraying the soul of a man and of a race. The genre in which both Douglass and Du Bois seek and achieve fresh space is autobiography, not historiography, even though the participant-observer posture of their hero-narrators militates against any rigid segregation of the two.

The question before us is: What types of autobiographical statements are achieved by Douglass and by Du Bois? As his syncretic language suggests, Douglass creates himself in time, in history; insofar as his language (discrete passages as well as the narrative as a whole) constricts, distills, or convolutes historical time and event, historical self becomes, as Albert Stone suggests, historical metaphor. The metaphorical quality of the creation is the key here, for while the historiographical (observer) qualities of the self-portrait insure a requisite measure of representativeness (that is, Douglass as a representative former slave), the metaphorical (participatory in the special sense of being introspective) qualities are finally those which lift the narrative beyond representativeness to self-portraiture. Thus, in terms of its place in Afro-American literary history, Douglass's narrative of a historical self is truly a fresh expression. Once raised to the level of literary art, it does not enter into kinship with other previous texts as much as it establishes its own bloodline.

The narrative manifestations of personal history in *The Souls* evolve in a different way. Du Bois's self-portrait has its historical aspects; indeed, an arresting feature of *The Souls* is its construction of history (public and private) with the barest reference to chronology. However literary these achronological statements may be, they are the stuff of allusion and reference, and not of the refining narrative energies that yield metaphor. In *The Souls* these energies lie elsewhere, in Du Bois's sustained evocation of the spiritual world of a race. This evocation is the volume's narrative creation beyond historiography; thus Du Bois's fashioning of a self beyond history —beyond his posture in time as a representative product of a particular uplift myth—necessarily involves the assumption of a spiritual posture in a spiritual space. While the autobiographical impulses in Douglass's *Narrative* render metaphor, those in *The Souls* fashion archetype; Du Bois's posture beyond history is that of a cultural archetype within the Afro-American *temenos* or cultural circle. In terms of its place in Afro-American literary history, Du Bois's narrative of a cultural archetype is a historical event, in that it identifies existing cultural expressions and postures far more than it initiates new ones. But, more to the point, it is the first true narrative expression of a distinctly Afro-American cultural immersion ritual, and it is in this sense the precursor text for such major narratives as *The Autobiography of an Ex-Coloured Man* and Jean Toomer's *Cane*.

JOURNEY INTO THE BLACK BELT

Du Bois's journey in *The Souls* from infancy in the Berkshires of western Massachusetts to adulthood amid the western hills of Atlanta, complete with symbolic disembarkings in Tennessee, Philadelphia, and that part of the Black Belt surrounding Albany, Georgia, is not simply the story line of the volume but also the narrative manifestation of Du Bois's cultural immersion ritual. What is extraordinary and absolutely fresh about this ritual is that, in terms of its symbolic geography, it is a journey both to and into the South. In the previous Afro-American narratives, the other great journey South—beginning, I might add, from an area in New York nearly adjacent to the Berkshires—is found in Solomon Northup's *Twelve Years a Slave*. But as Northup's repeated allusions to fire, heat, thirst, delirium, torture, and captivity suggest, that journey is hardly an immersion in a source of culture and of what Du Bois would term "race-spirit"; rather, it is a descent into hell, the very pit of which is in the narrative an area rather fittingly called the Red River region. To a degree, Booker T. Washington's southern journey from boyhood in West Virginia to adulthood in Alabama (including his all-important "stopover" in Hampton, Virginia) fashions a symbolic geography in *Up from Slavery,* especially when one envisions Tuskegee as the grove of the grail within the nether reaches of the Black Belt and recalls as well Washington's famous refrain and charge, "Cast down your buckets where you are!" But in that narrative Tuskegee is neither a grove nor a city on the hill; the terrain is not, as Du Bois says of his landscape, "full of history"; and the Jim Crow cars shackled to the trains traversing this merely cartographical space are hardly transports of or for *communitas.* (Indeed, Washington is in the parlor car or smoker and has done his best to place Frederick Douglass amid the baggage!)

Prior to *The Souls,* the seminal journey in Afro-American narrative literature is unquestionably the journey north. In many narratives this perilous assertion of mobility after the assault of bondage assumes the properties of an ascension ritual, especially when the journey is a quest for literacy as well as for freedom. In this way the Douglass *Narrative* of 1845 is, I believe, the paradigmatic narrative of ascent, identifying the requisite features or tropes of any ritualized journeys or pilgrimages in Afro-American narratives, whether they be of ascent or of immersion. I am most interested in two of these features: symbolic geography, which is my extension of what Victor Turner has termed "ritual topography"; and the final posture of the hero-narrator *vis-à-vis* the rituals and ritual ground which he has discovered and, in a sense, defined through his travels.

To begin with, I should mention that my working definition of symbolic geography, in all its obvious indebtednesses to the ideas of Professor Turner, focuses on the idea that a landscape becomes symbolic in literature when it is a region in time and space offering spatial expressions of social structures and ritual grounds on the one hand, and of *communitas* and *genius loci* on the other. The distinction between the two pairings has to do quite simply with time: social structures and ritual grounds exist in time, while spatial expressions of *communitas* and *genius loci* are, as Turner says of *communitas* alone, "moments in and out of time." The social structure confronting the Afro-American hero-narrator and most often providing the point of departure for his ritualized journey is, in a word, slavery, even though a contemporary phrase such as "institutionalized racism" may better describe the more subtle structures besetting the modern pilgrims. What interests me is the fact, confirmed by the narrative literature, that the confining social structure (slavery) is not a fixed geographic or symbolic space; it is not quite simply and powerfully "Georgia" or "Mississippi" (even though Mississippi has come to have a certain popular resonance in this century) but, in its various dimensions and symbolic meanings, many states and regions, including that nebulous but universally known realm referred to as "downriver." In the case of both the ascension and the immersion narratives, a fair portion of the hero-narrator's journey is through differing manifestations of social structure expressed in spatial terms. Maryland, with its ports and vistas of the white sails of the Chesapeake, is a symbolic space different from the red-clay interior of Georgia or the green Kentucky bluffs from which freedom in Ohio can be imagined; Savannah, Atlanta, St. Louis, and New Orleans are all "slavery cities" but far different symbolic spaces, and the same is true for "free cities" like Boston, Philadelphia, and New York. Symbolic geography in Afro-American narratives emerges less as a Turnerian ritual topography—"a distribution in space of permanent sacred sites"—and more as a structural topography in which seemingly permanent (to the Afro-American) social structures manifest themselves as sites for locus-specific variations upon a nearly universal race ritual.

Ritual grounds are those specifically Afro-American spatial configurations within the structural topography that are, in varying ways, elaborate responses to social structure *in this world,* or, paraphrasing Ralph Ellison, what other men call reality. The slave quarters are, I think, the prototypical ritual ground, not only because they constituted the first space within social structure redefined in some measure by Afro-Americans, but also because they serve as a spatial expression of the tensions and contradictions besetting any reactionary social structure, aggressive or latent, subsumed by a dominant social structure. The grand tension is that of self-initiated mobility versus self-imposed confinement: ritual grounds such as the slave quarters, the Black Belt, recent depictions of Harlem as a symbolic space, and even Washington's Tuskegee offer the exhilarating prospect of community, protection, progress, learning, and a religious life while often birthing and even nurturing (usually unintentionally) a sense of enclosure that may reach claustrophobic proportions. In short, Afro-American ritual grounds are quite frequently, in the final analysis, spatial expressions within a structured topography of the "double life, with double thoughts, double duties, and double social classes" giving rise to "double words and double ideals" that characterize what Du Bois describes to be the Negro's burden of "double-consciousness."

Because I use *communitas* as Victor Turner employs the term, I ought to let him define it:

> . . . communitas tends to characterize relationships between those jointly undergoing ritual transition. The bonds of communitas are anti-structural in the sense that they are undifferentiated, egalitarian, direct, extant, nonrational, existential, I-Thou (in Feuerbach's and Buber's sense) relationships. Communitas is spontaneous, immediate, concrete—it is not shaped by norms, it is not institutionalized, it is not abstract. Communitas differs from the camaraderie found often in everyday life, which, though informal and egalitarian, still falls within the general domain of structure, which may include interaction rituals. Communitas . . . is *de la vie serieuse* . . . part of the "serious life." It tends to ignore, reverse, cut across, or occur outside of structural relationships. In human history, I [Turner] see a continuous tension between structure and communitas, at all levels of scale and complexity. Structure, or all that which holds people apart, defines their differences, and constrains their actions, is one pole in a charged field, for which the opposite pole is communitas, or anti-structure, the egalitarian "sentiment for humanity" . . . representing the desire for a total, unmediated relationship between person and person, a relationship which nevertheless does not submerge one in the other but safeguards their uniqueness in the very act of realizing their commonness. Communitas does not merge identities; it liberates them from conformity to general norms. . . .

In terms of symbolic geography, a spatial expression of *communitas* is not so much a reaction to social structure within a structural topography (that is, a ritual ground) as it is an autonomous, fresh space *in* time in that it is anti-structure (or, in the context of this discussion, antislavery and its residuals), and *outside* time in that it is a space and in some sense a vehicle for extra-structural relationships. In Afro-American narrative literature, the progression from "reaction to structure" to "anti-structure" is not so much a leap as a bond; a ritual ground and a spatial expression of *communitas* may often occupy the same space, but on different terms. Du Bois's configuration of the Black Belt is a prime example here, suggesting that spatial expressions of *communitas* are often the figurative dimensions of those literal spaces previously identified as ritual grounds. The Du Boisian model suggests as well that spatial expressions of *communitas* in Afro-American letters are far more group oriented than individual oriented. When Du Bois describes, in the first chapter of *The Souls,* his ideal of a culturally pluralistic America,

> Work, culture, liberty,—all these we need, not singly but together, not successively but together, each growing and aiding each, and all striving toward that vaster ideal that swims before the Negro people, of human brotherhood, gained through the unifying ideal of Race; the ideal of fostering and developing the traits and talents of the Negro, not in opposition to or contempt for other races, but rather in large conformity to the greater ideals of the American Republic, in order that some day on American soil two world-races may give each to each those characteristics both so sadly lack. . . .

he expresses a mode of *communitas* that is as much or more "We-They" or "We-You (plural)" as it is "I-Thou." In *The Souls,* Du Bois's valiant search for spatial expressions of *communitas* thus involves nothing less than his envisioning fresh spaces in which black and white Americans discover bonds beyond those generated by social-structured race rituals.

However, the figurative spaces in the "charged field" are not exclusively spatial expressions of interpersonal relations or *communitas.* In Afro-American narrative literature, one finds as well depictions of spirit of place or *genius loci,* in which, as Geoffrey Hartman has remarked, the "local integrities" or "imagery of the tribe are given bounding outline." Such spaces figure highly in cultural immersion rituals, since the "weary traveler's" perception of the *genius loci* is the goal of the immersion ritual, if not always the concluding point of the narrative. In fully realized systems of symbolic geography, spatial expressions of *genius loci* somehow stand alone as spaces unto themselves, even though as expressions of spirit of place they depict place (ritual grounds), and as expressions of "race-spirit" or "race-message" (Du Bois's terms) they provide the currency of exchange, as it were, within the realm of *communitas.* The challenge in realizing such a system is immense, and it is precisely the challenge which Du Bois undertakes in *The Souls.*

Given these definitions of the types of symbolic geography, we may briefly describe the "charged field" in *The Souls,* which Du Bois calls simply "the American soil." Structural topography is differentiated in the narrative, but not to the same degree or in the same ways as in many slave narratives. Unlike the Douglass narrative or that of William and Ellen Craft, there is no clear social structural distinction expressed in spatial terms between the various Atlantic coastal states and their ports or cities. Du Bois's journey south is, figuratively, a journey into the color red: red for the heat and blood of the War, red for the clay soil of Georgia, red for the deposed and dispossessed Indian, red for the relentless sun upon the plantation field, red for the spilt blood and enduring bloodlines of black brethren under assault. The structural topography of *The Souls* is thus strung between two poles, the green and shadowy hills of the Berkshires and the red dust "full of history" of the Black Belt. The best way to comprehend it is to look at what constitutes the structural topography of the North and that of the South.

In the narrative, the North is fashioned as a composite of Berkshire County (more specifically, "south county" along the Housatonic), Massachusetts, Philadelphia, and, to a lesser degree, New Hampshire and New York City. As a region, urban spaces and rural reaches merge to become, on the one hand, a private space for birthing (Du Bois, his son), burial (again, the son), and linkage with kin (the great-grandmother and her Sorrow Song handed down), and on the other hand a public arena in which black Americans, including most obviously Du Bois, Alexander Crummell, and the fictional John Jones, experience mobility, only to be confronted in turn by circumference. The race rituals invariably involve education and what Du Bois terms "The Kingdom of Culture." The confrontation between the hero-narrator and "newcomer" girl at school who will not accept his greeting card is a momentary stay against mobility in his own birthing ground; likewise, but far more violent and final, Alexander Crummell's school is torn from its perch atop New Hampshire soil when local farmers hear of his presence in the classroom. The mature hero-narrator, once credentialed as a scholar and in Philadelphia after having completed a major research project there, speaks to deaf ears of the work to be done in studying the sons of masters and men in the South; and John Jones, in flight from all the South represents to him in terms of claustrophobia and responsibilities, is borne aloft by the glorious sights and rhapsodic sounds of a Manhattan temple of high culture, only to be grounded by the burden and history of race. Du Bois's North is thus brightly green with hope, private memory, and a certain mobility, and yet be-shadowed, mottled, and green with an infection, the cure for which is immersion in the darker and yet more vivid hues of ritual ground.

Hence, we go South. South to Tennessee, Atlanta, and the anti-pode of Berkshire County, Massachusetts—Dougherty County, Geor-gia. Literally speaking, these regions no more sum up the South in all its configurations than the Berkshires, Philadelphia and New York comprise the North. But they are the South of the narrative, and to-gether they seem to reproduce the social structure delineated in the North—but in reverse. The confinement, constriction, and sense of circumference that northern blacks eventually encounter is southern blacks' daily fare; likewise, the Northerner's relative mobility is something that the Southerner may hope for, something he may achieve, perhaps by boarding a train, perhaps by going to town—as if this will perpetuate the motion, cheer, and sense of community previously known as the special world of Saturdays.

Ritual grounds in *The Souls* are all in the South, and the princi-pal ones are the Black Belt and Du Bois's own personal construction of Atlanta. The Black Belt is presented in two phases, representing constructions that are as psychological as they are topographical. The first phase, outlined in chapter IV of the narrative and also, but to a lesser degree, in chapter X, is the region Du Bois terms "Tennes-see—Beyond the Veil." Tennessee is the first phase because, while the landscape is blessed with hill and dale, river and stream, and is thus not unlike Du Bois's native land to the eye, it is at the same time "out in the country" and "far from home." For Du Bois, it is a new social space, a new response to structure:

> I have called my tiny community a world, and so its isolation made it; and yet there was among us but a half-awakened common con-sciousness, sprung from common joy and grief, at burial, birth, or wedding; from a common hardship in poverty, poor land, and low wages; and, above all, from the sight of the Veil that hung between us and Opportunity. All this caused us to think some thoughts to-gether; but these, when ripe for speech, were spoken in various languages.

This "half-awakened common consciousness" and inability to speak in common tongue is what finally defines Du Bois's Tennessee

hamlet as ritual ground. The blessing and curse of its isolation fore-
bode the rougher forms of fractured communities encountered once
the land turns flat and red to the south.

The second and final phase of the Black Belt is not only situated further south, but also characterized by ritual grounds found in
what is, for the hero-narrator, a horrific harmony with a strange
topography. To get there, he travels "Out of the North," south
through "crimson soil . . . stretching away bare and monotonous
right and left," and southward still, below Macon, until the Black
Belt appears in full relief as a "strange land of shadows." Having
heard the varied yet partial speech of a black Tennessee hamlet, he
is not surprised by the "faint and half-intelligible murmurs to the
world beyond" that accoutre this symbolic space; indeed, they an-
nounce, however dimly, that he has found the land he sought, a land
where a history can be read but a future can barely be expressed.

The ritual ground which Du Bois fashions chiefly for himself in Atlanta is clearly a response to the Black Belt and is, in that
sense, a topography of response to two social structures, not one.
The western hill upon which Atlanta University and, more to the
point, Du Bois's study are situated "speaks" in clear tones of many
things: the continuity in Du Bois's personal sense of time and
space between those western Massachusetts hills that are his birthing and burial ground, and his present condition; the link forged
in his mind between his Atlanta classroom and his first school-
house amid the hills of Tennessee; the distance, desired one imagines
for reasons involving more than scholarly detachment, from his personal space to the flat terrain and tone of the Black Belt; the heights
and ever-soaring aspirations of Du Bois's particular myth of uplift; the articulate and prophetic posture fashioned against the deaf-
ness and myopia of most of the American academy of his day; and
the distance from his hill in the City of a Hundred Hills to those
breasts of land that spew the thin milk of Mammon and triumphant
commercialism. The hill is Du Bois's "high Pisgah" above the
"dull red hideousness" of a structural topography that is racially
both black and white. But it is also a construction that abets self-
isolation: the "fresh young voices" singing the songs of the generations must well up from "caverns of brick and mortar below" in
order for "the sunshine trickling down the morning into these high
windows" to be filled with song. Surely, this is a circuitous route

to union with a race and culture! In Du Bois's defense, one can only say that the fact that he went on to attempt to fashion topographies of *communitas* and *genius loci* suggests that he could at least envision symbolic spaces in which such matters would be resolved.

Spatial expressions of communitas in *The Souls* are repeatedly sketched, but for the most part unrealized. As I have mentioned, Du Bois issues his first call for a truly plural American culture in the narrative's first chapter, "Of Our Spiritual Strivings." The previously quoted passage in which the call is made goes on to read:

> We the darker ones come even now not altogether empty-handed: there are to-day no truer exponents of the pure human spirit of the Declaration of Independence than the American Negroes; there is no true American music but the wild sweet melodies of the Negro slave; the American fairy tales and folk-lore are Indian and African; and, all in all, we black men seem the sole oasis of simple faith and reverence in a dusty desert of dollars and smartness. Will America be poorer if she replace her brutal dyspeptic blundering with light-hearted but determined Negro humility? or her coarse and cruel wit with loving jovial good-humor? or her vulgar music with the soul of the Sorrow Songs?

To the modern reader, Du Bois's formula for *communitas* is a bit simplistic; Afro-American music is more pervasive than ever, but the same is true of certain rituals along the color line. More to the point, here is the shape and sense of Du Bois's appeal. Each example dwells on what whites may learn or acquire from blacks; and just as the examples help establish Du Bois as a very particular kind of race-conscious and self-conscious narrator, they forge as well a central narrative strategy: the creation of the illusion that a journey of immersion into the "deeper recesses" of the Black Belt conducted by a group of blacks and whites alike will indeed be a moment in and out of time, an occasion of *communitas,* a "ritual transition" to a true America.

Du Bois picks up the threads of this strategy when he fashions the Jim Crow car passage in chapter VII, "Of the Black Belt," and I must offer it once more—this time in its entirety:

> But we must hasten on our journey. . . . If you wish to ride with me you must come into the "Jim Crow Car." There will be no objection, —already four other white men, and a little white girl with her nurse, are in there. Usually the races are mixed in there; but the white coach is all white. Of course this car is not so good as the

other, but it is fairly clean and comfortable. The discomfort lies chiefly in the hearts of those four black men yonder—and in mine.

The glory of the passage is Du Bois's transformation of a despised and imposed conveyance, employed rather ingeniously to inflict the stasis of social structure upon blacks in motion, into something of a ritual vehicle for *communitas.* One assumes that Du Bois envisions this railroad coach rolling into the heart of the Black Belt as being not unlike Melville's whaling vessel rolling upon the seas of the White Whale; each is mobile in a nearly cosmic geography, each has a leader, a captain, an articulator as self-designated hero, but each has the egalitarian spirit of individuals jointly undergoing ritual transition as well. Yet there is this considerable problem: is the Jim Crow car outside structure and, hence, an anti-structure? Can it ever be? The answer seems to be a negative one, since the vehicle is, as I suggested before, of a nefarious design for the perpetuation of structure in instances where structure of site or place cannot hold sway. One expects, then, a spatial image of destination not simply in the interior of the Black Belt (indeed, we receive this many times) but more profoundly in *communitas* itself. Unfortunately, such an image is not forthcoming.

We receive instead, in chapter IX, a veiled depiction of an "unbrotherly" convocation of scholars in the City of Brotherly Love, and, in chapter XIV, the aforementioned construction of Du Bois's personal space in Atlanta. Given the triple choice of shaping the narrative so that it ends within a spatial image of a plural American culture or American anti-structure, or of an anti-structure replete with its guide or priest or custodian, or of an articulate hero removed from anti-structure (even though he can envision it) and ensconced in a private yet discreetly fenestrated space, Du Bois quite obviously chose the last. The most persuasive explanation for this choice is that, for Du Bois, the development of a prophetic voice—a voice that can call for *communitas*—was either more consuming or more important a task than the development of a prophetic geography. While this is disappointing, we cannot finally fault Du Bois or his narrative strategy, since the development of such a voice provides him with his grand opportunity to authenticate himself as an articulator of his race's "race-message to the world." In this way the narrative eventually yields to its autobiographical impulses.

While spatial expressions of *communitas* are more or less un-fulfilled in *The Souls,* those of *genius loci*—"spirit of place," "local integrities," "imagery of the tribe"—are, if not wholly successful, much more complete. For Du Bois, expressions of *genius loci* are "race-messages," and, culturally and historically, the "race-messages" of Afro-Americans have manifested themselves in the lilt and imagery of the Sorrow Songs. Thus, when they occur in *The Souls,* spatial expressions of *genius loci* bind spirit of song to spirit of place. The only "problem" with this strategy is that it defines the Afro-Ameri-can *genius loci* more by charting its circumference or "bounding out-line" than by attempting to gauge its interior; as a result, circum-ference is sometimes mistaken for interior—which is to say, the songs are mistaken for *genius loci.* Du Bois usually escapes this error, but a host of subsequent Afro-American writers do not. In their work, mere reference to song masquerades as a literary render-ing of *genius loci.*

In *The Souls,* spirit of song bound to spirit of place receives spe-cific attention in the "Veil" section. There we are told of the music that, along with the Preacher and the Frenzy, characterizes a camp-ground revival meeting behind the Veil (which is a ritualized space within an Afro-American ritual ground). Furthermore, at the be-ginning of chapter XIV ("The Sorrow Songs"), Du Bois describes Nashville's Jubilee Hall in the following way:

> Then in after years when I came to Nashville I saw the great tem-ple builded of these songs towering over the pale city. To me Jubilee Hall seemed ever made of the songs themselves, and its bricks were red with the blood and dust of toil. Out of them rose for me morn-ing, noon, and night, bursts of wonderful melody, full of the voices of my brothers and sisters, full of the voices of the past.

This is the stuff of symbolic geography; Jubilee Hall is not so much a local building as it is a locus-specific structure. Especially through the reference to the bricks "red with the blood and dust of toil," land-scapes, histories, and "tribal" images merge into a single construc-tion. To *see* Jubilee Hall is to know why the Sorrow Songs are alternately called Jubilee Songs, and to glimpse the Afro-American *genius loci.*

If the campground and Jubilee Hall represent the first two phases of Du Bois's spatial expression of *genius loci,* then the por-trait of his private realm in Atlanta is a third and final phase. In

"The Sorrow Songs," which is the "Veil" chapter where we see Du Bois's Atlanta best, language such as the following echoes and virtually reproduces his first chapter's call for a plural American culture: "Little of beauty has America given the world save the rude grandeur God himself stamped on her bosom. . . . And so by fateful chance the Negro folk-song—the rhythmic cry of the slave—stands to-day not simply as the sole American music, but as the most beautiful expression of human experience born this side the seas." The effect is that the first and final chapters share a specific subject and its accompanying language; in turn, the private landscapes the hero-narrator inhabits in each chapter figuratively blend to become a new space of grander construction. On one level, the new space ranges from the hills of Berkshire County, Massachusetts, to those of Atlanta, Georgia; on another, it is the "modal" stretch of racial memory, shared and private, occasioned by the Sorrow Songs. In the final chapter each wisp of song prefacing one of the narrative's chapters is identified as a bar or two from a "master" Sorrow Song. Thus, in a certain sense, each major text of the narrative is a literary improvisation upon a master trope of *genius loci,* a response to an essential call, a local topography subsumed by a "tribal" geography. These expressions plus those new mappings of Afro-American space mentioned above constitute the fullest dimensions of the geography of *genius loci* in *The Souls.*

Despite its majestic and hermetic appearance, this rendering of *genius loci* geography is not without its patches and seams. In the first place, Du Bois's effort to impose what is, in effect, a national identity upon Afro-America by locating its *genius loci* upon a broad expanse of American soil is not totally successful, partly because he cannot overcome the fact that what is national about Afro-America is that it is without dominion, and mostly because other aspects of his strategy militate against his vision. Although his portraits of local structures in space and time, such as Jubilee Hall and the campground revival, are persuasive, it is difficult to accept the same structure writ large. Du Bois does not sufficiently contextualize his "national" structure in a global landscape wherein national traits may be perceived as "local integrities." Furthermore, one never really gets over the fact that, even when the literal landscape from Massachusetts to Georgia becomes a figurative space, it is still *Du Bois's* space, the arena in which he fashions *his* life. If we ask whether Du Bois's composition of tribal space is indeed tribal, we can only reply with assurance that it is tribal *for him*. On one hand, Du Bois cannot be faulted: tribal images and "race-messages" must be tethered to a symbolic geography, and so he constructs one based on what he has experienced, imagined, and seen. But on the other he must be scored, since once again, as the final symbolic space of the narrative instructs, his autobiographical impulses dominate to the point where certain other narrative strategies are left undone, or perhaps done in.

My reference to the final symbolic space in *The Souls* brings me to the other topic of this discussion, Du Bois's final posture *vis-à-vis* the Black Belt. This becomes an issue when we realize that, despite all the narrative energies that have been directed toward fashioning a narrative of cultural immersion in an Afro-American ritual ground (the Black Belt), the hero-narrator's final positioning is elsewhere, in Atlanta, in what may be a ritual ground of only a private sort. What does this final posture signal? Is it meant to suggest a final phase to the immersion journey, and hence an affirming of Du Bois's personal ritual into Race? Or is it a new development, a removal, an act of distancing if not outright rejection? It is clear, I think, that Du Bois intends a positive and affirmative conclusion, but that his construction of a private ritual ground as a spatial expression of self- and race-consciousness conflicts to a degree with his intentions.

At base, the journey is a grand statement and majestic scheme. First, there is the descent south through topographies of social structure from Massachusetts to Tennessee. There Afro-American ritual grounds (Josie's hamlet, the campground revival) are first encountered and assayed. Then the journey continues southward still, and east, through additional regions of social structure until the land turns flat and red as one descends to that capitol of capital, Atlanta. On southward and now westward, travel continues in the Jim Crow car—dull with filth, yet bright with the hope of *communitas* envisioned in this world—down to the city of Albany, county of Dougherty, the courtyard of King Cotton, the heartland of the Black Belt. When Du Bois alights from the train at Albany and hires a buggy so that he might penetrate the backroads, the journey into the Black Belt enters its southernmost phase. Fittingly enough, the most distant point of his circular journey out from Albany is marked in space and time by a symbolic structure:

It seemed quite a village. As it came nearer and nearer, however, the aspect changed: the buildings were rotten, the bricks were falling out, the mills were silent, and the store was closed. Only in the cabins appeared now and then a bit of lazy life. I could imagine the place under some weird spell, and was half-minded to search out the princess. An old ragged black man, honest, simple, and improvident, told us the tale. The wizard of the North—the Capitalist —had rushed down in the seventies to woo this coy dark soil. He bought a square mile or more, and for a time the field-hands sang, the gins groaned, and the mills buzzed. Then came a change. The agent's son embezzled the funds and ran off with them. Then the agent himself disappeared. Finally the new agent stole even the books, and the company in wrath closed its business and its houses, refused to sell, and let houses and furniture and machinery rust and rot. So the Waters-Loring plantation was stilled by the spell of dishonesty, and stands like some gaunt rebuke to a scarred land.

The saga of this plantation is not without interest, but what is more compelling is Du Bois's seemingly unintended dismantling of certain plantation "myths." Coming as it does at the height of the "plantation tradition" in *fin de siècle* popular literature—and here it is useful to recall that *The Souls* was reviewed in the *Dial* along with Thomas Dixon, Jr.'s *The Leopard's Spots* under the heading, "The Case for the Negro"—this language provides what Du Bois liked to call "an unvarnished tale" of the postbellum South. Living in what remains of the slave quarters, the Negroes may be "ragged" and "improvident," but they are not the "wizards" who, flushed with Mammon's fever, cast the "spell of dishonesty" upon the land. Likewise, the black elder who intones this saga of florescence and fall is not a happy "uncle" going about the business of entertaining "massa's" children. To be sure, his tale is in some measure about creatures and briar patches; but his posture as a storyteller sustains certain traditions we have come to associate with the African *griot*. Although he is in this way a kind of priest or custodian of history and culture, he is not portrayed in any "varnished" way: he is as ragged, honest, simple, improvident, poor, and probably as dispirited as anyone else bound to that "scarred" space.

Contact with the "silent scene" of the Waters-Loring plantation ends Du Bois's journey south. When he writes, "somehow that plantation ended our day's journey," we sense that he has seen enough of the South's structural topography, and even of those Afro-American ritual grounds assembled in response to social structure, to last him a good while. Thus the journey north to Atlanta and a private space begins, first, through the southwest and northwest sectors of the county—the heart of the "Egypt of the Confederacy" represented spatially by the Swamp—back to Albany, then across southern and northern terrains to the City of Brotherly Love, where, in chapter IX, Du Bois delivers his plea to fellow scholars (white, to a man) to engage in "a conscientious study of the phenomena of race-contact," and finally on to Atlanta and to his study, where, bound to his race by bloodline, "tribal" song, and the passions of scholarship, Du Bois will indeed pursue the work he has just called for.

Of the many features to this final posture, which is clearly intended as a final phase and thus an integral part of the journey into the Black Belt, three interest me principally because they bear directly on how we read other, central narrative texts. To begin with, Du Bois's positioning of himself in his Atlanta University study contrasts sharply with whatever image we may have of Booker T. Washington ensconced in his office at Tuskegee. On one level, Du Bois achieves an implicit confirmation and summation of all his narrative has urged in terms of a philosophy of higher education (in contrast to Washington's vocationalism), including, one feels, the distinction between a university scholar and an institute principal. On another level, the contrast seems to involve certain literary and extraliterary notions of closure: according to Du Bois, a journey of immersion into the Black Belt must end on "higher ground," not in the establishment of what is, in effect, a cultural outpost. That Washington would of course argue a contrary view (and perhaps cry once again but with fresh meaning, "Cast down your buckets where you are") tells us much about the content *and* form of each man's narrative.

The second feature concerns immersion as well, but here the contrasting text is Jean Toomer's *Cane.* In *Cane,* immersion in the Black Belt seems at times to be a goal unto itself. Some of the most resonant passages occur when the narrator or persona *sees* the symbolic space, complete with its wisps of smoke, blood-burning moon, cane fields, cotton fields, train lines, and goat paths back to Africa. As Du Bois writes in chapter VII of the trip home from the Waters-Loring plantation, the sensory aspects of the Black Belt are also wonderful, but not consuming:

> Somehow that plantation ended our day's journey; for I could not shake off the influence of that silent scene. Back toward town we

glided, past the straight and thread-like pines, past a dark tree-dotted pond where the air was heavy with a dead sweet perfume. White slenderlegged curlews flitted by us, and the garnet blooms of the cotton looked gay against the green and purple stalks. A peasant girl was hoeing in the field, white-turbaned and black-limbed. All this we saw, but the spell [of dishonesty, of the Waters-Loring plantation] still lay upon us.

Du Bois sees the world of *Cane* but embraces the call from a different realm of his imagination. The resulting contrast between the near-fatal stasis of the voice in *Cane,* occasioned by the particular form of his immersion journey—recall here especially his cry from the pit of Halsey's shop, "But its th soul of me that needs th risin" —and Du Bois's final posture on "higher ground" in *The Souls* is a key not only to both narratives, but also to how the journey into the Black Belt has figured in the shaping of Afro-American literary history. Between the antipodes of soullessness and soulfulness erected by these two texts lies the space in which most other twentieth-century Afro-American "journey" narratives may be found.

While it is useful to contrast the final posture of Du Bois's hero-narrator with those of Washington's and Toomer's voices, the exercise doesn't suggest nearly enough of what Du Bois inaugurated in Afro-American letters. If I may call the journey into the Black Belt a "hibernation ritual" and describe Du Bois's hero's state of self- and race-consciousness as a "post-apprenticeship" or "post-hibernation" posture, then the kinship between Du Bois's "weary traveler" and Ralph Ellison's Invisible Man becomes ringingly clear. Of course, the Invisible Man's "higher ground" is a hole—clearly, a revision of Toomer's hero's shop pit, among other images —but then there is the music, the spirit of song bound to the spirit of place. Through these texts we know even better than before that "What Did I Do to Be so Black and Blue" is linked modally to the Sorrow Songs wafting up to Du Bois's study.

Truly, this formidable construction is spun not of gossamer, but of iron. Yet there are weaknesses, imperfections, if not precisely gaping holes and splitting seams. Why is the dead son buried in the North amid hills the hero will never live in again, far from the site so elaborately constructed for a lifework? Is "family" a sufficient reason, given the "national" dimensions Du Bois assigns to the Afro-American *genius loci?* When Du Bois places himself in his Atlanta study, especially after the Philadelphia episode, is he there more as a scholar in quest of his field of research, or more as a man rejoining kith and kin? What is desired is some blend of the two, and Du Bois seeks that blend by fashioning himself as one of the weary travelers. One senses, however (possibly because he *is* a weary traveler), that the study bathed in sunshine and song is a structure at once too perfect and too fragile—that it will not last. But perhaps this is only proper. If, as Ellison's hero remarks, "a hibernation is a covert preparation for a more overt action," then the fragility of Du Bois's final construction is nothing but an expression of encouragement for his hero to travel on.

BOOKER T. WASHINGTON'S LITERARY OFFENSES

While it has become a nearly myopic and certainly consuming custom to speak of Du Bois, Washington, and their differences in political terms alone, their literary differences are also considerable. Indeed, in *The Souls of Black Folk* one may see Du Bois's response to what he might have termed, ever mindful of Mark Twain's elegant barbeque of James Fenimore Cooper, the literary offenses of Booker T. Washington. In *The Souls,* Du Bois's response usually manifests itself in one of two ways: in expressions of "unvarnished" truths that counter those "dangerous half-truths" which Washington promulgated most effectively, or in the creation of larger, more sustained constructions that challenge not only what *Up from Slavery* shows to be Washington's abiding idea of narrative, but also the "speech and thought of triumphant commercialism" of which Washington was the turn-of-the-century black spokesman. In either case, we observe Du Bois wrestling with issues of Washington's influence. However, since he and Washington sought to write radically different types of narratives, our study of their literary rivalry must admit that questions of influence are not always those of intertextuality, or that "influence" need not always refer to an event in literary history wherein an antecedent text—here, *Up from Slavery*—fills and dominates an artistic space. For Du Bois, Washington's posture as the author of *Up from Slavery* is but one manifestation of his posture as a race spokesman; likewise, his literary influence is but a part of what appeared to be his outward or public indifference toward his culture's on-going quest for language and literacy. Thus, our working definition of influence in this instance must be at least as large as Du Bois's conception of the dilemma Washington presents, and, thereby must also be a construction that focuses more on a predecessor's control of language at large than on his control of language in text.

The "unvarnished truths" that Du Bois fashions are the most limited weapons in his strategy against Washington, partly because they come in direct response to phrases, passages, and motifs in *Up from Slavery,* and partly because they are rarely metaphors or conceits unto themselves. However, they do have a distinct place in the inner workings of *The Souls,* and of the many examples I would like to mention briefly five. In "Of Our Spiritual Strivings," for instance, Du Bois writes of the double-consciousness that plagues black Americans, and he includes as a pointed example the plight of the artisan: "The double-aimed struggle of the black artisan—on the one hand to escape white contempt for a nation of mere hewers of wood and drawers of water, and on the other hand to plough and nail and dig for a poverty-stricken horde—could only result in making him a poor craftsman, for he had but a half a heart in either cause. . . . " Here, Du Bois is making a concerted effort to demystify Washington's black construction of the archetypal American yeoman, a figure who is, of course, a primary "product" of Washington's vocationalism and myth of uplift. Insofar as remarks such as these augur Du Bois's probings into the inner or spiritual life of black folk, whether on the level of the "mass" or that of the "throbbing human soul," they initiate a central motif in *The Souls* which, taken as a whole, is a sustained response to Washington's language and text.

Another central motif is inaugurated when, in writing of the "bright ideals of the past," Du Bois revises a familiar Washingtonian bromide, "education of the hand, head, and heart," to read, "the training of brains and the training of hands." This subtle shift deftly opens up Washington's phrase so that it may refer to both the Negro college or university and to vocational schools. This kind of counterstatement is sustained later on in *The Souls,* when Du Bois repeatedly contextualizes Hampton or Tuskegee within the broad scheme of higher education for Negroes—"Fisk, Atlanta, Howard, and Hampton were founded in these days," i.e., the Reconstruction period—and reminds his readership that

> Colored college-bred men have worked side by side with white college graduates at Hampton; almost from the beginning the backbone of Tuskegee's teaching force has been formed of graduates

from Fisk and Atlanta. And today the institute is filled with college graduates, from the energetic wife of the principal [i.e., Washington's third wife, Margaret James Murray] down to the teacher of agriculture, including nearly half of the executive council and a majority of the heads of departments.

Given these remarks, it seems inevitable that Du Bois will respond to Washington's famous, mocking portrait in *Up from Slavery* of a black youth exploring a French grammar, delivering at least a shot or dig if not precisely an "unvarnished truth." This he does in the chapter on Washington when he writes: "And so thoroughly did he [Washington] learn the speech and thought of triumphant commercialism, and the ideals of material prosperity, that the picture of a lone black boy poring over a French grammar amid the weeds and dirt of a neglected home soon seemed to him the acme of absurdities. One wonders what Socrates and St. Francis of Assisi would say to this." Du Bois is incensed about Washington's posture toward language and, most likely, the issue of race *and* language. The partial truth confronted here involves a narrow idea of education, mobility, and literacy and a skewed conception of race leadership as it is bound, in an Afro-American context, to race spokesmanship. For this reason Du Bois refuses in other passages to sustain the popular opinion (put forth by James Creelman, among others) that Washington is the Moses of his people. Washington's posture as a leader must be acknowledged; however, to suggest that he led or is leading his people out of slavery in a New World Egypt, or that he, like Moses, is privy to the Word and hence a law-giver and a prototypic articulator is, for Du Bois, in the face of history and within the sound of Washington's veiled tongue, to go much too far. In his moment of greatest praise for the good principal, Du Bois endorses him as a successor and not an originator, as a "Joshua called of God and of man to lead the headless host." Contained within this praise is a pointed criticism, for Joshua led the Israelites into Canaan and brought them to the very den of great temptations and false gods, including Mammon, the arch-culprit in Du Bois's scheme, that high priest of "the dusty desert of dollars and smartness." In this way, certain seemingly random rhetorical features in *The Souls* begin to complement and fit with each other, like pieces in an elaborate puzzle. If Washington is indeed a Joshua and Atlanta is the city of Mammon, then the national space which Washington comes to control through his triumphant Atlanta Exposition Address is, for Du Bois, a literal and figurative Canaan infested with more problems than promises. But we must remind ourselves that this construction is both a criticism and a strategy. By assigning Washington to a troubled realm devoid of visionary language, Du Bois creates fresh space for his own narrative and, more precisely, for his ambitious construction of a personal prophetic voice.

Most of the examples given above are like verbal drops on the stone of Washington's text: they methodically wear away at particular phrases, passages, and terms, but they are hardly the stuff of a concentrated strategy against Washington's literary offenses. We get closer to a strategy when we observe Du Bois's sustained responses to Washington's treatment of what Raymond Williams calls, in another context, "key words." How an author employs certain terms that possess "tribal" or "local" stature and meaning, and thus are in some sense coded cultural references, will often tell us much about his posture *vis-à-vis* his audience, his inherited cultural and artistic traditions, and language itself. The "key words" I have in mind here are "slave quarters," "big house," "Reconstruction," "Black Belt," and "Jim Crow car." Like any literate reader of *Up from Slavery,* Du Bois doubtless observed that Washington's public tongue and resulting authorial posture repeatedly combine to obliterate the figurative properties and cultural resonances that, especially for Afro-Americans, shine forth from each of these impacted terms. To be sure, Washington offers modest definitions—the "slave quarters" are "the part of the plantation where the slaves had their cabins"; the "big house" is what "the master's house was called"; the "Black Belt" is variously "a part of the country . . . distinguished by the colour of the soil . . . the part of the South where the slaves were most profitable . . . the counties where the black people outnumber the white" —but these very definitions and what they suggest of Washington, the articulate race spokesman, are the issue. Du Bois's efforts to unvarnish Washington's simple yet successful mystifications of charged terms are attempts to renew what may be the "tribal," "local," cultural, and even historical referents contained within that language. Thus Du Bois contextualizes the slave quarters and big house within the literal and figurative space of the Black Belt, creating arresting images and spatial constructions of slaves huts still occupied and big houses tattered and abandoned, of the Waters-Loring plantation with its faint traces of parks, promenades, fields, and mills, of the big house on the brim of the Swamp near a road built by black chain gangs while they were surrounded by gnarled trees red, Du Bois imagines, with the blood of African and Indian dead. To understand this scene Du Bois tells us we must study Reconstruction, not in Washington's public terms of "the craze for Greek and Latin learning" and "the desire to hold office," but with a sense of the experiment that was the Freedmen's Bureau and with a vision of how and why former slaves could sing, amid the promise and the poverty, "My Lord What a Morning." And to arrive at this scene we must ride in the Jim Crow car. It is all one extraordinary image, all of a piece. Du Bois's sustained construction of this image through the rejuvenation of key words is probably the heart of his strategy for both exposing and liberating himself from the soulless double-tongue that forms Washington's public speech.

At the risk of suggesting further indebtedness to Professor Williams, I must point out that Du Bois also fashioned a sustained response to Washington's rhetoric concerning the perennial tension between country and city. This is no idle or subjective matter in either book; each man's veiled and explicit pronouncements convey his opinions on such issues as burgeoning capitalism, the revitalization of the South, labor, foreign immigration, black mobility and migration, and the era's blossoming nostalgia for what was supposedly a golden age when America had been not simply an agrarian but a pastoral realm. Portraits and opinions of country and city life in *Up from Slavery* and *The Souls* inform us of Washington's and Du Bois's public stances toward their era's unorganized yet potent counter-Reconstruction movement, and suggest how each man fashioned, and hence positioned, his text *vis-à-vis* the popular literary expressions of nostalgia authored by black (e.g., Paul Laurence Dunbar) and white (e.g., Thomas Nelson Page) writers alike.

Ever mindful of his monied public, who lived mostly in the urban North yet possessed country houses and country dreams, Washington in *Up from Slavery* takes care to vilify the city and extol the virtues of the soil. When he reaches Richmond while en route to Hampton for the first time, he describes his poverty and exhaustion, adding, "I had never been in a large city, and this rather added to my misery." He portrays Washington, D.C., where he briefly attended a Baptist seminary, as a bastion of superficiality and folly—as a place where "a large proportion" of "coloured people . . . had been drawn . . . because they felt that they could lead a life of ease there." Additional well-calculated remarks allow Washington not only to chastise further the urban black who has forsaken the South (thus drying up the well for those celebrated cast-down buckets), but also to assure certain readers of his position regarding improvidence amongst blacks, black officeholders, and federal "stewardship" of the race:

> I saw young coloured men who were not earning more than four dollars a week spend two dollars or more for a buggy on Sunday to ride up and down Pennsylvania Avenue. . . . I saw other young men who received seventy-five or one hundred dollars per month from the Government, who were in debt at the end of every month. I saw men who but a few months previous were members of Congress, then without employment and in poverty. Among a large class there seemed to be a dependence upon the Government for every conceivable thing. The members of this class had little ambition to create a position for themselves, but wanted the Federal officials to create one for them.

The sight of all this degradation in even the nation's capital occasions Washington's most effusive praise of the countryside:

> How many times I wished then, and have often wished since, that by some power of magic I might remove the great bulk of these people into the country districts and plant them upon the soil, upon the solid and never deceptive foundation of Mother Nature, where all nations and races that have ever succeeded have gotten their start—a start that at first may be slow and toilsome, but one that nevertheless is real.

The virtues of the country are extolled, but so are the tenets of Washington's myth of uplift. In a typical effort to placate both North and South, Washington lodges his complaints about urban life against both a former capital of the Confederacy (Richmond) and the Union's capital, but such precautions are finally unnecessary. For Washington and most of his readership, the country and the city are nonspecific geographies, except in the all-important sense that the country is essentially the South and the city is either in the North or an expression of northern values, systems, and spatial relationships besmirching the southern countryside.

Du Bois's attack on these sentiments focuses mainly on what he would have termed Washington's "varnished" portrait of the country and, in particular, the Black Belt. While sustaining Washington's opinion that "coloured people" in the South may be ignorant but generally not "degraded and weakened" in body "by vices such as are common to the lower class of people [black and white] in the larger cities," he amends this "partial truth" by describing, more precisely than Washington dares, the physical conditions in which southern black folk live:

> The size and arrangements of a people's homes are no unfair index of their condition. . . . All over the face of the land is the one-room cabin,—now staring at the dusty road, now rising dark and sombre amid the green of the cotton-fields. It is nearly always old and bare, built of rough boards, and neither plastered nor ceiled. Light and ventilation are supplied by the simple door and by the square hole in the wall with its wooden shutter. There is no glass, porch, or ornamentation without. Within is a fireplace, black and smoky, and usually unsteady with age. A bed or two, a table, a wooden chest, and a few chairs compose the furniture; while a stray showbill or a newspaper makes up the decorations for the walls. Now and then one may find such a cabin kept scrupulously neat, with merry steaming fireplace and hospitable door; but the majority are dirty and dilapidated, smelling of eating and sleeping, poorly ventilated, and anything but homes.

The glory of this description lies not so much in its nearly photographic attention to detail as in its insistent contextualization of fact. The spatial dynamics between cabin and road, cabin and field, and, perhaps most important, cabin and Big House place these structures in symbolic space and in a history bristling with motive, burden, aspiration, cause and effect. The fragile gaiety of a "stray show-bill" reminds us that even amid travail there are bright moments of pleasure, amusement, and trips to town (to Memphis or Montgomery, perhaps; not just to the county seat). The very idea of a newspaper tacked to a rough dark wall is not only true to life but, in this context, a poignant reminder of the Afro-American quest for literacy. It is difficult to envision a lithograph, daguerreotype, photograph, embroidered homily or other wall decoration that better expresses the dawn of freedom.

More to the point is Du Bois's implicit contention that many aspects of the national exaltation of the country are, quite simply, specious:

> Above all, the cabins are crowded. We have come to associate

crowding with homes in cities almost exclusively. This is primarily because we have so little accurate knowledge of country life. Here in Dougherty county one may find families of eight and ten occupying one or two rooms, and for every ten rooms of house accommodation for the Negroes there are twenty-five persons. The worst tenement abominations of New York do not have above twenty-two persons for every ten rooms. Of course, one small, close room in a city, without a yard, is in many respects worse than the larger single country room. In other respects it is better; it has glass windows, a decent chimney, and a trustworthy floor. The single great advantage of the Negro peasant is that he may spend most of his life outside his hovel, in the open fields.

What Du Bois leaves out here, and yet includes elsewhere in the Black Belt chapters, is some suggestion of how life in the "open fields" is of a piece with life in what are usually the remains of slave quarters; burdens, frustrations, and, above all, a nearly debilitating sense of enclosure or confinement are properties shared by these interior and exterior spaces. Although he inspects the Black Belt with the same keen eye that other observers of the era, such as Jacob Riis, brought to bear on urban ghettos, Du Bois goes a step further than those investigators: by comparing the conditions in which poor and struggling people actually live, North and South, city and soil, he links those conditions, fashioning what is finally an expression of a national dilemma. Needless to say, we have here in dim outline a vision that will inform Du Bois's politics in later years, for it takes only another brief look to see Mammon and one of his henchmen, the Wizard of the North, squatting in the tawdry shadows of tenements and cabins alike. In the context of *The Souls,* however, two things are very clear: Du Bois's exposé of urban and rural conditions supports his view that the South is as much a field for social scientific study as is the North; it also discredits the popular urban/rural distinctions that Washington publicly endorsed as an essentially false spatial expression of America's condition. For Du Bois, the issue is not the country versus the city but, as he explains many times, the problem of the color line.

While the color line is rendered and inspected continually in *The Souls,* Du Bois's discussion of it in "Of the Sons of Master and Man" is most appropriately mentioned here, partly because it chronicles the persistence of the line as blacks and whites moved into the twentieth century and into town, and partly because it sustains his demythologizing of the country and city. Both aspects of the

discussion appear in his remarks on the physical dwellings and neigh-
borhoods wherein reside the sons of master and man:

> It is usually possible to draw in nearly every southern community
> a physical color-line on the map, on the one side of which whites
> dwell and on the other Negroes. The winding and intricacy of the
> geographical color line varies, of course, in different communities.
> I know some towns where a straight line drawn through the middle
> of the main street separates nine-tenths of the whites from nine-
> tenths of the blacks. In other towns the older settlement of whites
> has been encircled by a broad band of blacks; in still other cases
> little settlements or nuclei of blacks have sprung up amid surround-
> ing whites. Usually in cities each street has its distinctive color,
> and . . . in the country something of this segregation is manifest in
> the smaller areas, and of course in the larger phenomena of the
> Black Belt.

These comments help initiate the grand theme, in modern Afro-
American letters, of what Ralph Ellison calls "invisibility." To be
sure, Du Bois rides his own particular hobby horse when he com-
plains that "the best of the whites and the best of the Negroes almost
never live in anything like close proximity," and that "both whites
and blacks see commonly the worst of each other"; he virtually abets
the national nostalgia for an agrarian, antebellum America by lamenting, "Nothing has come to replace that finer sympathy and love
between some masters and house servants which the radical and
more uncompromising drawing of the color-line in recent years has
caused almost completely to disappear." By when this latent elitism
is cast aside, it is clear that at the heart of his remarks is another
call for a culturally plural community or nation, one beyond the
geography of race ritual of either the country-city or the color-line
construction. There must be a "social going down to the people,"
a "generous acknowledgement of a common humanity and a common
destiny." For this reason—and with, I am sure, a clear sense of the
symbolic geography he has charted, as well as of the place of song
in that scheme—Du Bois concludes the chapter and indeed the
"white world" section of *The Souls* with the lines:

> "That mind and soul according well,
> May make one music as before,
> But vaster."

It is fitting to end this discussion of *The Souls* with a brief
inspection of Du Bois's rendering of the color line, for, in truth,

the color line manifests itself in every aspect of the narrative and is the barrier against which every feature of his narrative and rhetorical strategy strains. The "preliminary text" of *The Souls* was massively revised so that the "deeper recesses" of the "black-side" of the line might be fully seen. The immersion journey is initiated so that blacks may perceive their "race-message" to the world; Du Bois hopes whites might comprehend it as well, so that together, above the color line or Veil, they may forge a new community "in large conformity to the greater ideals of the American Republic." The narrative's symbolic geography is, above all, a remarkable expression of how Afro-Americans have persistently constructed real and imagined dominions, responding to spatial expressions of oppressing social structures which are always configurations and manifestations of the color line. Du Bois's response to Washington involves the line as well, since Washington's apparent adoption of "the speech and thought of triumphant commercialism" may be readily perceived as his public acquiescence to a national rhetoric that embalms the status quo with the oils of progress and what Walter Lippmann would later call "the acids of modernity." In sum, while the subject of *The Souls* is "the spiritual world in which ten thousand thousand Americans live and strive," the subject cannot be explored without continual reference to the color line which, in its literal, figurative, and spatial expressions, is the most persistent and yet debilitating bond between master and man and their near and distant kin.

The Souls is not a social scientific study or the verbal tracings of a muckraker; rather, it is a book of prophecy. In the narrative, data become metaphor, rough winds become melodious songs, swamps occasion meditations, and, through art, Du Bois may place his life and voice amid his culture's pantheon of named and nameless articulate heroes. While it can be said that all this marvelous activity comes in response to the relative prosaicness of Washington's authenticating narrative, such a statement doesn't begin to say enough about Du Bois's compulsion to *write*. *The Souls* is an act of private love and enthusiasm, made public through its author's genuine awe of the word.

PART TWO

The
Response

CHAPTER **4**

Lost in a Quest:
James Weldon Johnson's
The Autobiography of
an Ex-Coloured Man

I sat amazed. I had been turning classic music
into rag-time, a comparatively easy task; and
this man had taken rag-time and made it classic.
The thought came across me like a flash—It can
be done, why can't I do it? From that moment
my mind was made up. I clearly saw the way of
carrying out the ambition I had formed when
a boy.
> —James Weldon Johnson,
> *The Autobiography*
> *of an Ex-Coloured Man*

A friend told me
He'd risen above jazz.
I leave him there.
> —Michael S. Harper, "Alone"

By the time our journey through Afro-American narrative literature arrives at Johnson's *The Autobiography of an Ex-Coloured
Man,* first published anonymously in 1912, several assumptions about
the literature are presumed as given. One is that we have entered a
zone called the modern era or modernism, which means of course
that *The Autobiography* is a modern or modernistic text. Another
is that the term "narrative" has run its course in Afro-American letters and is now obsolete. The implication here is that *The Autobiography,* in part because it is a "modern text," either fits an established generic category—historiography, autobiography, or the novel
—or doesn't exist. The third assumption, which in effect rescues the
reader from the horns of the dilemma posed by the second, is that
there *is* something we can assuredly call an Afro-American novel,
and that by Johnson's time it had existed and prospered for at least

sixty years since William Wells Brown completed *Clotel; or, The President's Daughter.* The net effect of these assumptions is that, without bothering to fashion a working definition of literary modernism *in Afro-American letters* (can even one such definition be found in the critical canon?), and without recourse to what Geoffrey Hartman would call the "historical consciousness" of Afro-American narrative forms, *The Autobiography* is conventionally and routinely delivered unto us as a "modern novel," or, more boldly, as a "modern Afro-American novel." In retrospect, the only thing more extraordinary than this conception and delivery is the deliberate nurturing that has been bestowed upon this illusionary child.

In the course of this discussion of *The Autobiography,* and of my subsequent commentaries on texts by Richard Wright and Ralph Ellison, I remain ever mindful of Paul de Man's effective warning that "the question of modernity could . . . be asked of any literature at any time, contemporaneous or not." I will generally avoid using terms such as "modern," "modernism," and "modernity"; however, when such terms are employed, they will refer to a contour in Afro-American literary history that is characterized by textual events which revoice their antecedent narratives, or, in terms closer to the Afro-American *genius loci,* which *respond* to the post-textual *call* of those antedating texts. "Novel" is a more difficult term to establish in a fresh way, partly because it is so encrusted with nebulous definitions and partly because, if we take its etymology seriously, we cannot help being genuinely agitated by the question, "What *is* new?" In the case of *The Autobiography* (and *Invisible Man,* and possibly *Black Boy*) no discerning reader can call the book a novel and in the same breath agree that *Clotel* is also a novel. *The Autobiography* and *Clotel* are textual events of differing orders and differing degrees of newness. Like *Clotel* in its indebtedness to antislavery writings, *The Autobiography* identifies and collects from antedating texts—notably *Up from Slavery* and *The Souls of Black Folk,* but also the slave narratives—those key tropes which form the Afro-American literary tradition. In this way both texts are, as literary events, watersheds in literary history; and insofar as watersheds represent something new, they are new. However, *The Autobiography* differs from *Clotel* in that while *Clotel* is, as Jean Yellin has shown, little more than an anthology of borrowed expressions, *The Autobiography* attempts fresh renderings of its collected tropes in a work independent of an authenticating text. This suggests that *The Autobiography* is a generic narrative far more than it is a primary or ancillary text in an authenticating construction; indeed, that suggestion is bolstered when we recognize that *The Autobiography* is, like the Douglass and Du Bois narratives, a coherent expression of personalized response to systems of signification and symbolic geography occasioned by social structure. Yet when we recall the complete arc of the generic canonical story, culminating so magnificently and so hopefully with literal and figurative expressions of voice, literacy, bloodline, mobility, and personal space within racial-communal space achieved, we realize that Johnson has fashioned a narrative different from those of Douglass and Du Bois. What is telling here is that the Ex-Coloured Man's inability to create and assume a heroic or communal voice is predicated, for the most part, upon his adoption of the public language of a different narrative tradition: namely, that of the authenticating narrative initiated by certain slave narratives, and sophisticated almost singlehandedly by Washington's *Up from Slavery*. *The Autobiography* is at very least a synthesis of (and hence a watershed in) Afro-American narrative history, in that it fuses aspects of authenticating rhetoric to aspects of generic narrative form.

Here one could stop and ask whether this synthesis and all such syntheses create novels—but to do so is to run the twofold risk of fashioning yet another nebulous definition of the novel, and of ignoring the harder question of whether Johnson's text generates narrative energies that propel it beyond synthesis into a new narrative realm. At the end of this chapter I will attempt an answer to this question, but first I must suggest in what ways *The Autobiography* is a literary event.

INDEBTEDNESSES

Since the grand dialectic in *The Autobiography* binds multiple expressions of mobility to multiple expressions of confinement, it is no surprise that certain features of the text are rooted in slave narrative tropes and conventions. In some instances tropes and conventions are simply borrowed; in others—and this is where Johnson begins to fashion something new—aspects of slave narratives are not so much borrowed as improvised upon, much as the Ex-Coloured Man syncopates and "rags" Mendelssohn's "Wedding March." Perhaps the most notable borrowing from the slave narratives is the device of the authenticating preface, written in this instance by Johnson's publisher, Sherman, French and Co., and signed somewhat cryptically (but in capital letters) "THE PUBLISHERS." In slave narratives such prefaces conventionally affirm the former slave's authorship of his tale, make some effort to verify facts within that tale, and, insofar as they mount their own documented indictment of slavery's injustices, compete with the former slave's tale—his personal history—for control of the narrative as a whole. While *The Autobiography*'s "Preface" does not sustain all of these activities, it is nevertheless an authenticating text that seeks to position the tale's narrator in society and to shape the reader's opinion of his story. For example, the startling absence of any commentary about the author may be a rhetorical silence that abets the persona's own well-calculated omissions; it may even be an ingenious stratagem supporting his final posture as "an ordinarily successful white man who has made a little money." (The implication is that, unlike an *ex-slave,* an *ex-coloured man* may thrive without the alms of authorial verification.) But the overwhelming effect of the Ex-Coloured Man's lack of a history, place, name, or referential pronoun in the "Preface" to his life story is that he is portrayed less as a human being than as a fact, or, to borrow language from the "Preface," an integer within an "unascertainable number." Since the focus of the "Preface" is removed from the author, it falls on the reader and what he may "glimpse," "view," and be "initiated" into while reading *The Autobiography*. Predictably enough, despite the Ex-Coloured Man's mobility in both a black and a white world, the publisher is emphatically clear in stating that *all* such glimpses, bird's eye views, and initiations are of or into the black world. Indeed, according to the publisher, the glory of *The Autobiography* is its "composite and proportionate presentation of the entire [Negro] race." At very least, these gentle words to the reader seem to pursue two ancient strategies: to ignore, undercut, or render aberrant the narrative's glimpses, views, and opinions of the white world, while sustaining the integrity and even the social posture of the publisher *vis-à-vis* the tale's author in a manner commonly found in what I've previously called an eclectic or phase-one slave narrative. The "Preface" puts the Ex-Coloured Man in his place by acknowledging his mobility in two worlds, but authenticating the clarity of his vision in only one.

The final touches to this strategy are provided by the most peculiar feature of the "Preface"—its indebtednesses to Du Bois's *The Souls of Black Folk*. That Johnson is struggling with the example of *The Souls* while composing *The Autobiography* is, as I will discuss later, manifest almost to the point of embarrassment. That is to be expected, partly because *The Souls* saw print just four years before Johnson began work on his narrative, but mostly because *The Souls* is a seminal text in Afro-American letters. However, as the following language confirms, the author of the "Preface" (the publisher, if indeed not Johnson himself) cannot perform his task without echoing Du Bois as well:

> It is very likely that the Negroes of the United States have a fairly correct idea of what the white people of the country think of them, for that opinion has for a long time been and is still being constantly stated; but they are themselves more or less a sphinx to the whites. It is curiously interesting and even vitally important to know what are the thoughts of ten millions of them concerning the people among whom they live. In these pages it is as though a veil had been drawn aside: the reader is given a view of the inner life of the Negro in America, is initiated into the freemasonry, as it were, of the race.

For the most part, this is the heart of Du Bois's "The Forethought" in *The Souls*—"Leaving, then, the world of the white man, I have stepped within the Veil, raising it that you may view faintly its deeper recesses"—recast in a public rhetoric for matters of race most commonly assigned to the tactical genius of Booker T. Washington. While I doubt that this rather accurate expression of *The Autobiography*'s narrative and rhetorical indebtednesses is an *intended* dimension of the "Preface," it must be there for reasons related to the conscious and unconscious strategies confining the Ex-Coloured Man to his place. Since, for the average reader, the Washingtonian rhetoric unquestionably dominates the Du Boisian allusions, I judge that the strategy here is to create a rhetorical signal assuring that the Ex-Coloured Man, *as* an Ex-Coloured Man, and even as an Ex-Coloured Man thinking Coloured Thoughts, is nevertheless a Coloured Man of "proper spirit." The absurdity of the strategy is matched by that of the conditions creating it—and that is another, albeit a lesser, legacy of the slave narrative canon.

The other legacies appear in the tale itself, and are employed mostly to establish the layers of irony that pervade the text. One such legacy is suggested by the houses where the persona and his mother reside in both Georgia and Connecticut. Although he supposedly has only a "faint recollection" of it, the Ex-Coloured Man describes the Georgia dwelling in some detail:

> I can see in this half vision a little house—I am quite sure it was not a large one—I can remember that flowers grew in the front yard, and that around each bed of flowers was a hedge of vari-coloured glass bottles stuck in the ground neck down. I remember that once, while playing round in the sand, I became curious to know whether or not the bottles grew as the flowers did, and I proceeded to dig them up to find out; the investigation brought me a terrific spanking, which indelibly fixed the incident in my mind.

As the description continues, the focus remains upon exterior features—what is "behind the house," what is "back from the house," what delightful things "grew along the edge of the fence." Given these features, and certain well-calculated references to the "endless territory" of the vegetable garden, sumptuous blackberries, and the "patient cow," it is clear that the narrator is trying to convince the reader that the predominant qualities of this birthplace are pastoral and idyllic. However, this torrent of nearly rhapsodic pastoralism, which adumbrates many later passages in which romantic music is employed to buffer personal assault, must be contextualized in the passage as a *response* to the Ex-Coloured Man's aforementioned *initial* memory—of digging up the glass bottles and his subsequent "terrific" whipping.

As Robert Farris Thompson, the historian of African art, has explained to me, the "planting" of multicolored glass bottles, like the careful positioning of light-giving or light-reflecting objects such as mirrors and automobile headlamps in tombstones in southern black cemeteries, is unquestionably an example of what we've come to call, perhaps too glibly, an African survival in the New World. These objects express the "flash of the spirit," the "spirit embedded in glitter"; they "rephrase" the African (and more specifically, in many instances, Kongo) custom of "inserting mirrors into the walls or pillars of tombs" and of "displaying a mirror embedded in the abdomen" of statues "as a sign of mystic vision." To be sure, the front yard of the Ex-Coloured Man's first home is not a burial ground, but is a ritual space in that it is the place of his birth—a spatial expression of community into which he is born. When the Ex-Coloured

Man digs up the bottles—ironically, in order to "know whether or not the bottles grew as the flowers did"—he performs an innocent yet devastating act of assault upon a considerable portion of his heritage. That act prefigures his misdirected attempts to approach, let alone embrace, black American culture, including most obviously his desire to render the "old Southern songs" in "classical form." Such acts, in Thompson's articulation of African values, are "experiments with form at the expense of community." Little wonder, then, that the narrator's mother, in this first of several occasions where she postures as a custodian of those aspects of black culture confronting her son, spanked him so hard that the incident became "indelibly fixed" in his mind.

Unfortunately, while the Ex-Coloured Man remembers the event, he appears, in the course of the narrative, not to have learned from it—or, to put it another way, not to have read or comprehended its semiological meaning. Never do we sense that he knows, finally, *why* he was spanked; and he performs virtually the same transgression against black cultural and spiritual forms when he returns from Europe to uproot the old songs for what are, in effect, experimental purposes. Predictably enough, this second uprooting leads to another "terrific spanking"—namely, the psychological whipping he receives from witnessing the "nigger burning." While in the second instance he retreats to New York City, which is as much the City of Mammon for *The Autobiography* as Atlanta is for Du Bois's *The Souls of Black Folk,* the first instance of transgression, or at least the Ex-Coloured Man's depiction of it, occasions his removal to the interior spaces of the cottages, first in Georgia then in Connecticut, where he and his mother live. Despite the extraordinary mobility upon an international landscape (a mobility which is prompted by his racially ambiguous appearance, facility with several languages, and ease of gaining employment), the Ex-Coloured Man grows distrustful of open spaces, particularly in their American and southern configurations. Instead, he is confident of himself and his abilities only in strictly defined interiors such as parlors, clubs, and drawing rooms; there, usually by means of his musical abilities, he can at least initially control the socially required personal relationships by presenting himself as a man of talent.

All this helps explain why he is most exhilarated by Paris in general and by its outdoor cafés in particular. To be sure, the Ex-Coloured Man portrays Parisians (in contrast to Americans) as being relatively free from race prejudice, but that old bromide hardly does justice to the complexity of his feelings or his situation. Paris is the one landscape he roams without experiencing racial assault (the exception being his encounter with his white father and half-sister at the Opera—but that is an American dilemma brought to Europe). The outdoor cafés represent an exquisite commingling of exterior and interior space; that milieu allows him the excitement of exploring an outdoor territory while controlling, or at least experiencing an illusion of control of, a discrete social setting. The Ex-Coloured Man's love of Paris and its amphibious spaces partially explains his relative ease in Manhattan: for him, as for others, New York is a city of interior spaces. Perhaps because it is an island, even its out-of-doors is more a boundaried space within the reach of benign and malignant human orchestration than it is an "endless territory," especially of the prototypical American persuasion.

But we mustn't lose sight of the similarity between the Ex-Coloured Man's initial retreat into the interiors of his boyhood cottages—from which he seems to emerge only for school, music lessons, and duets of one sort or another with radiant young women—and his final flight to New York. If New York, in all its multiple expressions of gambling, intemperance, and violent miscegenetic relations, is Mammon's city, then the narrator's boyhood homes, replete with the jingle and flash of his absent white father's lucre amid the thick pall of his black mother's woeful circumstance, is Mammon's natal lair. What the narrator recalls most vividly from his Georgia home's interior are those transient accoutrements, those flashes and gleams of shined leather and polished gold, that came and went as his father billowed into and out of his and his mother's lives. These gleaming *objets materiel* stand in bold and horrific relief as Mammon fetishes, when compared to the spirit-in-glitter phrased and rephrased by the multicolored bottles implanted in the yard. Clearly, the Ex-Coloured Man has made a choice when, upon leaving his Georgia birthplace, he accepts his father's gift of a ten-dollar gold piece that is fashioned to a string around his young neck. Despite the obvious allusions here to collars, shackles, and nooses, the Ex-Coloured Man's sole remark (in retrospect, from what we wish to assume is a posture of wisdom and maturity) is: "I have worn that gold piece around my neck the greater part of my life, and still possess it, but more than once I have wished that some other way had been found of attaching it to me besides putting a hole through it."

By the time the Ex-Coloured Man and his mother arrive in Connecticut, his alienation from landscapes (occasioned, one assumes, partly by the terrible spanking in Georgia and partly by his mother's overprotectiveness in the face of her circumstances) is so complete that he can only describe his new home in terms of its interior furnishings: "My mother and I lived together in a little cottage which seemed to me to be fitted up almost luxuriously; there were horse-hair covered chairs in the parlour, and a little square piano; there was a stairway with red carpet on it leading to a half second story; there were pictures on the walls, and a few books in a glass-doored case." Later, after the narrator's father visits the cottage and is overwhelmed by his son's renderings of rhapsodic melodies, this lovely domicile is graced by a new piano of considerable tone and worth. Of this event the narrator remarks, presumably with his Mammon fetish still fast about his neck, "there momentarily crossed my mind a feeling of disappointment that the piano was not a grand." Although he attempts to soften this with a line of pious rhetoric—"The new instrument greatly increased the pleasure of my hours of study and practice at home"—the damage is done. We know that, even in retrospect, the Ex-Coloured Man has not yet comprehended or "read" the events of his personal past.

I have gone on at some length about these homes and how they prefigure other features in *The Autobiography* in order to demonstrate the extent to which Johnson has borrowed a particular legacy from antislavery literature, elaborated upon its implications and potential narrative strategies, and set it in motion within the bounds of his text. The legacy to which I refer is the haunting image of the snug cottage in the clearing. To cite two examples, that cottage is the lure forsaken by Linda Brent (Harriet Jacobs) when she refuses to submit to the lecherous Dr. Flint in *Incidents in the Life of a Slave Girl* (1861), and it is the payment (one hopes only the down payment) received by Henry Bibb's wife near the end of his narrative, once she becomes her master's favored concubine and in that way halts, once and for all, Bibb's valiant forays into slave territory in quest of her deliverance. While the construction of this image in antislavery literature rarely goes beyond the literal assembly of such cottages (after all, one need not cross the portals or light the hearth to envision the moral sore that festers there), Johnson's constructions begin with the cottages not only finished and furnished, but also inhabited, both by the kept woman and by the inevitable issue of her protracted liaison. His purpose is not to expose this once common or tacitly accepted persuasion among males of the South's "best blood," but to accept that persuasion as what Du Bois would call an unvarnished fact of life along the color line and then assign to it, in the course of a fresh narrative, those human complexities that it will undoubtedly bear (and bare), including certain modal expressions of relations between master and slave, their children, and those children's children as well. In this way the Ex-Coloured Man's boyhood homes do not so much echo as recast a primary trope in antislavery literature. If this makes *The Autobiography* a modern text in Afro-American letters, then so be it.

Much the same argument can be brought to a discussion of the various journeys in *The Autobiography*. The antecedent trope for the black mother's and racially ambiguous son's journey north from Georgia, complete with its inland leg to Savannah and sea leg up the Atlantic coast, is William and Ellen Craft's perilous escape from bondage. Moreover, the Ex-Coloured Man's trip south from Atlanta to Jacksonville in the cramped quarters of a Pullman linen closet is clearly an inversion (of nearly grotesque proportions) of Henry "Box" Brown's celebrated crating and shipping of himself north to the City of Brotherly Love. And when the Ex-Coloured Man flees the scene of the "nigger burning' (in which the chaining of the victim to a post occasions, in part, his fear and shame of being shackled to an inferior race), buys a ticket to New York on the "overground" railroad, and, once there, "grows" a disguise and changes his name, his flight is a fresh but skewed expression of every antedating ascent from bondage in the Afro-American canon. The point is not so much that Johnson portrays his narrator as being different, but that he enables us to perceive the fullest dimensions of these differences by juxtaposing certain features of the narrator's character and experiences against a host of canonical images. In every case the self-centered, hermetic, and idiosyncratic qualities of the Ex-Coloured Man's perils and travails present him as being less than heroic. They sustain the heroic proportions of the canonical types and tropes by offering what is, in effect, a negative example

of them. Thus *The Autobiography*'s posture in Afro-American letters depends as much upon its implied definition of the hero as upon
its explicit study of a non-hero. Indeed, this counterpoint is just as
central to the narrative as is that between the expressions of mobility
and confinement.

So far I have stressed those features of action and setting that
are found both in *The Autobiography* and in antislavery literature,
but language must be mentioned as well. While there are a number of
points of comparison, including the various biblical allusions, Johnson's use of what I've previously called a rhetoric of omission seems
to be the most pertinent here, principally because it fuels the aforementioned contrapuntal machinery of the narrative. In the Douglass
Narrative of 1845, especially at the beginning of chapter XI, Douglass lends a certain extraordinary credence to the communal and
archetypal aspects of his tale and authorial postures by eloquently
omitting the details of his escape to freedom; he does not want to
"run the hazard of closing the slightest avenue by which a brother
slave might clear himself of the chains and fetters of slavery."
Through this omission Douglass achieves a full measure of authorial
control over his narrative, because he defines a body of knowledge
possessed by him and unknown to the ancillary voices (principally
those of William Lloyd Garrison and Wendell Phillips) circling within
and without his tale. Douglass inaugurates a rhetoric and narrative
strategy so powerful in the context of Afro-American literary history, and more specifically still in the context of that history's leit-
motif of the quest for authorial control, that it becomes something
of a requisite trope for succeeding narratives of its kind. In *The
Autobiography* the most notable rhetorical omissions appear at the
beginning and end of the narrative. In the first instance, the Ex-
Coloured Man is careful not to name the Georgia town where he
was born "because there are people still living there who could be
connected with this narrative"; in the second, which begins the final
chapter, he is most assiduous about being "brief" and "skipping" and
"jumping" and providing "meagre details" because he is now thoroughly ensconced in New York, and he dreads the possibility of
unraveling his position or that into which his children have been
born. This is all effective writing that tends to authenticate the narrator's tale and elicit readers' sympathy for his circumstances,
but it doesn't screen the fact that the personal arena of concern to

which these rhetorical ploys are brought is not on the same scale of Douglass's. Even though matters of physical, psychic, and social mobility are at stake in both narratives, what the Ex-Coloured Man protects through his strategies is finally too personal and idiosyncratic to sustain significant communal resonances. While Douglass's rhetorical omissions serve to obliterate social structures and race rituals, the Ex-Coloured Man's omissions appear to be designed only for the exploitation of those structures and rituals; on one hand, a race is freed, while on the other, a material world is propped up for the immediate comfort of a racially ambiguous few. The point is not so much that the Ex-Coloured Man comes off again as a less than heroic figure, but that we are aware of his limitations because of the various ways—involving actions and, in this last example, language —in which *The Autobiography* aggressively invites comparison with major antecedent Afro-American texts. Although the comparisons made thus far between *The Autobiography* and certain slave narratives sketch its narrator's character, for a full portrait we must add those shadings and hues provided by the narrative's indebtednesses to *Up from Slavery* and *The Souls of Black Folk*.

In his informative biographical study, *James Weldon Johnson: Black Leader, Black Voice,* Eugene Levy makes the following remarks about *The Autobiography*'s literary indebtednesses:

> Johnson was the first black writer to use the first-person narrative in fiction. He had before him the nonfictional models furnished by Douglass and Washington. As a student at Stanton School he had won a copy of *The Life and Times of Frederick Douglass,* and after reading it he added Douglass to his list of heroes. . . . By 1906, as a friend of Washington, he was also thoroughly familiar with *Up from Slavery*. Both works are written in a simple, straight-forward prose style generally free of rhetorical flourishes; in both, the narrator seems to detach himself from the experiences he describes; and both authors make frequent asides to comment directly on the significance of particular incidents to the American racial situation. It seems clear that *Up from Slavery,* more than any other literary influence, led Johnson to the use of the pseudo-autobiography.

As I have discussed before in the chapter on *Up from Slavery,* the precursing text with which Washington struggled while composing his most famous narrative is none other than the *Life and Times of Frederick Douglass*. That Johnson was apparently influenced by features of both of these texts—texts which already spoke to one another as opposing events in Afro-American literary history—constitutes, I think, a remarkable example of *transitio* and *traditio* in literary history, one that is well worth further study in another context. In this way, Professor Levy's remarks are most helpful; in other ways they are not. At the heart of his opening sentences are problems created by simplistic and limited working definitions of "fiction" and "nonfiction." Obviously, the language there does not allow for what is nonfictional in fiction, or for what is fictional in nonfiction, especially autobiographies. When these complexities of form, content, and authorial posture are taken into account, it is clear that his remarks are rather glib and one dimensional. If we agree that autobiographical statements are, by definition, fictions imposed upon a given personal history (theoretically, a nonfiction) in which what is singularly personal is the author's control over *which* fiction is imposed on his history, then we cannot submit that Douglass's and Washington's models are nonfictional any more than we can say, given the host of generic, authenticating, and autobiographical narratives antedating *The Autobiography*, that Johnson was "The first black writer to use the first-person narrative in fiction." Since, as Levy notes, Johnson himself admitted in later years that "he had not written [*The Autobiography*] with the *intention* of producing a 'piece of fiction,' " perhaps it is more accurate to say (if indeed we must sustain the enterprise of locating whatever a given black author did first) that Johnson was the first black writer (we can think of) who successfully employed first-person narration in a narrative where nonfiction imposes on fiction far more than fiction (in accord with the models provided most notably by Douglass and Washington) impinges on nonfiction.

Levy's phrase "rhetorical flourishes," in his remarks on Douglass's and Washington's prose styles, is also bothersome, primarily because it is not completely clear what kind of bond is implied between "rhetoric" and "flourish." Surely he does not mean to suggest that the terms are synonymous; that would suggest that if Douglass's and Washington's prose styles are "generally free" of flourishes, they are also devoid of rhetoric—a judgment that is a common mistake of many readers. If, as Levy claims, "*Up from Slavery* . . . led Johnson to the use of the pseudo-autobiography," it is because Johnson came to be as influenced by the example of Washington's rhetoric as by narrative's autobiographical impulses. In both *Up from Slavery* and *The Autobiography,* the narrative balance between participation and observation is skewed toward observation; thus both narrators create what I will term a rhetoric of detachment in their tales. Furthermore, this rhetoric performs much the same function in both narratives: In *Up from Slavery* it combines with the accumulating power of Washington's burgeoning résumé to express the domination of the past by the present; in *The Autobiography* it reveals almost singlehandedly how the unambiguousness of the Ex-Coloured Man's outward posture in the present (he is an ordinary white man who has made a little money, and who plans to remain so) dominates his interpretation of his ambiguous past and controls his actions, if not all of his thoughts, in the present.

On the other hand, whereas Washington's narrator is quite comfortable with, and derives a certain power from, his posture and rhetoric of detachment, this is much less the case for the Ex-Coloured Man. Here we begin to see a fundamental difference between the two narratives, a difference that clarifies the point at which Johnson stopped borrowing from Washington and started creating something new within the Afro-American narrative canon. In *Up from Slavery,* the narrator's posture and rhetoric of detachment serve as literary means to certain specific *extraliterary* ends. Above all, that posture never transcends its status as a strategy or a technique to become a subject, or *the* subject, in *Up from Slavery.* In contrast, the Ex-Coloured Man's posture and rhetoric of detachment are literary means to a literary end: Johnson's exposition of his narrator's character. His posture and rhetoric are a subject in *The Autobiography* not only because the Ex-Coloured Man's character is bound to the language with which he attempts to interpret the past, but also because the only meaningful development in the narrative is the accumulation of events and forces that prompt him to submit to (far more than to choose) the ennui of which his rhetoric is an expression. Just as he builds upon the familiar yet haunting image of the snug cottage in the clearing, an image also found in exposés of the immoralities of male slaveholders, Johnson takes the rhetoric of detachment (of which Washington is the prime practitioner) less as a given than as a thing to be explored, as well as used, in the course of a narrative. And while Washington's example instructs that rhetoric is a powerful mask, Johnson's own considerable imaginative energies lead him to inquire in his narrative whether this mask does not, indeed, affect its wearer as well.

Much of this comes clear when we look at a passage that is heavily indebted to Washington's style of rhetoric but which also, in the end, assumes Johnson's stamp. Such passages abound, but few are more developed or more interesting than the one in which the Ex-Coloured Man remarks on the furor over *Uncle Tom's Cabin:*

> This work of Harriet Beecher Stowe has been the object of much unfavorable criticism. It has been assailed, not only as fiction of the most imaginative sort, but as being a direct misrepresentation. Several successful attempts have lately been made to displace the book from Northern school libraries. Its critics would brush it aside with the remark that there never was a Negro as good as Uncle Tom, nor a slave-holder as bad as Legree. For my part, I was never an admirer of Uncle Tom, nor of his type of goodness; but I believe that there were lots of old Negroes as foolishly good as he; the proof of which is that they knowingly stayed and worked the plantations that furnished sinews for the army which was fighting to keep them enslaved. But in these later years several cases have come to my personal knowledge in which old Negroes have died and left what was a considerable fortune to the descendants of their former masters. I do not think it takes any great stretch of the imagination to believe there was a fairly large class of slave-holders typified in Legree. And we must also remember that the author depicted a number of worthless if not vicious Negroes, and a slave-holder who was as much of a Christian and a gentleman as it was possible for one in his position to be; that she pictured the happy, singing, shuffling "darky" as well as the mother wailing for her child sold "down river."

If these excessively balanced remarks are meant to reflect the "perspective" on life in the black and the white worlds that the Ex-Coloured Man supposedly gleaned from reading Stowe's novel, then we need not wonder why he is so tentative and embattled, or why he seems incapable of interpreting or "reading" the significance of most events in his life. His circumstance obviously confirms the theory that one kind of illiteracy breeds another. As far as indebtednesses to Washington are concerned, the most overt example is probably the Ex-Coloured Man's echoing of Washington's "Mars Billy" anecdote and other stories which, in their depiction of slaves and ex-slaves mourning the death of a master or honoring a specific trust, bolster Washington's arguments for southern whites to cast down their buckets amongst the black folk. Washington retells these tales because he has a plan for revitalizing the South in general, and the Black Belt in particular. But when the Ex-Coloured Man pursues a similar vein and remarks on those "old Negroes" who left their fortunes to former masters' living kin, his statement appears gratuitous and, most certainly, bereft of the kind of goal-directedness that underlies Washington's seemingly straightforward commentary.

This issue of story-telling of one form or another as a means to an end continues when we turn to what is really the heart of the matter of Washington's influence—the Ex-Coloured Man's rhetoric of detachment. In the above passage, the narrator first creates the illusion that he has an opinion, that he is willing to debate those who have a contrary view, and that he is about to offer his opinion in a substantial way. Then, after segregating *Uncle Tom's Cabin*'s critics into a class ("Its critics")—which suggests that he has sighted his adversary and is primed for the kill—he bravely launches a salvo with the words, "For my part. . . ." But for reasons having to do exclusively with the Ex-Coloured Man's radical degree of detachment from any cultural base for opinion-making, his salvo has the substance and velocity of a gradeschooler's spitball. We have every reason to expect that a narrator bound by sympathy and bloodline to Afro-America, one who is only too aware of the history of assault upon the race, and who declares (as the Ex-Coloured Man does) that Frederick Douglass is one of his heroes, would take greater issue with his opponents' charge that there never was a slaveholder as bad as Legree than with their claim that there never was a Negro as good at Uncle Tom. But alas—the opposite is true. To be sure, he suggests that "there was a fairly large class of slave-holders typified in Legree"; but this remark is buried between his speculations on "good" Negroes and his acknowledgment, for purposes of fairness and objectivity, of Stowe's depiction of "worthless if not vicious Negroes." One can only assume that part of the Ex-Coloured Man's strategy is to suggest that Stowe's critics are one-sided in their views, and therefore irrational, while he, the narrator, has a balanced view and is thus a reasonable person. He accomplishes this fairly well; but eventually, as the passage's final sentence attests, the seams in his construction expose themselves and, in turn, expose him. Only an exaggerated sense of balance—which is to say, a sense crazily adrift from its moral site and source—could first extract from *Uncle Tom's*

Cabin and then champion an illusionary symmetry between the stereo-
type of the "shuffling 'darky'" and the type of the slave mother whose
child has been sold away. Shortly thereafter the Ex-Coloured Man
concludes, in a tone calculated to convey his fairmindedness, that
"it is [not] claiming too much to say that *Uncle Tom's Cabin* was a
fair and truthful panorama of slavery"; but, as we know from the
preceding language, he has not fashioned a vigorous and persuasive
argument to support that claim. Indeed, more often than not what
he cites as evidence of fairness and truthfulness in Stowe's novel
are examples of how his own personal and, in some cases, skewed
racial reveries balance out on the ledger of his mind.

As these remarks suggest, Johnson has his narrator intone a
rhetoric akin to Washington's, but he also has the rhetoric turn back
upon its speaker in such a way that his character is exposed as his
argument, in all its failings, is advanced. While this new development,
occasioned by improvisation upon a seminal linguistic model in a
given literary tradition, creates fresh space for *The Autobiography* in
Afro-American letters, it does not remove the text from that canon.
On the contrary, as far as the Ex-Coloured Man's rhetoric of detachment is concerned, Johnson repeatedly appears to argue that
one cannot fully comprehend the devastating aimlessness portrayed
when a compromising public tongue becomes a figure's private con-
fessional speech without knowing how Washington, in contrast, employed such a tongue *only* in the public arena and *only* to advance
a grand plan for communal uplift.

The last point I wish to make by way of "improving upon"
Professor Levy's remarks is that I am astonished at his omission of
Du Bois's *The Souls of Black Folk* from his list of literary influ-
ences on *The Autobiography*. In reading *The Autobiography,* one
must take care not to confuse the Ex-Coloured Man's opinions with
Johnson's; but late in the book Johnson probably speaks through
his narrator when he declares: "the opportunity of the future Negro
novelist and poet [is] to give the country something new and unknown, in depicting the life, the ambitions, the struggles, and the
passions of those of their race who are striving to break the narrow
limits of traditions. A beginning has already been made in that
remarkable book by Dr. Du Bois, *The Souls of Black Folk*." Clearly
this is not another aside on the state of Afro-America but an admission of literary indebtedness. At very least, the point is made

that *The Souls* influenced Johnson's decision to attempt a narrative about "something new and unknown"—in this case, an "ex-coloured" man who is probably more of a Du Boisian "weary traveler" than a Douglassonian hero-as-metaphor or a Washingtonian hero-as-authenticator. This particular influence of *The Souls* is readily seen, largely because it is not predicated upon any need to judge the book as a literary form. But the form—or, more precisely, the generic aspirations—of *The Souls* undoubtedly affected Johnson's conception of *The Autobiography,* and his writing of it as well. Obviously, *The Souls* is a first-person narrative with autobiographical impulses; but, more important in terms of the model it offered Johnson, it presents a more overt and radical commingling of nonfiction and fiction than any that can be observed in texts by Douglass and Washington. Indeed, as I will suggest later on, Johnson is virtually incapable of composing those southern episodes in his narrative where nonfictional (social scientific) and fictional (pseudo-autobiographical) threads interweave without specific recourse to Du Bois's antedating volume.

In the parlance of jazz, many of Johnson's opening riffs are improvisations upon Du Bois's basic melody in *The Souls.* Within the first chapter it is established that the Ex-Coloured Man, like Du Bois, was born a few years after the Civil War; that he spent his boyhood in a Connecticut village not unlike Du Bois's Great Barrington, Massachusetts; that, like Du Bois, he knew the "old songs" long before he came to know something of America's rituals along the color line; and that he learned, as did Du Bois, through a seemingly frivolous episode at school that he was black and therefore different, but nevertheless acceptable as a classmate and neighbor on certain, usually unspoken, terms. In both narratives these configurations of setting and experience, entwined with an awakening race consciousness, ·occasion remarks on the peculiar and debilitating psychology with which American Negroes seem to be afflicted from birth. Here Johnson's debt to Du Bois is so obvious that one first wonders why a footnote is not appended. At the beginning of chapter II, after the Ex-Coloured Man confesses with characteristic overstatement that "that fateful day in school . . . wrought the miracle of my transition from one world into another," adding that "From that time I looked out through other eyes, my thoughts were coloured, my words dictated, my actions limited by one dominating, all-pervading idea," he goes on to explain this condition in these terms:

And this is the dwarfing, warping, distorting, influence which operates upon each and every coloured man in the United States. He is forced to take his outlook on all things, not from the view-point of a citizen, or a man, or even a human being, but from the view-point of a *coloured* man. It is wonderful to me that the race has progressed so broadly as it has, since most of its thought and all of its activity must run through the narrow neck of this one funnel.

Clearly, these words echo Du Bois's famous description in *The Souls* of the Negro's "double-consciousness": "It is a peculiar sensation, this double-consciousness, this sense of always looking at one's self through the eyes of others, of measuring one's soul by the tape of a world that looks on in amused contempt and pity." But what are finally more significant than the echoes are the subtle ways in which the Ex-Coloured Man's seemingly unintended revisions of Du Bois's thoughts and language begin to reveal his character.

While Du Bois laments the fact that the American Negro seems psychically bereft of a "true self-consciousness," he never goes so far as to suggest, as does the Ex-Coloured Man, that the Negro's resulting "outlook" is somehow subhuman or inhuman. Furthermore, while Du Bois very deliberately describes a duality accosting the Negro ("One ever feels his two-ness,—an American, a Negro"), the Ex-Coloured Man radically reduces this to a nearly grotesque oneness: "the view-point of a *coloured* man." Finally, unlike Du Bois, who concludes by mining even further the "recesses" of an archetypal soul within the Veil and praising the Negro's "dogged strength" in the face of what is, in effect, an imposed schizophrenia, the Ex-Coloured Man ends with vapid remarks about the race's broad progress—remarks that are as shrill with false cheer as they are devoid of substance and earnestness. Given these points of contact between the pronouncements of Du Bois's and Johnson's narrators, I am willing to credit Johnson with the extraordinary ability to reveal his narrator's character in at least two sophisticated ways at once. On one hand, the Ex-Coloured Man exposes his extreme fear, shame, and utter distaste for things "coloured"—hence, for that considerable part of himself that is black—when he very nearly states that the Negro is not a citizen, a man, or even a human being. This, one might say, is the distinctly literal level of his self-exposure. On the other hand, if we consider the Ex-Coloured Man's remarks to be revisions of Du Bois's ideas—not in the sense of improvements or misreadings for purposes of appropriation and authorial control within the literary tradition, but in the sense of misreadings due to deficiencies of vision and character—then we may say that the Ex-Coloured Man also exposes himself in a virtually figurative way. I have spoken before of the Ex-Coloured Man's chronic inability to "read" the events of his life; here we observe, even more than in the aforementioned passage on *Uncle Tom's Cabin,* his illiteracy *vis-à-vis* a verbal text. In *The Autobiography, The Souls* is the verbal manifestation of the Afro-American *genius loci.* If the Ex-Coloured Man cannot read *The Souls,* then he cannot possibly gain immersion in the soul and spirit of Afro-America. Illiteracy *vis-à-vis* a "master" verbal text is thus a grand trope for displacement from the *genius loci.*

Before we are far into the second chapter of *The Autobiography,* the Ex-Coloured Man's deficiencies of vision and character are almost completely sketched. The rest of the narrative is little more than a nearly deterministic statement of what logically happens to a young man who *never* overcomes a type of illiteracy whenever confronted by either a tribal text (notably, *The Souls*) or context (constructed initially and figuratively by the Georgia yard aglitter with "flashes of spirit"). As an Afro-American narrative type, *The Autobiography* is essentially an aborted immersion narrative. With high expectations and a growing awareness of what he *ought* to be, the Ex-Coloured Man makes two journeys to the South, to regions including his Georgia birthing-ground; but these pilgrimages never become rituals, and the pilgrim never achieves a personal tongue beyond a borrowed public rhetoric. Moreover, immersion and rebirth occur only in the perverse sense that a baptism by the fire of a nigger burning and an ascent to Mammon's city grotesquely complete the shape, if not the substance, of an immersion ritual's narrative arc. With all this in mind, it is not surprising that echoes and revisions of *The Souls* continue in *The Autobiography,* and appear with particular clarity and import in those episodes where the Ex-Coloured Man ventures south. Indeed, in these instances the most effective feature of Johnson's narrative strategy is the comparison he aggressively encourages us to make between Du Bois's questing narrator and his own.

The comparison begins in a major way in chapter IV of *The Autobiography,* where the Ex-Coloured Man draws heavily on Du Bois's narrator's antecedent language (at the beginning of chapter

VII of *The Souls*) while describing the Georgia landscape which emerges as he travels south to Atlanta. The parallels—and discrepancies—between these descriptions are so numerous and striking that I shall quote from each at length. *The Souls* reads:

> Out of the North, the train thundered, and we woke to see the crimson soil of Georgia stretching away bare and monotonous right and left. Here and there lay struggling, unlovely villages, and lean men loafed leisurely at the depots; then again came the stretch of pines and clay. Yet we did not nod, nor weary of the scene; for this is historic ground. Right across our track, three hundred and sixty years ago, wandered the cavalcade of Hernando de Soto, looking for gold and the Great Sea. . . . Here sits Atlanta, the city of a hundred hills, with something Western, something Southern, and something quite its own, in its busy life. And a little past Atlanta, to the southwest, is the land of the Cherokees, and there, not far from where Sam Hose was crucified, you may stand on a spot which is to-day the centre of the Negro problem,—the centre of those nine million men who are America's dark heritage from slavery and the slave-trade.

The echoing and yet contrasting passage in *The Autobiography* is as follows:

> The farther I got below Washington, the more disappointed I became in the appearance of the country. I peered through the car windows, looking in vain for the luxuriant semi-tropical scenery which I had pictured in my mind. I did not find the grass so green, nor the woods so beautiful, nor the flowers so plentiful, as they were in Connecticut. Instead, the red earth partly covered by tough, scrawny grass, the muddy, straggling roads, the cottages of unpainted pine boards, and the clay-daubed huts imparted a "burnt up" impression. Occasionally we ran through a little white and green village that was like an oasis in a desert.
>
> When I reached Atlanta, my steadily increasing disappointment was not lessened. I found it a big, dull, red town. This dull red colour of that part of the South I was then seeing had much, I think, to do with the extreme depression of my spirits—no public squares, no fountains, dingy streetcars, and, with the exception of three or four principal thoroughfares, unpaved streets. It was raining when I arrived and some of these unpaved streets were absolutely impassable. Wheels sank to the hubs in red mire, and I actually stood for an hour and watched four or five men work to save a mule, which had stepped into a deep sink, from drowning, or, rather, suffocating in the mud. The Atlanta of today is a new city.

The parallels between these two descriptions—in content, diction, syntax, and the symbolic use of the color red—are obvious; however, the discrepancies between the two are, I think, more interesting and to the point. Both men are assaulted by the "crimson soil," but while Du Bois responds to temporary immobility with expansive images of immersion in time and space ("this is historic ground"), the Ex-Coloured Man submits to this immobilizing force and offers embellishing images of his stasis, for which the "impassable" streets of Atlanta are a vivid expression. These contrasting images of immersion —in history on one hand, and mud on the other—tell us much about each narrator's gut-level response to the South as a culture's ritual ground. They also suggest the true dimensions of their inherited (if not always assumed) postures as questing, articulate heroes. There is no doubt about Du Bois's narrator's strenuous effort to assume the mantle: the landscape is strange and "unlovely," but he can see that it both stretches and straggles (the Ex-Coloured Man dwells only on the "straggling," and appropriates that very term from *The Souls*). Because he can envision the myriad points of a wonderful compass charting territories of race and culture, time and space, he becomes what Richard Wright proclaimed the Afro-American voice should strive to be—a guide to our daily living. In contrast, the Ex-Coloured Man's vast removal from the speech and responsibilities of the articulate hero is best expressed by his anecdote about witnessing the rescue of a mule from a sink of Georgia mud. In the context of *The Autobiography* as a whole, the incident prefigures the terrifying nigger-burning; in both instances the Ex-Coloured Man is not a guide but a bystander—an observer in the most unambiguous sense, who is transfixed and inarticulate before the horror conjured by his momentary yet acute empathy with either victim. As American history and literature both inform us, the suffocating mule and the burning Negro are partners in a centuries-old cultural dialectic that still haunts and punishes us. However, the Ex-Coloured Man cannot see this in his past, for he clearly lacks a fully interpretative or historical mind. His imagination is self-directed and present oriented. When he sees a mule stuck in a muddy road or a terrified black man burning while chained to a post, he can identify with the victim but not see *through* the victim—even in retrospect—to the underlying historical and racial tropes. The Ex-Coloured Man is a seer of surfaces, which helps explain why he becomes a master of disguises, far more than a student of prophecy. In the face of tribal texts and contexts advancing an archetypal protean posture, the Ex-Coloured Man becomes more and more of a chameleon.

While the nearly asphyxiated mule leaves the Ex-Coloured Man speechless and mired in his own psychic mud (so much so that he actually spends an hour studying the dilemma without lending a hand), other features of southern life, including the social and economic classes he observes among the Negroes of Jacksonville and the quality of food and shelter in the Black Belt, prompt a great deal of commentary. One supposes that these passages, appearing principally in chapters V and X, are what the publishers had in mind when they praised *The Autobiography*'s "composite and proportionate presentation of the entire [coloured American] race"; but in truth they are low points in the narrative, where simplistic sociology and thin fictional impulses take turns trying to sustain each other. The most one can say about the narrator's remarks on Jacksonville and the rural Black Belt is that they confirm our suspicions: he is instinctively an elitist for whom lower-class black folk are animal-like, "offensive" and "desperate" or "dull" and "simple," and those in the upper classes are colored yet "refined" and fairly interesting. While in Jacksonville, however, the narrator avoids relegation to either of these classes by falling in with, and in effect becoming, one of the Cuban-American cigar-makers. The resulting narrative thread is bare from the start, but here Johnson probably wants to establish supportive attitudinal bases for several subsequent episodes in his narrator's life. For example, given the Ex-Coloured Man's unsympathetic depiction of the lowest class of Jacksonville Negroes, we should not be startled when he describes the "wretch" who is about to be burned as "a man only in form and stature" with "every sign of degeneracy stamped upon his countenance." In a sense, the Ex-Coloured Man has despised and feared this man ever since he laid eyes on his *type* in Jacksonville years before. Thus, when a twist of his imagination informs him that the world views him, too, as a man only in form and stature—that is, if he announces himself a coloured man—and he flees across the color line to New York, we are meant to understand the full, if perverse, historical dimensions of his shame. Similarly, we are encouraged to make historical connections between the Ex-Coloured Man's initial plunge into racial ambiguity as a bilingual "Cuban" in Florida and his final posture as a white, multilingual businessman in New York, and between his interest in the refined yet racially committed colored upper class and his fear that he has sold his birthright. The threads are there but, as suggested earlier, Johnson does not discover the proper weave.

These problems are not inconsiderable, but they merely shroud the heart of this particular narrative failure which, like Johnson's successes, involves his indebtednesses to Du Bois. To begin with, the Ex-Coloured Man's sociological expositions are not original; his study of Jacksonville's Negro community merely rehashes Du Bois's observations in chapter IX of *The Souls* ("Of the Sons of Master and Man"). In the case of his lament that the best of each race never gain a meaningful or heartfelt communion with each other, he pirates both language and sentiment. Similarly, the Ex-Coloured Man's remarks upon the state of affairs in the Black Belt's rural reaches are clearly indebted to both "Of the Sons of Master and Man" and its preceding chapter, "Of the Quest of the Golden Fleece." All this is nothing new; as I have already suggested, one of Johnson's key narrative strategies is the illumination of his narrator's failings through presentations of his misreadings and non-readings of "tribal" texts and contexts—the former including most obviously and most consistently *The Souls*. What *is* new is that these particular echoes and revisions do not reveal the Ex-Coloured Man in any consummate way, principally because the strategy of playing the Ex-Coloured Man's ambiguous stature off Du Bois's narrator's heroic stature is stunted by the Du Boisian voice's purposely less than heroic posture as a participant-observer social scientist. Once Du Bois's protean voice assumes an objective or scientific posture (a posture that almost masks Du Bois's own ambivalences about southern black life), Johnson can no longer portray the Ex-Coloured Man as simply the inverse of Du Bois's wayfarer. Any suggestion of a powerful, emotional immersion in black life at its cultural fount in the South on the part of the Ex-Coloured Man will dismantle all we've come to know about his character and will render the outcome of the narrative an improbable contradiction. Since the shades of distinction between Du Bois's narrator's "scientific" rhetoric and the public tongue of the Ex-Coloured Man are so mute, Johnson's only recourse within his narrative strategy is to suggest that his narrator is less heroic or archetypal than Du Bois's by having the Ex-Coloured Man be just a little more obsessed with surfaces, and hence more assaulted and shamed by the conditions he observes.

But this is not a satisfactory way to construct a fresh narrative out of the shards of a narrative tradition. Johnson's dogged pursuit of his strategy in a situation requiring new narrative approaches ultimately reveals more about his artistic indebtednesses and dependencies than about his central character.

On the other hand, the episode in which the Ex-Coloured Man visits a "big meeting" is also patterned upon incidents and commentary in *The Souls* (see especially Du Bois's chapter X, "Of the Faith of the Fathers"). It offers reassuring evidence that Johnson can interweave nonfictional and fictional threads with great facility when the nonfictional subject matter—here, the interplay of the preacher, the singing leader, and black sacred music—is of greater interest to the Ex-Coloured Man and, one imagines, to Johnson as well. Early in the episode the narrator remarks that he found "a mine of material" for his musical compositions at the big meeting; the rest of his commentary, complete with annotated transcriptions of the words to "master" Sorrow Songs such as "Swing Low" and "Steal Away," bears this out. His use of the word "mine" is telling, because it sustains all that we know of his inherent Mammonism and all that we've come to suspect about how he will view a ritualized manifestation of artistic traditions once he stumbles upon it. The Ex-Coloured Man seeks neither communion nor succor; he comes not to embrace but to extract. The big meeting is, for him, a mine riddled with ore, not a welcome table laden with food for body and soul. Nevertheless, the overall implication of the episode is that the Ex-Coloured Man has been genuinely stirred by both word and song. For this reason his commentary may be described in part as a revision of antedating passages in *The Souls,* a revision that selects portions of "Of the Faith of the Fathers" and "Of the Sorrow Songs" and binds them into a single, abbreviated statement. With this in full view, Johnson's indebtednesses to Du Bois again become abundantly clear. However, Johnson does more than just borrow from Du Bois in this instance, partly because his own special knowledge of preachers, sermons, singing leaders, and song allows him to improve upon Du Bois's earlier commentary, and partly because he is able to capitalize on what I believe to be a lapse in Du Bois's narrative.

To be sure, the Du Boisian voice is marvelously subjective and self-conscious in both a personal and racial sense, in the Sorrow Songs chapter. But in "Of the Faith of the Fathers," where he visits his first campground or revival meeting, he is first and foremost a scientific observer. His initial remarks on "The Preacher, the Music, and the Frenzy" do not immediately advance the narrative's immersion ritual, prompting instead a rather dry and, in many parts of the argument, suspect analysis of Afro-American religious practice, North and South. In light of *The Soul*'s ultimate drive and direction as an immersion narrative, it could be argued that Du Bois should have revised "Of the Faith," as he did so many of the essays that became chapters in his volume, with an eye to enhancing the full import of the revival experience. But he did not, and his narrator remains to the end conspicuously uninvolved and even unmoved. While Johnson begins the big meeting episode with intimations of the Ex-Coloured Man's detachment and paucity of racial and moral sentiment—he first views the meeting as an opportunity to "mine" or "catch the spirit of the Negro in his relatively primitive state"—he ends by taking advantage of Du Bois's lapse and portraying the Ex-Coloured Man as being moved for the first time (save perhaps in those youthful moments when his mother sang and played the old songs) by Afro-American spiritual and creative expressions:

> As I listened to the singing of these songs, the wonder of their production grew upon me more and more. How did the men who originated them manage to do it? The sentiments are easily accounted for; they are mostly taken from the Bible; but the melodies, where did they come from? Some of them so weirdly sweet, and others so wonderfully strong. Take, for instance, "Go down, Moses." I doubt that there is a stronger theme in the whole musical literature of the world. And so many of these songs contain more than mere melody; there is sounded in them that elusive undertone, the note in music which is not heard with the ears. I sat often with the tears rolling down my cheeks and my heart melted within me. Any musical person who has never heard a Negro congregation under the spell of religious fervour sing these old songs has missed one of the most thrilling emotions which the human heart may experience. Anyone who without shedding tears can listen to Negroes sing "Nobody knows de trouble I see, Nobody knows but Jesus" must indeed have a heart of stone.

This is Johnson at his best. We are made aware of the Ex-Coloured Man's considerable enthusiasm through an abrupt change in rhetoric; the language here is far more personal than public. However, the more he attempts to wax eloquent, the more he irreparably exposes himself. When, for example, he accounts for the songs' sentiments by stating that "they are mostly taken from the Bible," he again shows himself to be an ahistorically minded seer of surfaces, even though in this instance the surfaces he views are most resonant and metaphorical. To be sure, sentiments in the Sorrow Songs *are* taken almost exclusively from the Bible; but the Ex-Coloured Man never comprehends the singular racial-historical experience that occasioned the adoption of biblical allusion and reference in the first place. He can hear an echo and read a reference, but that is all. The Ex-Coloured Man's embarrassing self-exposure is compounded when he suggests that he has been so terribly moved by his experience because he is a sensitive, "musical person," and that other "musical" persons are missing something if they haven't yet heard Negroes sing the Sorrow Songs. *That* argument is ludicrous to the point of being painful. In sum, while Johnson's object here is clearly to bring his narrator as close to the figurative site of the Afro-American *genius loci* as he will ever come, and hence to buoy him up before the nigger-burning brutally tears him down and sends him fleeing to the City of Mammon, he also reveals that those uplifting emotions and sentiments are skewed and impure. While it is tempting to fault Johnson for being so singleminded in his pursuit of a strategy that plays his narrator off that of an ever-looming prototype, we must finally praise him and thoughtfully consider his achievement. Even more than *The Souls, The Autobiography* forces a rereading of Afro-American literature in order for its wayfaring narrator to come alive, to be heard and seen. And *we* must do the hearing and seeing, since the Ex-Coloured Man is lost in his quest and cannot even hear or see himself.

ANTICIPATIONS: RACE, MUSIC, AND MAMMON

While *The Autobiography*'s indebtednesses to antecedent texts (especially *Up from Slavery* and *The Souls of Black Folk*) tell us much about how Johnson fashioned "something new and unknown," they tell only a partial story of his narrative's literary past. The rest of the story involves *The Autobiography*'s literary future, and especially its literary present. Only by discovering this literary present may we assume that the narrative achieves enough integrity to begin to predict a literary future. In this regard one feature of *The Auto-*

biography stands out from the rest: its uncompromising study of race and music in the world of Mammon. This feature constitutes a nearly sacrilegious inversion of those hallowed tropes in Afro-American art which remain responsible for the culture's abiding belief in the essential oneness of its music and tribal integrity. While it certainly can be argued that the feature is to some degree an indebtedness, since it inverts preexisting tropes found in the writings of Dunbar, Du Bois, and others, the quality of the inversion is such that the feature finally must be assigned to a new category, namely, that of "anticipation." In this particular instance, the distinction between an indebtedness and an anticipation is quite specifically that between a literary feature that inverts and one that demystifies a preexisting trope. To be sure, the line between these two activities can be quite fine, but that is part (and probably most) of the point: the line is fine because indebtednesses and anticipations *both* exist in a given text's literary present.

I want to suggest here that *The Autobiography*'s demystification of the "sacred" bond between Afro-America's music and its tribal integrity is not only part of the "something new," creating fresh space for the narrative in Afro-American letters, but also a feature anticipating certain prominent tropes and expressions in the literature to come. Indeed, once the music is heard in Mammon's lair as well as in cultural ritual grounds such as the Black Belt, both the sacred and secular (if not exactly profane) strains in the music and the discrete subcultures enveloping each become artistic subjects, especially in periods such as those following the publication of *The Autobiography,* when there is an interest in a literary social realism. While it can be argued that Johnson "broke the new wood" for subsequent Afro-American (and American) literary ventures, it also can be said that he almost singlehandedly created a great deal of havoc. When Afro-American literary critics in the 1920's (including especially Du Bois) roundly condemned those vivid portraits of Negro America's urban underbelly in the "renaissance" writings of Claude McKay, Langston Hughes, and others, they sustained, albeit from their own point of view, a peculiarly American notion of degeneracy and sordidness which achieves its greatest frenzy in the face of spatial configurations of music, interracial liaison, and intemperance such as the Negro cabaret. In *The Autobiography* the Club where the Ex-Coloured Man is first introduced to ragtime music and "coloured Bohemia," as well as to his future patron and "the rich widow," inaugurates all such spatial configurations in modern Afro-American letters. It does so because it is not so much a setting as a symbolic space.

The significance of Johnson's invention becomes clear when we not only look forward in literary history to the literature fashioned by Jean Toomer, Langston Hughes, Claude McKay, and Sterling Brown, but also turn back once again to texts by Du Bois and Washington. *The Souls of Black Folk* and *Up from Slavery* are seminal texts in Afro-American letters partly because each contributes to the series of symbolic spaces in the tradition. In the case of the former, there is first and foremost the Black Belt, but also the consummate construction of Du Bois's Atlanta study; in the latter, the chief symbolic space is Tuskegee itself. Coming hard upon the heels of these volumes, *The Autobiography*'s novel and in many ways abrasive assertion is that the Ex-Coloured Man's Club, in all its external and internal complexities, is a compact world unto itself, a world of no less significance and resonance in Afro-American art and life than that readily assigned to Du Bois's and Washington's more agreeable constructions.

While the club is catacomb-like and occasionally a setting for intemperance and violence, it is less an inferno and more an Afro-American ritual ground where responses to oppressing social structures are made and in some measure sustained by "tribal" bonds, as they are in Du Bois's Black Belt. The main floor of the Club is divided into two large rooms. In the back room is the piano that introduces the Ex-Coloured Man to new forms of Afro-American music, and areas for performances, buffets, and dancing. In the parlor, carpets and lace curtains help establish a particular atmosphere and tone, but the significance of the space is most accurately and directly conveyed by the fact that "the walls [are] literally covered with photographs or lithographs of every coloured man in America who [has] ever 'done anything.'" As the Ex-Coloured Man continues his description, we learn that this visual pantheon includes a marvelous array of heroes—athletes, entertainers, and (not surprisingly) Frederick Douglass—that it is as much a new expression of Afro-American heroism as the Club is a fresh symbolic space. The Club's gallery of heroic images transports us back to the single tattered handbill adorning the rough walls of the Negro hut sketched with such eloquence by Du Bois, as well as forward to such recent constructions as Bigger's "gallery" in his quarters at the Daltons' in Wright's *Native Son,* the array of homely treasures in the Harlem eviction episode in Ellison's *Invisible Man,* and the family tree of real and adopted kin in Michael Harper's *Nightmare Begins Responsibility.* At the very least, this journey affords us a nearly prophetic vision of a race's history of response to assault. But in truth, just as "something new and unknown" is launched in Afro-American letters by the radical juxtaposition of Du Bois's study and the Ex-Coloured Man's Club, the full measure of our visionary experience as readers is triggered by the parlor with its gallery, *in communion* with the back room with its matériel for ritual dance and song. Plagued as he is with a particular kind of illiteracy, the Ex-Coloured Man cannot "read" the Club's deep structure, and hence experience the "spiritual race message" and history brimming forth from this highly accoutred and orchestrated vessel. But we are meant to perform this literate act, if for no other reason than to achieve the proper spirit in which to receive certain representatives of the pictured heroes once they enter the Club and, in effect, come to life.

As the Ex-Coloured Man's description of the Club unfolds, he sketches many sporting types, including "the most popular jockey of the day," who earned $12,000 a year but spent "about thirty times that rate." However, his most pertinent remarks regarding aspects of black heroism in Mammon's world involve the entertainers for whom the Club is something of a practice area, audition hall, and guild lodge rolled into one. Of these, the most important are "the younger and brighter men" who often discussed "the time when they could compel the public to recognize that they could do something more than grin and cut pigeon-wings," and especially the minstrel who "whenever he responded to a request to 'do something,' never essayed anything below a reading from Shakspere [*sic*]." Given the topic of discussion that obsessed the younger performers, and the Ex-Coloured Man's remark that the minstrel, in his ambition to be a tragedian, did indeed "play a part in a tragedy," it seems clear that when Johnson composed this passage he thought of well-known poems by his good friend Paul Laurence Dunbar—"The Poet," "We Wear the Mask," and possibly "Sympathy." More to the point, however, is Johnson's particular use of Dunbar's tropes in his own literary work. Whether the lines speak of caged birds singing, jingles in a broken tongue, or of masks and who is the seer and who the seen, the Dunbar poems are finally less concerned with specific *fin de siècle* issues such as the accuracy of Negro dialect and the influence of "plantation" literature than with the abiding crisis involving the Afro-American artist's pursuit of authorial control. When certain Negro performers come to the Club and, in effect, reenact and rephrase Dunbar's expressions, we may say that Johnson clearly establishes two major points involving both his narrator and the most remarkable symbolic space in *The Autobiography*. First, much of what makes the Club a significant Afro-American ritual ground is that it is an intricate space wherein authorial control is not only discussed, but also aggressively pursued. Again the relationship between the Club's parlor and back room figures prominently in Johnson's strategy: the communion between the two rooms is but a spatial expression of the bond between artful acts in the present and a sense of tradition shaping past, present, and future into a single continuum. In the Club, an Afro-American artist may refine, direct, and hence gain a measure of control over his or her talent through contact with fellow "weary travelers" past and present, known and unknown, gathered around a table or portrayed upon a wall. This, and not the lure of drink, revelry, and the transgression of racial taboos, is the true source of the Club's power and position in the Negro world of Johnson's narrative.

The second point is that once the Ex-Coloured Man becomes a nearly famous ragtime piano player, he also becomes, without really knowing it, one of the many black performers at the Club who must wrestle with questions of authorial control—especially as those questions persistently relate to a sense of self. Given Johnson's construction of this symbolic space, based as it is upon a profound comprehension of Afro-American artistic traditions, one imagines that if the Ex-Coloured Man realized for even a single moment that Frederick Douglass was staring at him from the parlor while he was improvising ingenious rags in the back room, *The Autobiography* could end right then and there. But the point is that the Ex-Coloured Man is a performer without control and, quite probably, out of control. Alienated from the deepest bonds of his race, he learns to play the music without reference to who is "in the other room"—he becomes a musical technician bereft of an artistic soul. It is inevitable that the Ex-Coloured Man will be as much drawn to the white slummers—who appear to appreciate him and his music more than any of his other admirers—as they are attracted to him. Caught as he is in a kind of illiteracy that argues that technique can pass for art, it is also inevitable that the Ex-Coloured Man will unwittingly mistake the modulation and exploitation of race rituals along the color line for proper relations between artist and audience. The disastrous consequences of these mistakes are expressed in the narrative when th Ex-Coloured Man is almost killed in the Club by the wealthy white widow's "other" black lover, and when he is forced to play for his "second" white father for hours on end—often in the middle of the night. In *The Autobiography,* as elsewhere, the most unsettling outward expression of the condition plaguing the Ex-Coloured Man occurs whenever the subtle and potentially honorable bond between artist and audience is grotesquely skewed, and art becomes something transiently novel, amusing, or soporific.

Given the Ex-Coloured Man's nearly obsessive attraction to interiors after he receives the whipping for digging up the "spirit in glitter" in the yard of his birthplace, the greatest of *The Autobiography*'s many ironic touches must be the fact that the essence of black life and song, for which he searches so energetically in the "outdoors" of the Black Belt, was readily available to him earlier, in the confines of the Club's resonating rooms. Had he been in tune with these resonances, not only could he have filled many a notebook; he could also have achieved contact with artistic traditions and concerns which would have focused and directed his compositions in such a way that he would have indeed become, for himself as well as his race, a Negro composer. In this way Johnson's initial construction of the Club seems to be a fresh and assertive configuration, in conflict with more established "tribal tropes" such as the Black Belt. But such is not the case: on the contrary, the Black Belt of *The Autobiography* is not a wasteland devoid of cultural resonances, but the homeland and ritual ground of a preacher extraordinarily named John Brown, and a master-singer known to all as Singing Johnson from whom the Ex-Coloured Man, in his limited way, learns much. Clearly, in Johnson's view, the Ex-Coloured Man could have learned all of what he thinks he ought to know in *either* symbolic territory. What we must see, as students of Afro-American narrative, is that this fresh assertion is part of what places *The Autobiography* on the literary map.

All in all, the hallowed dialectic between race and music which yields the most revered expressions of the Afro-American *genius loci* in much of the literature preceding and following *The Autobiography* is an alien idea for the Ex-Coloured Man—or at least an idea that is subsumed by his personal opinion of what are more pertinent constructions. For him, the modulation and occasional exploitation of America's race rituals are persistently more important than true and honest contact with his race, and so a bond between music and race ritual is seen to be more useful and valuable than one between music and race itself. Since the Ex-Coloured Man is in this way always *upon* the color line, and not truly on either side of it, even in his most joyful moments as a "black" music-maker, Johnson's full and complete nightmare vision of race and music in Mammon's world is ultimately quite clear. As far as Afro-American music is concerned, what distinguishes the heights of Pisgah from the mire of the dusty desert has less to do with genres and traditions (ragtime versus the Sorrow Songs) than with how the music is approached, perceived, and used. When Johnson renders this point by presenting his narrator as being more preoccupied with his white patrons—which is to say, with taboos and materialism—than with the kinfolk, present and portrayed, who constitute his other audience, he transports his narrative into realms never before explored.

If *The Autobiography* is a modern Afro-American text, it is so because tropes such as the Club revoice tropes such as the Black Belt, and because new territories, including the ambiguous domain between America's black and white world, are finally explored. In my estimation, Johnson's peculiar allegiances to past examples of sociological reportage retard *The Autobiography,* making it ultimately something less than a novel. But given his abiding interest in how fact imposes upon fiction, it is clear that he is up to something different from what Douglass, Washington, and even Du Bois pursue in their autobiographical narratives. For this reason it may be said that *The Autobiography* is on the verge of achieving generic stature— much as its narrator, albeit for very different reasons, is perpetually on the verge of seeing sign and event and himself. In light of Johnson's statement that he was not attempting a novel in the conventional sense of the term, we cannot fault him for almost achieving something that was not his goal. With a steady eye on what had come before in Afro-American letters, Johnson pursued and found both a form and voice that are, if not absolutely new and unknown, very peculiar. The task of *fully* describing and weighing these peculiarities remains before us still.

CHAPTER 5

Literacy and Ascent:
Richard Wright's *Black Boy*

I was poised for flight, but I was waiting for
some event, some word, some act, some
circumstance to furnish the impetus.
                    —Richard Wright, *Black Boy*

> He leaps, board wings clum—
> sily flapping, big sex
>   flopping, falls.
>
> The hawk-hunted fowl
> flutter and squawk;
>   panic squeals in the sty.
>
> He strains, an awk-
> ward patsy, sweating strains
>   leaping falling. Then—
>
> Silken rustling in the air,
> the angle of ascent
>   achieved.
> —Robert Hayden, "For a Young Artist"

In the preceding chapter, we saw how a modern or epiloging text—*The Autobiography of an Ex-Coloured Man*—achieves a place for itself in the Afro-American narrative tradition by binding the rhetorical conventions of the authenticating narrative to the narrative impulses of the immersion ritual and creating what is, in effect, an aborted narrative of immersion. In this chapter we shall discover how another modern text—Richard Wright's *Black Boy* (1945) —achieves a comparable integrity within the tradition by fusing a different set of conventions and impulses from the authenticating form to the narrative properties of the ascension ritual, creating what is fundamentally a narrative of ascent that authenticates another, primary text by the same author. *Black Boy* has the responsibility of revoicing Wright's own *Native Son* as well as harking back to certain primary tropes in the Afro-American narrative canon, and the fact that *Black Boy* meets both of these responsibilities is cause enough (although not the most often cited cause) for the narrative's great fame.

Of course, the "official" and sanctioned authenticating text for *Native Son* is not *Black Boy,* but the pulsing and affecting shorter piece, "How 'Bigger' Was Born." Written within a few months after *Native Son* saw print in 1940 and promptly published by *Harper's,* "How 'Bigger' Was Born" soon replaced *Native Son*'s original and innocently vapid preface by a "white guarantor" (Dorothy Canfield Fisher), and in that way took over the responsibilities of not only introducing but also authenticating Wright's greatest novel. On its surface, this development had all the marks of a great personal and artistic triumph: the opportunity for Wright to introduce his own text suggests a high level of earned and sanctioned authorial control. But while "How 'Bigger' Was Born" answered one question—how Wright came to know Bigger—it unintentionally posed another: How did Wright come to escape *becoming* a Bigger?

At first glance, this latter question appears exceedingly irrelevant and extraliterary, but it is not—primarily because of the compulsions in Afro-American letters that prompt the question, and because the question need not be answered (as the example of *Black Boy* attests) in a nonliterary way. Despite Wright's brave assertion in "Blueprint for Negro Writing" (1937) that "tradition is no longer a guide," there can be no doubt that tradition guided him: in the 1940's, after he finally read most of the corpus of Afro-American literature, and became aware of, if not thoroughly imbued with, the demands of its tropes and traditions, Wright had to write *Black Boy* (indeed, all of *American Hunger*) because "How 'Bigger' Was Born" is not a full and complete authentication of *Native Son,* and neither text authenticates the extraordinary articulate self that lies behind them. Once that self *was* authenticated in *Black Boy,* Wright could expatriate to France (or just about anywhere, save Mississippi) and pursue new projects, including new modes of writing. And that is exactly what he did.

In "How 'Bigger' Was Born," Wright deftly sketches the various "Biggers" he encountered in Mississippi, Memphis, and Chicago who collectively provided the wellsprings, as it were, from which he drew the archetypal Bigger Thomas. Of course, missing in that essay is Wright's acknowledgment of the Bigger who resides in the shadows and deeper recesses of his own personal past, the Bigger who once had a powerful grip on the thoughts, actions, and even the debilitating inarticulateness of Wright's daily life as a youth. In *Black Boy* Wright finally makes this acknowledgment or confession, and his remarks are often as self-serving as they are informative. For example, in chapter III of *Black Boy* we discover that Wright's own youthful experiences gave him a firsthand knowledge of the cockiness and restlessness that typically characterize streetcorner or pool-hall gangs like Bigger Thomas's in *Native Son*. Wright did not have to draw exclusively upon his experiences as a WPA-sponsored youth worker in a south side Chicago Boys' Club—as reported in "How 'Bigger' Was Born"—in order to capture the prevailing ambiance of Bigger's world. The following passage from the beginning of the chapter describes Wright's own coterie of restless and pubescent seekers, but the feelings, rituals, and persons sketched are hardly unique to Wright's childhood:

> Having grown taller and older, I now associated with older boys and I had to pay for my admittance into their company by sub-scribing to certain racial sentiments. The touchstone of fraternity was my feeling toward white people, how much hostility I held toward them, what degrees of value and honor I assigned to race. None of this was premeditated, but sprang spontaneously out of the talk of the black boys who met at the crossroads. . . . We had somehow caught the spirit of the role of our sex and we flocked together for common moral schooling. We spoke boastfully in bass voices; we used the word "nigger" to prove the tough fibre of our feelings; we spouted excessive profanity as a sign of our coming manhood; we pretended callousness toward the injunctions of our parents; and we strove to convince one another that our decisions stemmed from ourselves and ourselves alone. Yet we frantically concealed how dependent we were upon each other.

Clearly, these words describe Bigger Thomas's world in Book I of *Native Son,* a world that Wright evidently once shared, modally if not literally, with his most famous protagonist. But this passage is not nearly so much about shared (and, hence, authenticated) ex-perience as it is about profound differences in degrees of literacy, or the chasm between literacy and its absence. The passage is unique to *Black Boy* because of the voice displayed, rather than the detail deployed; the voice is that of a former "Bigger" who has transcended both a woeful circumstance and an illiterate self. Put another way, the voice displayed in *Black Boy* is that of an Afro-American articulate hero who has learned to read the "baffling signs" of an oppressing, biracial social structure.

Wright's compulsion to exhibit his hard-won literacy is amply documented as the chapter continues. He glosses or annotates what he remembers to be the kind of conversation in which his gang perennially engaged.

"Hey." Timidly.
"You eat yet?" Uneasily trying to make conversation.
"Yeah, man. I done really fed my face." Casually.
"I had cabbage and potatoes." Confidently.
"I had buttermilk and black-eyed peas." Meekly informational.
"Hell, I ain't gonna stand near you, nigger!" Pronouncement.
"How come?" Feigned innocence.
" 'Cause you gonna smell up this air in a minute!" A shouted accusation.
Laughter runs through the crowd.

"Man, them white folks oughta catch you and send you to the zoo and keep you for the next war!" Throwing the subject into a wider field.
"Then when the fighting starts, they oughta feed you on buttermilk and black-eyed peas and let you break wind!" The subject is accepted and extended.
"You'd win the war with a new kind of poison gas!" A shouted climax.
There is high laughter that simmers down slowly.

"Man, them white folks sure is mean." Complaining.
"That's how come so many colored folks leaving the South." Informational.
"And, man, they sure hate for you to leave." Pride of personal and racial worth implied.
"Yeah. They wanna keep you here and work you to death."
"The first white sonofabitch that bothers me is gonna get a hole knocked in his head!" Naive rebellion.
"That ain't gonna do you no good. Hell, they'll catch you." Rejection of naive rebellion.
"Ha-ha-ha . . . Yeah, goddamit, they really catch you, now." Appreciation of the thoroughness of white militancy.

"Yeah, white folks set on their white asses day and night, but leta nigger do something, and they get every bloodhound that was ever born and put 'em on his trail." Bitter pride in realizing what it costs to defeat them.

"Man, you reckon these white folks is ever gonna change?" Timid, questioning hope.

"Hell, no! They just born that way." Rejecting hope for fear that it could never come true.

"Shucks, man. I'm going north when I get grown." Rebelling against futile hope and embracing flight.

"A colored man's all right up north." Justifying flight.

"They say a white man hit a colored man up north and that colored man hit that white man, knocked him cold, and nobody did a damn thing!" Urgent wish to believe in flight.

"Man for man up there." Begging to believe in justice.

Silence.

Wright's recomposition of these exchanges and his reading of them as the signs of a culture from which he has triumphantly removed himself constitute a moment heretofore unheralded in *Black Boy* and, quite likely, in Afro-American narrative letters as a whole. Johnson's Ex-Coloured Man proves to be incapable of expressing a single retrospective thought, partly because his development as an individual is essentially an illusion, and partly because his tongue is bound to an ahistorical rhetoric. In contrast, Wright's persona is, along with Frederick Douglass's, the essential retrospective voice in the tradition. Whereas James Weldon Johnson draws on the example of Booker T. Washington's *intentional* minimalization of the distance between past and present, creating a narrator who *unintentionally* pursues such minimizing activities through his language, Wright takes the other path and fashions a voice who, if anything, exploits the reach between past and present. The reasons for this act of exploitation are clear and extend beyond the confines of *Black Boy*'s narrative line. The past is the southern Black Belt bound to the northern ghetto by the aimlessness and inarticulateness of the Biggers in us all, while the present is, in the terms *Black Boy* affords, the increasingly unchartable realm of the articulate survivor.

And so the grand narrative strategy of *Black Boy* is set in motion. Expressions of literate mobility slowly take form, then accompany, and then supersede expressions of illiterate immobility; the new triumphing expressions gain their greatest resonance when we perceive how they counterpoint certain major antedating images in

Native Son. While the preceding example regarding Bigger's and Wright's gangs and their coded speech suggests the kind of mobility Wright eventually achieves through language, we mustn't overlook the fact that mobility, for Wright, is very much a physical matter as well. He wanted to improve his mind, and he nearly worshipped the mysteries of language that afforded "new avenues of feeling and seeing"; but he also wanted to get the hell out of Dixie. All this is captured magnificently, I think, in the theater episode late in *Black Boy*, which the careful reader must counterpoint with that in *Native Son*.

The episode in *Black Boy* depicts Wright's short career as a movie theater ticket-taker. In that capacity, and because of an abiding desperation for enough money to leave what he calls elsewhere "the gross environment that sought to claim [him]," he conquers his fears and joins in a scheme to re-sell tickets and pocket the profits. Of course, the theater is a "colored" theater; as such, it takes its place in a continuum of symbolic constructions in Afro-American letters, including the various theaters in Toomer's *Cane* and the once-elegant Regal in which Bigger Thomas and his soulmates view "The Gay Woman" and "Trader Horn." What makes this theater episode a relatively fresh expression in the canon is the same thing that creates the counterpoint between it and the antedating event in *Native Son*. In *Native Son* Bigger is in the theater, viewing the celluloid flotsam of what Wright calls "a culture not a civilization," and although he and his brethren pose questions and issue taunts, they are far more encased by than removed from the cultural images flashing before them. On the other hand, in *Black Boy* Wright is outside the theater, removed from a technological culture's crudest propaganda; he is desperately but bravely putting together the last few dollars needed to buy the only kind of ticket that interests him and *should* interest Bigger—that train ticket (so magnificently a fresh expression of Douglass's "protection" pass) to what he hopes will be a better world. In terms of the orchestrated dialectic between Wright's two greatest works, this particular episode in *Black Boy* revises a major moment in *Native Son* by affirming that arresting images of illiterate immobility and literate mobility may be contextualized in the same symbolic space.

In this way, before embarking for Europe and his second great journey in quest of a civilization and not a culture, Wright erected the antipodes of the black world upon which his best literature is strung. It is a rather complete world when seen whole, chiefly because it is ordered less by political persuasion and economic law than by a quintessentially Afro-American notion of literacy in communion with artistic vision. When his oeuvre is viewed in this way, it seems remarkable that so many writers and critics (encouraged, perhaps, by certain celebrated remarks from Baldwin and Ellison) have persisted in the essentially Du Boisian enterprise of exposing the "partial truth" broadcast by *Native Son,* when it is clear that Wright "completed" that "truth" eventually. In the long run, the charge that a writer of Wright's talent should have been able to present the literate and illiterate (and mobile and immobile) dimensions of the world he knew in the harmonic as well as dissonant tropes of *one* exquisite expression may tell us less about aesthetic value than about those moments in literary history when aspects of intertextuality are largely forsaken, when the compulsions of a given tradition function more as dictates than as guidelines. Blinded as we have been by the searing light of *Native Son,* we have rarely seen how *Black Boy* completes that novel; nor have we always seen how *Black Boy* revoices certain precursing tropes in Afro-American letters, tropes that reach back at least as far as the slave narratives. In the former instance, the narrative performs the duties of an authenticating narrative, while in the latter it assumes the shape and fiber of a narrative of ascent. These activities are not distinct in image and episode, because they are not distinct or opposing activities in the narrative as a whole. For Wright as for others, including most notably Frederick Douglass, literacy and ascent are the interwoven contours of the road to freedom. Every expression of literacy in *Black Boy* that revises an expression of illiteracy in *Native Son* inevitably advances the narrator's ritualized ascent. This, if nothing else, assures a space for *Black Boy* in the Afro-American narrative tradition.

As in all the great Afro-American narratives of ascent, a primary feature of *Black Boy* is Wright's persona's sustained effort to gain authorial control of the text of his environment. The first phase of such an effort is always the identification of the enveloping culture's "baffling signs," which are to be read and, in some sense, transcended by the questing figure. In *Black Boy* the three catalogs of boyhood remembrances that provide such welcome relief from the relentless depiction of assault are also the means by which Wright can enumerate his culture's coded references in a concentrated way. The first catalog appears in chapter I; it is sorely needed even at that early point in the narrative, because it offers a legato bridge after Wright's furious opening riff on how, when he was four, he almost burnt the house down, and as a consequence was beaten until he lost consciousness and wandered day and night, in dream and without, in a "fog of fear." This catastrophic childhood event immediately calls to mind that which begins *The Autobiography of an Ex-Coloured Man,* and one can make useful comparisons between the two. Both narrators conduct experiments with forms that are primary expressions of family or community: in *Black Boy,* Wright fires the fluffy white curtains, but behind this lies his wanton mischief with the hearth; in *The Autobiography,* the Ex-Coloured Man uproots the "spirit in glitter." Furthermore, while both are soundly beaten for their violations, the Ex-Coloured Man retreats from the outdoor arena of his crime to the interiors of his boyhood cottages, while Wright's persona reverses this movement and flees from his home to outside. These two opposing treatments of a primary scene come into sharper focus when we observe the ways in which they speak to one another. The utter finality and completeness of the Ex-Coloured Man's dedication to knowing, and hence controlling, the world signified by his boyhood interiors is clarified by Wright's comparable ambition to know and control a world that initially has no definition, other than that it is outside and beyond a taut and bepeopled structure afflicting him.

It is virtually foretold that, when each narrative continues, the Ex-Coloured Man will identify the enveloping and engaging signs of his interior world (the glittering coins, the soft shined leather, the first of several pianos), while Wright's persona will list the equally significant signs belonging to an exterior space. Wright's catalog begins this way:

> Each event spoke with a cryptic tongue. And the moments of living slowly revealed their coded meanings. There was the wonder I felt when I first saw a brace of mountainlike, spotted, black-and-white horses clopping down a dusty road through clouds of powdered clay.
>
> There was the delight I caught in seeing long straight rows of red and green vegetables stretching away in the sun to the bright horizon.
>
> There was the faint, cool kiss of sensuality when dew came on

to my cheeks and shins as I ran down the wet green garden paths in the early morning.

There was the vague sense of the infinite as I looked down upon the yellow, dreaming waters of the Mississippi River from the verdant bluffs of Natchez.

The list builds in much the same evenhanded way, laying languorous image upon languorous image until we come upon the first (and only) sign involving kin—a sign that places someone who theoretically should be a part of the oppressing interior structure outside that structure, and indeed out-of-doors: "There was the experience of feeling death without dying that came from watching a chicken leap about blindly after its neck had been snapped by a quick twist of my father's wrist."

After this, the catalog of remembrances is characterized far more by small terrors and afflictions than by enrapturing pleasures and balms:

There was the thirst I had when I watched clear, sweet juice trickle from sugar cane being crushed.

There was the hot panic that welled up in my throat and swept through my blood when I first saw the lazy, limp coils of a blue-skinned snake sleeping in the sun.

There was the speechless astonishment of seeing a hog stabbed through the heart, dipped into boiling water, scraped, split open, gutted, and strung up gaping and bloody.

There was the hint of cosmic cruelty that I felt when I saw the curved timbers of a wooden shack that had been warped in the summer sun.

There was the cloudy notion of hunger when I breathed the odor of new-cut bleeding grass.

And there was the quiet terror that suffused my senses when vast hazes of gold washed earthward from star-heavy skies on silent nights. . . .

In this way Wright inaugurates the anti-pastoral strain in *Black Boy*. There is no mistaking the extent to which his feelings toward his father (in the context of the narrative) are at the heart of this development. Unlike the Ex-Coloured Man, who pursues his father's signs, if not precisely his father, after the latter leaves him and his mother almost paradoxically comfortable but adrift, Wright's persona rejects all that his father signifies. Especially after the father abandons his family, fails in his own flight and ascent to Memphis, and returns to work the Mississippi soil as a sharecropper, the son considers him the first of several elder kinsmen who are "warnings," not "examples." All this cannot be said explicitly in the catalog, but the positioning of the father outdoors (recall here that the father is the only one who can *see* and capture Richard after he flees outside and under the house during the fire) and the sudden change in the remembrances after this positioning tell us much and anticipate the first chapter's closure.

The Ex-Coloured Man gains momentary control over his father by playing the piano exquisitely—only to be controlled in turn (as the new expensive piano that soon arrives suggests) by his father's "signs." Likewise, Wright's voice seeks a measure of control over (and distance from) his father by effectively and defiantly declaring war on the most clear and obvious implied meanings in his father's daily address—as if such assaults might somehow dim the feverish glow of the premonition his father embodies. All this is made most evident in the famous kitten episode, wherein Wright's father, desperate for sleep after night work, is kept awake by the "loud, persistent meowing" of a stray kitten. He angrily yells, " 'Kill that damn thing!' . . . 'Do anything, but get it away from here!' " Young Richard responds, we will recall, by fashioning a noose and stringing up the kitten. The kitten's deathly gyrations—"It gasped, slobbered, spun, clawed the air frantically"—transport us back to the "leap" into death of the chicken whose neck was snapped by his father's hand. Ironically, Wright bests his father but reenacts an unsavory memory of him in the process.

At this point, aspects of the afflicting, and mostly female, interior world of *Black Boy* assert themselves—his mother devises a punishment that is as devastating psychologically as the first punishment was physically—but, as the chapter continues, the father remains the focus of Wright's youthful wrath. After the father leaves his wife and children to fend for themselves, Wright's persona soon remarks, "As the days slid past the image of my father became associated with my pangs of hunger, and whenever I felt hunger I thought of him with deep biological bitterness." While the immediate source of this bitterness is a grievous circumstance in the present, it is fed by hidden, less immediate energies. Modally, the image of the father being, while in Memphis, a pitifully inadequate provider is but a link in a chain of highly charged figurations that begins with the chicken-killing and ends with the sorrowful sight of him "standing alone upon the red clay of a Mississippi plantation, a sharecropper, clad in ragged overalls, holding a muddy hoe in his gnarled, veined hands." Collectively, the images present Wright's youthful impressions of immobility, hunger, and death. As his father appears in his memory's eye, with hoe in hand like some diminished king still grasping his impotent scepter, the Wright in *Black Boy* recoils from the death-in-life signaled by the red clay soil, much as Du Bois's and Johnson's narrators did before him, and seeks a realm characterized at least in its nearest reaches by flight, sustenance, and survival. Speaking in retrospect, a quarter-century after his first Memphis years, Wright's persona puts the matter this way:

> As a creature of the earth, he [his father] endured, hearty, whole, seemingly indestructible, with no regrets and no hope. He asked easy, drawling questions about me, his other son, his wife, and he laughed, amused, when I informed him of their destinies. I forgave him and pitied him as my eyes looked past him to the unpainted wooden shack. From far beyond the horizons that bound this bleak plantation there had come to me through my living the knowledge that my father was a black peasant who had gone to the city seeking life, but who had failed in the city; a black peasant whose life had been hopelessly snarled in the city, and who had at last fled the city —the same city which had lifted me in its burning arms and borne me toward alien and undreamed-of shores of knowing.

With these unrelenting words, Wright's persona does not so much slay his father as bury him alive. The jangling present that they once shared with such great discomfort is swiftly dismantled: for the father, the present is "a crude and raw past" that imprisons him; for the son, it is a vibrant future of living and knowing that sets him free. Just as they no longer share the same pulse of time, it is clear that they also no longer inhabit the same space, the same point of departure. The race has been run, and the plantation-bounding horizons that entomb the beaten man do not touch, let alone encompass or intersect, the "area of living" to which the victor has ascended. With the literal and figurative geography of *Black Boy* clarified in this way, the narrative's anti-pastoral strain—rooted as it is in similar motifs in antedating narratives—is finally unveiled and writ large. Furthermore, the city, a new and far more hopeful social structure erected upon what had been the site of departure for father and son alike, evolves and assumes an aggressive posture in the narrative's machinery, in triangular competition with the oppressing domestic interior and the ambiguous but unsnaring out-of-doors. Once the particular attractions of urban life for a truly questing figure are thus established, Wright's persona's flight to larger, grander, and hopefully more promising urban situations (such as Chicago) seems not just likely, but inevitable. (In real life, as we say, Wright's flight to Chicago, then to New York, and then to Paris was just as determined and heroic; and it is interesting to note, given the associations just discussed, that he did not live "upon the land" again until he expatriated to France.)

The second catalog appears fairly early in Chapter II of *Black Boy*. As suggested in the catalog's opening phrase—"The days and hours began to speak now with a clearer tongue"—this catalog is meant to represent a later stage along the path to literacy, beyond that in which events "spoke with a cryptic tongue." Nevertheless, many of the entries, especially at the beginning of the catalog, record the wonders and pleasures young Richard continues to discover outdoors. In that way they are virtually interchangeable with similar items in the first catalog:

> There was the breathlessly anxious fun of chasing and catching flitting fireflies on drowsy summer nights.
> There was the drenching hospitality in the pervading swell of sweet magnolias.
> There was the aura of limitless freedom distilled from the rolling sweep of tall green grass swaying and glinting in the wind and sun.
> There was the feeling of impersonal plenty when I saw a boll of cotton whose cup had spilt over and straggled its white fleece toward the earth.

With the eighth entry, however, where Wright describes "the drugged, sleepy feeling that came from sipping glasses of milk," the catalog begins to focus loosely but distinctly upon signs of food and sustenance that occasionally assume manna-like qualities:

> There was the slow, fresh, saliva-stimulating smell of cooking cotton seeds.
>
> There was the puckery taste that almost made me cry when I ate my first half-ripe persimmon.
> There was the greedy joy in the tangy taste of wild hickory nuts.
> There was the dry hot summer morning when I scratched my

bare arms on briers while picking blackberries and came home with
my fingers and lips stained black with sweet berry juice.

There was the relish of eating my first fried fish sandwich, nib-
bling at it slowly and hoping that I would never eat it up.

There was the all-night ache in my stomach after I had climbed
a neighbor's tree and eaten stolen, unripe peaches.

After leaving Memphis with his mother, young Richard finally got
something to eat while living briefly with his Granny and Grandpa
Wilson in Jackson. For this reason it is quite appropriate to say that
the signs cataloged above not only represent a large portion of what
was "enchanting" about the post-Memphis world of Granny's house
(he will reverse his opinion about her domain as the narrative prog-
resses), but also respond to the signs of that aspect of his American
hunger imposed by his father's many failures. Physical hunger in the
past is not the only catalyst for these images of sustenance; while in
the Wilson home, amid the plenty and pleasure of Nature's full fare,
Wright learns of another hunger when Ella, the schoolteacher boarding
with the family, whispers to him, after much cajoling, the story of
Bluebeard and His Seven Wives.

As Ella relates the tale, young Richard is transported to another
world—a world that is not charted by the vital geometry of food or its
absence:

> She whispered to me the story . . . and I ceased to see the porch,
> the sunshine, her face, everything. As her words fell upon my new
> ears, I endowed them with a reality that welled up from somewhere
> within me . . . . The tale made the world around me be, throb, live.
> As she spoke, reality changed, the look of things altered, and the
> world became peopled with magical presences. My sense of life
> deepened and the feel of things was different, somehow. . . . My
> imagination blazed. . . . When she was about to finish, when my
> interest was keenest, when I was lost to the world around me,
> Granny stepped briskly onto the porch.

Students of Afro-American narratives in general and of Frederick
Douglass's 1845 Narrative in particular need not wonder about what
Wright is experiencing, or about what comes next. At the heart of the
episode is the ancient call of literacy's possibilities, occasioned by the
narrator's first fleeting glimpse of the vibrant word—and the equally
ancient response of admonition or suppression, made by a representative of the most immediate oppressing social structure. When Granny

Wilson abruptly appears upon the scene, shouting that Ella is an "evil gal," that Richard is "going to burn in hell," and that what Ella and Richard are doing is "the Devil's work," she becomes for us (albeit within the confines of a black world) the latest manifestation of the archetypal oppressor initiated in Afro-American letters by Frederick Douglass's Mr. Auld. Indeed, this bond between Granny Wilson and Mr. Auld, which vilifies her far more than any oath we can imagine, is reinforced, perhaps unwittingly or subconsciously, by Wright's curious aside on how "white" Granny looked when she was angry: "My grandmother was as nearly white as a Negro can get without being white, which means that she was white. The sagging flesh of her face quivered; her eyes, large, dark, deep-set, wide apart, glared at me. Her lips narrowed to a line. Her high forehead wrinkled. When she was angry her eyelids drooped halfway down over her pupils, giving her a baleful aspect." More to the point, however, is the fact that Granny Wilson, like Mr. Auld before her in the tradition, interrupts and effectively bans as evil a fundamental activity in the narrator's quest for literacy. The "hunger" her behavior prompts in Richard is, in his telling of it, of a piece with the "torment" plaguing Douglass at a comparable point in his career.

The word of caution suggested above probably should be made more explicit: in reading *Black Boy* and observing its indebtednesses to tropes established by the slave narratives, we must remind ourselves that what places *Black Boy* in the tradition is not Wright's "enslavement" (which, despite its horrors, is finally not of the same weight and scale as, say, Douglass's), but the debt-laden rhetoric he brings to the task of describing it. With this in mind, we may thrill at Wright's concluding remarks about the Bluebeard episode, akin as they are to Douglass's declaration of his discovery of "the pathway from slavery to freedom"; yet at the same time we can recognize and measure them as part and parcel of a rhetorical strategy:

> Not to know the end of the tale filled me with a sense of emptiness, loss. I hungered for the sharp, frightening, breath-taking, almost painful excitement that the story had given me, and I vowed that as soon as I was old enough I would buy all the novels there were and read them to feed that thirst for violence that was in me, for intrigue, for plotting, for secrecy, for bloody murders. So profoundly responsive a chord had the tale struck me that the threats of my mother and grandmother had no effect whatsoever. They read my insistence as mere obstinacy, as foolishness, something that

would quickly pass; and they had no notion how desperately serious the tale had made me. They could not have known that Ella's whispered story of deception and murder had been the first experience in my life that had elicited from me a total emotional response. No words or punishment could have possibly made me doubt. I had tasted what to me was life, and I would have more of it, somehow, someway . . . I burned to learn to read novels and I tortured my mother into telling me the meaning of every strange word I saw, not because the word itself had any value, but because it was the gateway to a forbidden and enchanting land.

As the chapter continues, young Richard learns the full consequences of hungering after words, and of employing them without knowing all that they might mean or imply. I refer here, of course, to the bathing scene, wherein Richard reminds Granny to be sure to kiss his behind after she has toweled it off—a scene that is as darkly hilarious as those in the slave narratives, where an unknowing slave effectively asks his master to do the same and is beaten within an inch of his life. One such consequence is that Ella is blamed and forced to move, and that an avenue to reading and knowing—to sustenance of a particular sort—is thereby closed to Richard. The second catalog of signs to be read (and in that sense savored) is thus a response to multiple kinds of hunger; images of tasting and eating are but tropes for the pleasures of reading newly found minute particulars. Despite all the admonitions the narrator hears or discovers regarding how "forbidden and enchanting" lands often bear strange fruit, the episode involving Ella and Granny concludes on a hopeful note, because the catalog of signs at its end posits a familiar but nonetheless exhilarating correlation between manna and the word.

The third catalog also appears in chapter II of *Black Boy,* and is in some ways the most interesting of the three. The events leading up to the catalog depict a perennial concern—Wright's hunger as a boy, especially during those times when he, his mother, and his brother are not living with kin—and also a more immediate crisis, the death of his dog, Betsy. As often happens in *Black Boy,* these two dilemmas are bound as one. A week earlier, young Richard had been unable to bring himself to sell Betsy for money for food; with the dog's death, that possibility is irrevocably closed to him. The episode is important in the narrative because Wright's persona learns at least two lessons from it. The obvious one is expressed quite simply and directly by his mother's sole remark, " 'You could have had a dollar. But you can't eat a dead dog, can you?' " The less obvious (but perhaps more important) lesson is that stubbornness expressed outwardly and somewhat ingeniously by an insistence upon the literal meaning of words is still stubbornness. Something links the Betsy episode with the earlier events in which young Richard hangs a kitten, supposedly at his father's behest. In each instance the persona attempts to assert a sense of pride and self-worth by insisting upon the literal meaning of words: He told me to kill the kitten, didn't he? The ninety-seven cents the white woman offered me for Betsy wasn't a dollar, was it? But those attempts always lead to little more than the animal's death and the evocation of his mother's wrath. Clearly, in each case the persona has some elementary idea of how to manipulate words and meaning, but no idea of how to control the contextualizing event.

Here the narrative machinery of *Black Boy* oils itself and, in a sense, exposes itself, allowing us in turn to both construct and partially deconstruct the narrative as a whole. What is exposed, I believe, is the feigned innocence that must lie behind any scheme of vindictive literalness, no matter how simple or spontaneous. If the persona is capable of assuming such a posture, then our belief in his actual innocence and his subsequent inability to pursue certain kinds of verbal strategies is undercut. The obvious counterargument is that the innocence feigned in the kitten and Betsy episodes does not compromise the person's character—that, indeed, it displays his character by portraying his willingness, even as a youth, to fight a losing battle for a good if personal cause. But that leaves us where we began. The fact remains that *Black Boy* requires its readers to admire Wright's persona's remarkable and unassailable innocence in certain major episodes, and to condone his exploitation of that innocence in others. This, I think, is a poorly tailored seam, if not precisely a flaw, in *Black Boy*'s narrative strategy.

What is oiled is that part of the machinery which presents the evolution of Wright's persona's quest for authorial control. As I have suggested before—and as the 1845 Douglass *Narrative* instructs —authorial control of a personal history is achieved when the author's persona not only becomes the definitive historian (or fictionizer) of his past, but also finds a voice that is articulate enough to at least modulate, if not absolutely control, the pressing forces of a hostile environment. In *Black Boy* the kitten and Betsy episodes, marked as they are by the persona's youthful attempts to modulate or control person and event through language, represent the point of departure for whatever measure of authorial control the persona will achieve in his quest for literacy and freedom. In this way the third catalog of the narrative assumes a special weight and meaning: after the failures and rebuffs resulting from his inability to sell Betsy upon his own terms (monetary, but also verbal), young Richard is prompted quite naturally to speculate on what he may control—and on what terms.

> If I pulled a hair from a horse's tail and sealed it in a jar of my own urine, the hair would turn overnight into a snake.
> If I passed a Catholic sister or mother dressed in black and smiled and allowed her to see my teeth, I would surely die.
> If I walked under a leaning ladder, I would certainly have bad luck.
> If I kissed my elbow, I would turn into a girl.
>
> If I heard a voice and no human being was near, then either God or the Devil was trying to talk to me.
> Whenever I made urine, I should spit into it for good luck.
>
> If I covered a mirror when a storm was raging, the lightning would not strike me.
> If I stepped over a broom that was lying on the floor, I would have bad luck.
> If I walked in my sleep, then God was trying to lead me somewhere to do a good deed for Him.

While entries such as these unquestionably present the narrator initiating or embodying certain causes for certain effects, we must be aware (as Wright was undeniably aware) of the narrow limits of a world in which such acts have great meaning. On one hand, the catalog champions sign-reading of a fundamental sort, and that is an important step up the ladder to literacy for the sign-reader. On the other, the catalog can be seen as a mere listing of folk beliefs or events into which the narrator projects his own hypothetical participation—the point being that opportunities for personal modulation or control of events are nil, because the sequence and *form* of the "folk event" are always prescribed and hence pre-known. The fact that immersion in the enactment (or reenactment) of a "folk event" creates only an illusion of authorial control gives us pause in reading this catalog; but even more germane is the argument which Wright sustains in his own way, in "Blueprint for Negro Writing," that literacy *vis-à-vis* superstition rarely has any bearing on literacy *vis-à-vis* the word. With all this in mind, the purpose and place of the third catalog in *Black Boy*'s narrative strategy becomes ringingly clear, especially when we remind ourselves of Wright's other famous dictum in "Blueprint" that what is national (or "folk") in our lives must first be embraced in order to be transcended. The catalog marks that point on the path to literacy at which Wright's persona becomes proficient in the initiation and dispensation of "tribal" interpretations of the environment, and at which the persona may quite understandably rationalize such a proficiency by arguing, "Because I had no power to make things happen outside of me in the objective world, I made things happen within. . . ." But of course this way-station on the path is far more a point of departure than a destination: once the persona embraces and knows the signs and tongue of his "folk" world, he can only relinquish the quest and be defined by that world or, especially if he aspires to literacy *vis-à-vis* the word, courageously travel on. That Wright's persona will indeed travel on is made clear by two points on which the chapter ends. First, he returns to school; second, he sights for the very first time an airplane soaring in the sky. True to his limited experiences, and perhaps to the "reading" level documented by the catalog, the narrator's response is, " 'It's a bird . . . I see it.' " At that point—a point which affects much of the Afro-American canon to come—a man lifts our hero up upon his shoulder and solemnly enlightens him by saying, " 'Boy, remember this, . . . you're seeing man fly.' "

The three catalogs in the opening chapters of *Black Boy* are three systems of signs to be read en route to literacy. Once he reads them, young Richard knows something of the delight and terror, range and limitation, and literacy and illiteracy of the world into which he is born. Once that world is read and in that sense embraced, he is not just prepared but fated for the fresh space to be gained by additional knowing and seeing. All this is substantiated and reinforced in a wonderful way by the already discussed passage in the very next chapter, where Wright re-creates and glosses a typical conversation conducted by his boyhood gang. The entire conversation is a fourth catalog in the narrative in which every entry is, before it is glossed, a sign of the oppressing culture that necessarily must be read, and in that sense controlled to some degree, by anyone aspiring to be a literate survivor. In the first catalog Wright's persona is assaulted by the signs; in the second the assault continues, but is defused somewhat by the countering idea that signs may be read as well as felt; in the third the persona attempts to control the signs by entering them, but, since they are of a particular tribal sort, acts of entry are not full and complete acts of reading and control. In what I am calling the fourth catalog, each gloss is the kind of articulate response to a cultural sign that the persona has been working toward all along (by gathering a word hoard, finding a voice, discovering a perspective, seeing, feeling). The glory of Wright's construction is that the catalogs depict a progression not only from muteness to voice, and from stasis before assault to mobility found in response to assault, but also from "formless forms" bereft of counterpoint to highly formal ones rich with counterpoint—especially of an Afro-American persuasion. In the third catalog the "If/then" formula of the inherited and essentially static folk beliefs or events establishes the idea of counterpoint as an aspect of literacy in a fundamental, if not entirely invigorating, way; but it is in the fourth catalog, where response becomes a matter of personal articulation, that counterpoint is not simply enacted formulaically but sung. Here we may finally take the next step beyond Ralph Ellison's now classic definition of Richard Wright's blues (that, like any covering cherub, has guided us but inhibited us for so long) and locate that blues in a discrete counterpointing linguistic structure within the narrative. In the fourth catalog, each unit of exchange between an adolescent's wail or bark of misery bound to humor, and a mature voice's *reading* of the signs contained therein, is a blues stanza rendered improvisationally in literary terms; the articulate response is, of course, the requisite coda to the whole unit. The achievement of these improvised blues stanzas, at a time when most Afro-American writers (including Langston Hughes) were barely doing more than "transcribing" the blues on to the printed page, is remarkable in itself. But even more extraordinary is the fact that Wright, in this one rare, rhythmic moment in his art, could make those stanzas say so much. The key, I think, lies in the fact that each stanza is initiated in the past (the youthful wails, barks, growls, and riffs) and completed in the present (the mature voice's gloss). In this exaggerated way, Wright reminds us that reading—the completion of the stanza, as it were—depends on seeing and knowing and gaining perspective, and that art—once again, the completion of the stanza—is equally dependent upon the discovery of a mature voice. If *Black Boy* were an immersion narrative, it could end right here, and glory in the fact that indigenous art forms so vigorously and yet so partially sung in our hero's youth finally have been completed. But of course *Black Boy* is not an immersion narrative, but one of ascent. The great satisfaction which Wright's persona receives from singing the blues with skill is that, in direct contradiction to one famous blues line, he *can* get out of "them blues" *alive*.

In the preceding sections of this chapter I have mentioned some of the tropes and conventions found originally in the slave narratives and sustained in *Black Boy*. This section—which could be entitled "Reading, Writing, and Ascent"—focuses on another strain of indebtedness in the narrative, one that is rooted far more in turn-of-the-century literature than in what came before. The strain to which I refer links *Black Boy* to antedating texts such as Sutton Elbert Griggs's *Imperium in Imperio,* Du Bois's *The Souls of Black Folk,* and Johnson's *The Autobiography of an Ex-Coloured Man,* and establishes *Black Boy* as an antedating text for many recent narratives, including Ellison's *Invisible Man* and Toni Morrison's *The Bluest Eye.* What all these narratives share (or rather, participate in) is a primary scene in Afro-American letters: the schoolroom episode, which is often accompanied by its chief variant, the graduation episode. The significance of this scene has less to do with the extraordinary frequency of its appearance or even with its "logical" place in a prose literature dominated by autobiographical and *Bildungsroman* impulses, and more to do with how it characterizes and shapes—in literary terms— a discernible period in Afro-American literary history. Schoolroom and graduation episodes in Afro-American literature begin to assume their proper stature when we recall not only the laws and race rituals that enforced a people's illiteracy (*vis-à-vis* the written word) but also the body of literature, including most obviously the slave narratives, that expresses again and again the quest for freedom *and* literacy achieved regardless of the odds, regardless of the lack of sanctioned opportunities such as school attendance. When familiar images in the early narrative literature, such as that of a Frederick Douglass or a William Wells Brown having to dupe white urchins in order to learn the rudiments of reading and ciphering, give way to fresh if not altogether joyous expressions of black youths in one-room schoolhouses, high schools, institutes, colleges, and even universities, then we may say truly that a primary configuration in the tradition is being systematically revoiced, and that these expressions are almost singlehandedly creating a new contour in the tradition's history. To place *The Souls of Black Folk* or *Black Boy* in this contour, for example, is to say more about either text (especially about their relations to one another) than can be said when they are relegated to categories largely imposed by other disciplines, such as "literature of accommodation" and "literature of protest."

One point to be made regarding Richard Wright's participation in these activities is that his greatest novel, *Native Son,* is totally bereft of any schoolroom or graduation episode—unless one wishes (somewhat perversely) to assign those properties to the cell or courtroom scenes, or to Bigger's "tutorials" with Attorney Max. In contrast, *Black Boy*'s middle chapters are one sustained schoolroom episode; furthermore, the graduation episode that completes chapter VIII is unquestionably a major event in the narrative, and perhaps *the* event young Richard seeks when he earlier confides that he is "waiting for some event, some word, some act, some circumstance to furnish the impetus" for his flight from what he calls elsewhere "that southern swamp of despair and violence." The resulting contrast between the two volumes should not be viewed in any qualitative way—for example, the absence of the schoolroom scene from *Native Son* does not categorically make it a superior or inferior work of literature. But it should be examined, nevertheless, if for no other reason than to receive its suggestion of the full reach of the Afro-American landscape charted by Wright's oeuvre. Once this reach or territory is explored (and the space between Bigger's world and Wright's persona's world is indeed of continental proportions), the glories and failures of Wright's transtextual artistic vision become newly manifest. The glory is primarily and fundamentally the territory itself, a space full of nightmare and misery that is finally bounded only by the seemingly limitless horizons of living and knowing. The failure is essentially that Wright's antipodal construction of the landscape unwittingly positions his supreme fiction of himself—not just as a man or even as an articulate survivor, but as an artist—*within* an antipode, and hence removes it from whatever mediating postures might be available to him. Much has already been said about this particular failure or dilemma; Ralph Ellison and George Kent explore this issue in their own way when they remark respectively that "Wright could imagine Bigger, but Bigger could not possibly imagine Richard Wright," and that Wright's "deepest consciousness is that of the exaggerated Westerner." My interest here, however, lies less with investigating Wright's resulting posture as an artist and more with exploring the way-stations and stretches of road that constitute the pathway to whatever posture Wright's persona in *Black Boy* achieves. And it seems clear that the persona's school experiences provide a proper place to begin.

Since the world of *Black Boy* is so relentlessly hostile, we should not be surprised to discover that most of young Richard's learning situations are pockets of fear and misery. Certain features of the schoolroom scene, such as the persona's first efforts to acquire a (written and spoken) voice, are sustained here and there, providing a few bright moments. However, when these features occur, they are usually contextualized in the narrative as the spoils of bitter battles; their piercing light may be attributed as much to the flash of weapons as to the lamp of learning. Wright's persona is so embattled in his school experiences partly because, until he enters the Jim Hill School at the age of twelve, most of his schooling occurs at home or in classrooms that are formidable extensions of that horrific and inhibiting domestic world. When Ella (who is, we recall, a schoolteacher) clandestinely tells young Richard the spirited tale of Bluebeard, transporting him to new worlds beyond whatever he had previously dreamt and felt, the porch where they sit becomes momentarily a schoolroom complete with globe, primer, and, most important, a teacher sensitive to a child's hunger for knowledge. But that porch is first and foremost—as well as finally—Granny Wilson's porch, and Granny, with her particular ideas about the extraordinary reach of the Devil's hand, seems always just beyond the doorway, ready to pounce upon any "mischief" invading her domain. Another construction of this situation is offered when Aunt Addie returns from the Seventh-Day Adventist Religious School in Huntsville to open her own church school. Unfortunately, young Richard has no choice but to matriculate there. From the start, it is clear than things couldn't be worse if the class were taught by Granny Wilson herself: Richard and Addie square off right away, and when the battle of wills leads to a pitched free-for-all, replete with biting and kicking, in which Richard brandishes a kitchen knife in much the same fashion that he will later grab a razor blade in each fist to ward off his Uncle Tom, we cannot possibly be surprised to learn that Addie stopped calling on Richard in class, and that "Consequently [he] stopped studying."

Not all of Richard's "home learning" in *Black Boy* is this violent or unfulfilled. The rare moments of learning from kin are provided by his mother, usually during those brief interludes when they are living neither with his father nor with Granny Wilson—the prime representatives of the narrative's oppressing exterior and interior spaces. Quite typically, given Wright's drive to achieve literacy *vis-à-vis* the word, the best example of his mother in a teaching role involves diction—the choice of certain words for certain conditions and circumstances. And, quite appropriately, given the violent world of the narrative, the words he learns to use are "whip" and "beat" and, less directly, "boy" and "man:"

> . . . when word circulated among the black people of the neighborhood that a "black" boy had been severely beaten by a "white" man, I felt that the "white" man had had a right to beat the "black" boy, for I naively assumed that the "white" man must have been the "black" boy's father. And did not all fathers, like my father, have the right to beat their children?
> . . . But when my mother told me that the "white" man was not the father of the "black" boy, was no kin to him at all, I was puzzled.
> "Then why did the 'white' man whip the 'black' boy?" I asked my mother.
> "The 'white' man did not *whip* the 'black' boy," my mother told me. "He *beat* the 'black' boy."
> "But why?"
> "You're too young to understand."

To be sure, young Richard does not understand completely—but when does one ever pick up a grain of truth, in or out of school, and understand it completely upon first hearing? Sad as it may be, it is through exchanges such as this one that young Richard is taught about his environment, his place in it, and about *how* words mean as well as *what* they mean. Although his mother is unquestionably a part of the domestic structure afflicting and oppressing him, she is also, possibly because she is his mother, the best teacher his circumstances afford him: she explains words, she tells him stories, she helps him learn how to read. For this reason—and perhaps, too, because his semi-invalid mother often appears to be as ensnared by the household as he is—

young Richard cares for her, is not violent with her, and grieves for her in his own stolid way during her many illnesses. Still, there is an underlying tension between Richard's deep feelings for his mother and his compulsion—based not on whim or fancy, but on a rather accurate assessment of his circumstances—to take his neophyte stories and sketches outside the home, to show them to others including, in the first instance, an incredulous neighbor woman who most certainly turns out not to be the surrogate mother, aunt, or grandmother that Richard is obviously searching for. The abiding presence of this dilemma offers one more reason why Richard must leave the South— and take his mother with him. While flight may not allow mother and son to recapture those special moments when the home was a site of learning, it will at least extract them from Granny's lair and allow them to begin again.

Significant schooling outside the home environment in *Black Boy* begins only when young Richard enters the Jim Hill Public School. The only earlier public school experience reported in the narrative occurs in Memphis, shortly after his father "disappears." Richard's brief report serves mainly to depict the point of departure for his ascent, first and most immediately in his school world and then in the larger circumferences of his life beyond the South:

> I began school at Howard Institute at a later age than was usual; my mother had not been able to buy me the necessary clothes to make me presentable. The boys of the neighborhood took me to school the first day and when I reached the edge of the school grounds I became terrified, wanted to return home, wanted to put it off. But the boys simply took my hand and pulled me inside the building. I was frightened speechless and the other children had to identify me, tell the teacher my name and address. I sat listening to pupils recite, knowing and understanding what was being said and done, but utterly incapable of opening my mouth when called upon. The students around me seemed so sure of themselves that I despaired of ever being able to conduct myself as they did.

In this way, in a context removed from the domestic interior, Wright's persona initiates a motif that we know from the slave narratives: the ascent to find a voice which can, among other things, guide conduct and name itself. But the ascent is not immediately forthcoming; all of the episodes described above involving Granny Wilson and Aunt Addie—episodes marking young Richard's forced return to the domestic interior—intercede between his all-too-few days at Howard

Institute and his three years at the Jim Hill School. When he finally
reenters the school world, his longing to begin the ascent has become
an unfathomable energy, and his hunger for learning and for exploring
the realm beyond Granny Wilson's doorstep is even more acute than
his perpetual desire for food. Indeed, as he tells of his first days at
Jim Hill School and of his willingness to go without his usual miserable
fare at home in order to see "a world leap to life," he remarks, "To
starve in order to learn about my environment was irrational, but so
were my hungers."

Although this may suggest that the school world of *Black Boy*
is, in comparison to the narrative's other structural spaces, a kind of
paradise, such is hardly the case. In fact, the school world is truly the
second circle of Wright's southern hell, just as the oppressing domestic
interior is the first circle, and the white world of the narrative, to
which young Richard will be introduced shortly, is the third. The
school world is not as physically violent as the domestic interior, but
it has its own array of punishments and afflictions which display themselves fully in both of the signal episodes in which Wright's persona
takes a symbolic step toward freedom and literacy.

In the first episode, young Richard writes a short story ("The
Voodoo of Hell's Half-Acre") which the mature Wright describes in
retrospect as being "crudely atmospheric, emotional, intuitively psychological." The youth instinctively shows it to someone outside the
hostile environments of home and school, the editor of the local Negro
newspaper. The happy result is that the story is printed—young Richard has indeed come far from that day when he shared his first sketch
with a neighbor. But any joy or inspiration that he experiences is
quickly stifled by what he calls elsewhere "the tribe in which [I] lived
and of which [I was] a part." After family, schoolmates, and teachers
pummel him with their questions and condemnations, he is left thoroughly alone and abused—"I felt that I had committed a crime"—but
charged all the more with the self-generated energy needed to continue
his ascent. It is quite significant that the episode ends with Wright's
persona's first expression of the North as a destination and a symbolic
space, and that his emerging fantasy of what he will do there involves
acts of literacy on a grand scale: "I dreamed of going north and writing books, novels. The North symbolized to me all that I had not felt
and seen; it had no relation whatever to what actually existed. Yet,
by imagining a place where everything was possible, I kept hope alive

in me." These imaginings keep young Richard valiantly on the move for many years, but their immediate and much-needed effect is to offer him enough resilience to endure another year of tribal rigors at home and at school.

During the next year (and chapter) of the narrative, young Richard takes his second symbolic step toward freedom and literacy while at Jim Hill School, and that step is described in the graduation episode. While the first step involving his storywriting may be said to be an indebted and inverted rendering of the Ex-Coloured Man's reception as a youthful artist within his community, the graduation episode is a comparably indebted and inverted expression of many prior moments in the literature, but especially perhaps of that day in 1841 when Frederick Douglass rose to the podium and found his voice in Nantucket. In each of Wright's episodes, his inversion of antecedent expressions is not total—"The Voodoo of Hell's Half Acre" is probably no less flawed than the Ex-Coloured Man's youthful interpretations of romantic melodies, and Wright's persona's graduation speech is certainly no worse than Bernard Belgrave's in *Imperium in Imperio* or Shiny's in *The Autobiography*. But that is not the point. It is rather that Wright seems intent upon revising certain abiding expressions within the literary tradition of communal succor and of potential immersion in community, in order to place *Black Boy* within the ranks of the narrative of ascent. Put another way, his effort is to create a persona who experiences major moments of literacy, personal freedom, and personal growth while in a kind of bondage, and yet who maintains in a very clear-headed way his vision of a higher literacy and a better world.

As one might expect, the heart of the graduation episode is not the delivery of speech or its reception—that would suggest that communal bonds between speaker and audience are possible, and that the persona is satisfied with the stage of literacy he has achieved. Rather, the episode focuses on the series of tempestuous events that precede the "great day." Of these, none is more important than young Richard's conversation with the principal of the Jim Hill School. The scene that ensues should be familiar to students of Afro-American literature, because the principal is clearly an intermediate manifestation of a character type most visibly inaugurated by Jean Toomer in *Cane*'s figure of Hanley, and most formidably completed (for the moment) by Ralph Ellison in *Invisible Man*'s Bledsoe. In that scene young Richard is forced to choose between his principal and his principle:

whether to accept and read a speech "ghost written" by a "bought" man, or to go ahead with a speech written by himself, on his own, and probably in the same tattered but secretly dear notebook that produced "The Voodoo of Hell's Half-Acre." He chooses the latter course, and there ensues a predictable response amongst the tribe— from the principal on down to his schoolmates and, at the level of his home life, his worn-out and retired kinsman, Uncle Tom. After the barrage of assaults and cajolings, including bribes, Richard doggedly pursues his righteous course and describes the resulting event in this way:

> On the night of graduation I was nervous and tense; I rose and faced the audience and my speech rolled out. When my voice stopped there was some applause. I did not care if they liked it or not; I was through. Immediately, even before I left the platform, I tried to shut all memory of the event from me. A few of my class-mates managed to shake my hand as I pushed toward the door, seeking the street. Somebody invited me to a party and I did not accept. I did not want to see any of them again. I walked home, saying to myself: The hell with it! With almost seventeen years of baffled living behind me, I faced the world in 1925.

Several aspects of this statement interest me greatly, and I would like to offer two additional quotations from other sources by way of beginning to remark upon them. The first is quite recognizably from the 1845 Douglass *Narrative:*

> But, while attending an anti-slavery convention at Nantucket, on the 11th of August, 1841, I felt strongly moved to speak. . . . It was a severe cross, and I took it up reluctantly. The truth was, I felt my-self a slave, and the idea of speaking to white people weighed me down. I spoke but a few moments, when I felt a degree of freedom, and said what I desired with considerable ease. From that time until now, I have been engaged in pleading the cause of my brethren— with what success, and with what devotion, I leave those acquainted with my labors to decide.

The second quotation, as much a part of the tradition as the first, is from Langston Hughes's "The Negro Writer and the Racial Mountain," published in *The Nation* in 1926, within a year after Wright's persona made his commencement speech at the Jim Hill School:

> We younger Negro artists who create now intend to express our individual dark-skinned selves without fear or shame. If white

people are pleased we are glad. If they are not, it doesn't matter.
. . . If colored people are pleased we are glad. If they are not,
their displeasure doesn't matter either. We build our temples for
tomorrow, strong as we know how, and we stand on top of the
mountain, free within ourselves.

By citing these very different passages, I want to suggest that the voice
Wright's persona assumes—the voice found and honed presumably
through experiences such as those surrounding and including the graduation—is very much in the Afro-American heroic grain. The hard-
won freedom that Wright's persona acquires from the ordeal of the
entire valedictory event is, at root, much the same as the "degree of
freedom" Douglass's voice experiences while addressing the throng.
Furthermore, while Wright's persona has neither reached the top of
his idea of the "racial mountain" nor designed the temple to be situated in that space (that "Blueprint" will come twelve years later), he
clearly shares Hughes's conviction that one must ascend beyond the
"low-ground" of oppressive—interracial and intraracial—social structures to gain one's voice on one's own terms and, in that sense, be free.
Like Du Bois before them, Wright and Hughes both seek the heights
of a "Pisgah" soaring above the "dull . . . hideousness" of a structural
topography that is racially both black and white.

What is new about Wright's rendering of this familiar event is
not the voice achieved, but the positioning of the event in the narrative
itself. Unlike Douglass, Wright is not trying to end his narrative; instead, he is attempting to move his persona from one world of the
narrative to another. He does not want to suggest (as Douglass does)
that the achievement of voice may yield even a fleeting sense of personal ease and of community, for that would disruptively suggest that
his persona has found a measure of comfort and stability in the very
world he is about to leave. And so Wright's persona moves on with
his stride unbroken—handshakes are barely acknowledged, invitations
to parties are cast aside—and with only one small anchor fixing the
occasion in official time: he mentions the year, and it is 1925. One
notes this latter point partly because, in accord with the Du Boisian
model in *The Souls,* few dates are recorded in *Black Boy,* and partly
because 1925 is such a watershed year in Afro-American literature.
What this suggests about the graduation episode in *Black Boy* is that
Wright is concerned not only about positioning the event in the narrative itself, but also about placing the event in Afro-American literary

history. At the very time when the New Negro "renaissance" was under full sway in Harlem (*The New Negro,* edited by Alain Locke, made the pages of *Survey Graphic* in 1925) and, tangentially, in places such as Washington, D.C. (let us not forget Georgia Douglas Johnson, Jean Toomer, Sterling Brown, and Edward "Duke" Ellington), Richard Wright was belatedly but triumphantly graduating from the Jim Hill School and, according to the exquisite fiction of his personal history, thinking much the same thoughts that a bona fide renaissance hero (Langston Hughes) would publish within a year.

Wright gets the maximum mileage out of the graduation episode, and he does so in accord with his particular vision of how he must revise and at the same time honor tradition in order to assume a place within it. His revision of Douglass's model episode allows his persona to travel on, having achieved a voice and vision comparable to Douglass's; and with his revision of Afro-American literary history *vis-à-vis* 1925 he makes a place for himself within that history well before any of his major texts were written—let alone, saw print. With these ingenious undertakings completed, it is hard to believe that *Black Boy* has not run its course—although, in a very real sense, it has only just begun.

Given all of the affinities we have discovered between a modern text like *Black Boy* and a slave narrative like Frederick Douglass's 1845 *Narrative,* we must ask whether Wright merely duplicates narrative strategies inaugurated by the slave narratives, or whether he employs those strategies as a foundation for his own expressions of assault and ascent. This fascinating question liberates us from the need to examine further such obvious narrative features as the quest for freedom and literacy and the requisite mystification of the North, and directs us toward what turn out to be *Black Boy*'s most controversial passages. By and large, these are the passages in which Wright's persona aggressively demystifies the "black world" of the narrative or rejects what is tribal in his life. While this feature is unquestionably anticipated by certain slave narratives (recall here Frederick Douglass's distant and nearly cold-blooded attitude toward his fellow slaves in his opening chapters), Wright's revoicing of the motif is so strident and sustained that we may say that he is striving to create something new.

The slave narratives contain countless acts of rejection of the "black world" as it is configured by life in the slave quarters and among kin. However, these acts are nearly always presented by the narrators as difficult compromises that the fleeing slave must make, and as additional expressions of slavery's assault upon the slave family and community. When it is made clear, for example, that neither Henry Bibb nor William Wells Brown can successfully escape to freedom while bringing loved ones in tow, we are encouraged to grieve for their lot and to admire the courage and determination that prompt them to cut even the most tender bonds, leaping for what may be only an idea of a better life. Indeed, the Bibb and Brown narratives are so successful in this regard that when Bibb's wife resignedly becomes her master's favored concubine (complete with her own cottage in the clearing) and when Brown's mother is ruthlessly sold downriver, we hardly blame Bibb or Brown for being far away and free; instead, we grieve all the more for their continuing hardship.

While Wright's persona in *Black Boy* does what he can (as soon as he can) to have his mother accompany him in his northward ascent, the narrative's energies and strategies are not directed toward suggesting that this is a great triumph by black humanity over oppressive social forces, or that the flight north involves any sort of conflict or compromise occasioned by tribal feelings. On the contrary, *Black Boy* picks up where Douglass's 1845 *Narrative* leaves off, rationalizing the flight to freedom by portraying the "black world" known to the persona as another phase and form of slavery. Wright uses the new resulting portrait for its own narrative ends. Nowhere in the slave narratives do we find a passage comparable to the following famous one in *Black Boy,* partly because Wright is consciously and aggressively attempting to clear a space for himself in Afro-American letters:

> After I had outlived the shocks of childhood, after the habit of reflection had been born in me, I used to mull over the strange absence of real kindness in Negroes, how unstable was our tenderness, how lacking in genuine passion we were, how void of great hope, how timid our joy, how bare our traditions, how hollow our memories, how lacking we were in those intangible sentiments that bind man to man, and how shallow was even our despair. After I had learned other ways of life I used to brood upon the unconscious irony of those who felt that Negroes led so passional an existence! I saw that what had been taken for our emotional strength was our negative confusions, our flights, our fears, our frenzy under pressure.

The passage goes on for another paragraph and includes language that anticipates everything the persona will soon say about his search for a civilization and not a culture: "Whenever I thought of the essential bleakness of black life in America, I knew that Negroes had never been allowed to catch the full spirit of Western civilization. . . ." But by the end of the quoted section, Wright has already made his point and exposed his underlying concerns. Some readers might argue that Wright is attempting to "shock" his way into Afro-American literary history, and, to a degree, they have a point. But the fact of the matter is that Wright's extraordinary assertions have less to do with his opinion of how to arrest the attention of an American reading public than with his abiding struggle to define himself in relation to the most persistent spectres in both his private and his literary imagination: his father, Bigger Thomas, and the "Bigger" in his past.

One notes a strange but distinct and exacting correspondence between the above-quoted passage and that earlier one in which Wright's persona recalls and pities his father's condition as a Mississippi sharecropper twenty-five years after his failure in Memphis. The opening phrases of both are specifically fashioned to distance the persona, in time and achievement, from the black "specimen" he is about to dissect. "After I had outlived the shocks of childhood, after the habit of reflection had been born in me" is but a restatement of "A quarter of a century was to elapse between the time when I saw my father sitting with the strange woman [in Memphis] and the time when I was to see him again, standing alone . . . a sharecropper. . . ." In the earlier passage, the persona goes on to describe his father as a "black peasant" (and hence, for Wright, a denizen of America's trough). Given the fact that the persona senses some lingering bonds with his father ("I could see a shadow of my face in his face . . . there was an echo of my voice in his voice"), there is no mistaking why such extraordinary and virulent energies are used to condemn the father to a well-bounded time frame and geography: Wright wants his father out of his life, shelved in the space he has created for him. My suggestion here, prompted in part by the proximity of the passages to one another, is that the new or second passage can be easily read as yet another strident attempt by Wright's persona to condemn and obliterate the haunting image of his father. Every failing with which Negro America is charged is, at base, a failure he has witnessed within his family circle; each phrase employing the word "our"—our tenderness, our joy, our traditions, our memories, and especially our despair, our negative confusions, our flights, our fears, our frenzy—is fundamentally in reference to his relations with his kin, his father in particular. Surely Wright's persona has his family and father as much as his race in mind when he concludes the second half of his remarks: "And when I brooded upon the cultural barrenness of black life, I wondered if clean, positive tenderness, love, honor, loyalty, and the capacity to remember were native with man. I asked myself if these human qualities were not fostered, won, struggled and suffered for, preserved in ritual *from one generation to another* . . ." (italics added). With these words, kin and a culture are summarily dismantled as a price willingly paid so that a once-distant civilization may be envisioned and achieved.

Of course, whenever Wright, even in the creation of his autobiographical narrative, broods upon the cultural barrenness of black life, images of Bigger Thomas soon appear in our minds, and apparently in his as well. I have suggested before that one reason why Wright had to write *Black Boy* was so that he could lay to rest the question of how he escaped becoming a Bigger. While the passage being discussed does not precisely answer that question, it does offer one of Wright's strategies for displacing himself from Bigger's world. The issue of whether life in Negro America is as stunted as Wright's persona proclaims it to be is finally irrelevant, since the passage describes the black world of Wright's oeuvre in general, and of *Native Son* in particular. Indeed, the passage is something of a key to a full and complete understanding of all that Bigger represents: unlike his author (or at least his author's fiction of himself), Bigger never "outlives" the "shocks of childhood." As the cell-block scenes so convincingly report, he never acquires the "habit of reflection." The failures amongst Negroes involving real kindness, tenderness, genuine passion, great hope, joy, traditions, memories, and all the rest of Wright's bristling list are as rampant as the rats in Bigger's world; "the unconscious irony of those who felt that Negroes led so passional an existence" is clearly Wright's signal concerning how he wants us to receive the words and deeds of Mary Dalton, Jan, and possibly Attorney Max; and finally the phrase "our negative confusions, our flights, our fears, our frenzy under pressure" is but a compressed revoicing of what we know of Bigger's life, a line that virtually restates the title of each book within *Native Son*—Fear, Flight, Fate. While this "key" to *Native Son* is useful, the passage as a whole is finally even more useful to its author as a rhetoric (if not wholly a rite) of purgation or exorcism. One suspects, however, that the dim outline of all *three* of Wright's demons—his father, Bigger Thomas, and the Bigger in himself (or at least his past) who is almost simultaneously resurrected and buried in *Black Boy*—will always be before him. Even when he methodically dissects and shelves both Biggers and his father in the same morgue of his imagination, he is but reenacting Bigger Thomas's disposal of both the idea and the remains of Mary Dalton and Bessie. By writing *Black Boy* Wright may have learned that demons can reside in one's actions, as well as in one's mind.

At the beginning of this section I remarked that passages such as the one under discussion are controversial, and this is evident from the response they have occasioned amongst the writers who follow Wright in the tradition. Ralph Ellison, James Baldwin, Ernest Gaines, Cyrus Colter, Toni Morrison, James Alan McPherson, Al Young, Leon Forrest, Alice Walker, Gayl Jones, and Ishmael Reed are among the fiction writers who immediately come to mind, whose best work dispels the deathlike chill of Wright's (albeit rhetorical) vision of Negro America; in the context of this discussion, what I take to be Ellison's response interests me most. I should say at once, with Ellison's phrase "antagonistic cooperation" in mind, that the conversation between literary sensibilities which I am about to suggest has less to do with "anxieties of influence" (a subject which has been energetically explored *vis-à-vis* Wright and Ellison by Joseph Skerrett) and more to do with how one contour in literary history occasions another. The distinction forwarded here is one that Ellison himself encourages when he tutors Irving Howe, in "The World and the Jug," by explaining: ". . . perhaps you will understand when I say he [Wright] did not influence me if I point out that while one can do nothing about choosing one's relatives, one can, as artist, choose one's 'ancestors.' Wright was, in this sense, a 'relative'; Hemingway an 'ancestor.'" As his remarks continue, Ellison embellishes his distinction between "relative" and "ancestor" in general, and between Wright and Hemingway in particular, to a point where his final word on the subject is that Wright, as a "relative," was "a Negro like myself, and perhaps a great man"; Hemingway, as an "ancestor," was "in many ways the true father-as-artist of so many of us who came to writing during the late thirties." The phrase "father-as-artist" undoubtedly rings some critics' chimes, but I for one am quite unwilling to declare that I know the melody or the hour. I am more interested in the fact that Ellison is attempting a plausible explanation for his assertions, an explanation that is far more personal and atextual (and therefore, as history has shown, more vulnerable to attacks from the intelligentsia and not-so-intelligentsia) than necessary. Had Ellison gone ahead and pinpointed a textual source for the "antagonistic cooperation" between his art (and artistic sensibility) and Wright's, he could have avoided some of the confrontations that afflicted him in the 1960's. He did not have to look very far: the passage in *Black Boy* which is under discussion is a (perhaps *the*) textual source that clarifies Wright's and Ellison's artistic relationship, and it seems likely that Ellison was aware of the passage, since he quotes the second half of it in "Richard Wright's Blues."

While there can be no doubt that much or all of Wright's damning list of the Negro's shortcomings rankles Ellison, the crowning affront has to be: "After I had learned other ways of life . . . I saw that what had been taken for our emotional strength was our negative confusions, our flights, our fears, *our frenzy under pressure*" (italics added). I have suggested before that what Wright is up to here is, in part, a deliberate re-creation of the "black world" of *Native Son* (complete with references to the novel's section titles), prompted by a desire to distance his questing, articulate persona ("After I had learned other ways of life") from that world, and hence from Bigger Thomas. I want to suggest now that Wright is also about the task of defining a contour in literary history and placing himself in it—for certainly that is one momentous potential effect of his self-serving revision of Hemingway's famous credo, "grace under pressure." Once Wright bravely revoices that phrase as "frenzy under pressure" while planting obvious allusions to his most celebrated novel, not only is Afro-American life peremptorily typed, and possibly stereotyped, but a distinct idea of Afro-American literature—complete with maps of its foundations, abiding tropes, and central texts—is also aggressively launched. At the heart of either radical construction is the apparent conviction that Hemingway's creed must be turned inside out before it has any relevance to Afro-American life or art. This, I believe, is unquestionably a source-in-text for Ellison's differences with Wright, not simply because one of Ellison's "ancestors" has been mugged, but more profoundly because the idea of Afro-American life and art promulgated by Wright's assertions effectively excludes *his* life and art.

All in all, the relationship between Wright and Ellison is not unlike that between Washington and Du Bois. In either case, the issue is not whether the younger artist believes that the established figure is truly committed to the partial truthfulness of his rhetoric. Du Bois never argued that; and Ellison makes a point of writing, in "Richard Wright's Blues," that "Wright knows perfectly well that Negro life is a by-product of Western civilization, and that in it . . . are to be discovered all those impulses, tendencies, life and cultural forms to be found elsewhere in Western society." Nor does either Du Bois or Ellison assert that the narratives displaying Washington's and Wright's rhetorics (*Up from Slavery* and *Black Boy,* even more than *Native Son*) are such formidable artistic creations that they leave little or no space in Afro-American letters for their own work and that of others. Du Bois and Ellison are terribly proud men, but each would argue that the partial truths from which *Up from Slavery* and *Black Boy* derive their power occasion more good literature than they stifle. Both Du Bois and Ellison rightly came to feel that the older writer's rhetoric was quickly and disastrously becoming a race's and nation's language at large, instead of remaining one of many languages in text; which is to say, the rhetorics of Tuskegee and of Protest, as the latter came to be called, assumed tyrannical holds upon a nation's idea of a race's and culture's humanity. In response, in *The Souls of Black Folk* Du Bois reworked numerous features of *Up from Slavery* which I have already cited, and in *Invisible Man* Ellison obviously recast certain components of *Black Boy*—the persona's father, grandfather, and school principal, as well as his encounters with Mrs. Moss and young Harrison from the rival optical company. In Du Bois's and Ellison's cases, what we witness is not artistic envy—partly because the arena is not exclusively that of art—but "antagonistic cooperation" creatively forged between literary texts and kinsmen. To their credit, Du Bois and Ellison appear to have realized that the creation of such conditions—much like a properly functioning system of checks and balances—is fundamental to a nation's health, and possibly a step toward the ideal of *communitas* that lies beyond the lockstep of interracial and intraracial rituals. Aware that language at large must be a medley of many tongues, they raised their voices accordingly.

CHAPTER 6

Literacy and Hibernation:
Ralph Ellison's *Invisible Man*

I'm not blaming anyone for this
state of affairs, mind you; nor merely
crying *mea culpa*. The fact is that
you carry part of your sickness within
you, at least I do as an invisible man.
I carried my sickness and though for
a long time I tried to place it in the
outside world, the attempt to write
it down shows me that at least half
of it lay within me.
    —Ralph Ellison, *Invisible Man*

Anochecí Enfermo Amanecí bueno
(I went to bed sick. I woke up well.)
—Jay Wright, *Dimensions of History*

By the time we travel beyond the major work of Richard
Wright, Afro-American literature's narrative tradition is still very
much alive—even though the texts are rarely termed "narratives"
by writer or reader, or consciously placed in an ongoing artistic
continuum. However, after Wright it is also clear that the possibilities
for significant revoicings of the ascent and immersion narratives (and
their accompanying rhetorics) are virtually exhausted. This is not
to say that ascent and immersion narratives do not appear in our
recent literature; nor is it to say that Afro-American writers are no
longer fascinated with creating rhetorics of racial soulfulness and
soullessness. Indeed, in the last decade the abiding fascination with
rhetorics of the former type has become so pronounced that in some
quarters it is seen to be an Artistic Movement, and even an Aesthetic. Be this as it may, the fact remains that, after *Black Boy* in

particular, the situation is such that any actual forwarding of the "historical consciousness" of Afro-American narrative must involve some kind of escape from the lockstep imposed by the tradition's dominant and prefiguring narrative patterns. In theory, the logical first stop beyond the narrative of ascent or immersion (a stop which need not be any more generic, in a conventional sense, than were the preceding stops) is one that somehow creates a fresh narrative strategy and arc out of a remarkable combination of ascent and immersion narrative properties. In theory, attempts to achieve such remarkable combinations are possible in Afro-American letters any-time after the appearance of *The Souls of Black Folk* in 1903. In practice, however, very few Afro-American narrativists appear to have comprehended the opportunity before them, let alone fashioned combinations of merit and of a certain energy.

In *The Autobiography of an Ex-Coloured Man,* for example, James Weldon Johnson clearly demonstrates that he has some idea of the symbolic journeys and spaces which the new narrative will require, but his dedication to troping the Du Boisian nightmare of immersion aborted—which, in his hands, is fundamentally a com-mitment to expressing a new narrative content—precludes his achieving a new narrative arc. In writing *Cane,* Jean Toomer takes further than Johnson did the idea of binding new narrative content to new narrative form; but the success of his effort is questionable, since a new narrative arc never really emerges from his aggressive yet orchestrated display of forms and voices. The absence of such an arc is a further indication of Toomer's inability to detail his persona's final posture outside the realms of ascent and immersion. Without this requisite clarification, *Cane* appears to be an inventive text that can evoke, but not advance, the historical consciousness of its parent forms.

Before *Invisible Man,* Zora Neale Hurston's *Their Eyes Were Watching God* is quite likely the only truly coherent narrative of both ascent and immersion, primarily because her effort to create a particular kind of questing *heroine* liberates her from the task (the compulsion, perhaps) of revoicing many of the traditional tropes of ascent and immersion. Of course, Hurston's narrative is neither en-tirely new nor entirely "feminine." The house "full ah thoughts" to which Janie ascends after her ritualized journey of immersion with Teacake into the "muck" of the Everglades (recall here Du Bois's swamp in both *The Souls* and *The Quest of the Silver Fleece*) is clearly a private ritual ground, akin in construction if not in accoutrement to Du Bois's study. And Janie's posture as a storyteller—as an articulate figure knowledgeable of tribal tropes, (a feature probably overdone in the frame, but not the tale, of *Their Eyes*) and in apparent control of her personal history—is a familiar and valued final siting for a primary voice in an Afro-American narrative. Still, there is much that is new in *Their Eyes*. The narrative takes place in a seemingly ahistorical world: the spanking new all-black town is meticulously bereft of former slave cabins; there are no railroad trains, above or underground, with or without Jim Crow cars; Matt's mule is a bond with and catalyst for distinct tribal memories and rituals, but these do not include the hollow slogan, "forty acres and a mule"; Janie seeks freedom, self-hood, voice, and "living" but is hardly guided—or haunted—by Sojourner Truth or Harriet Tubman, let alone Frederick Douglass. But that world is actually a fresh expression of a history of assault. The first two men in Janie's adult life (Logan Killicks and Jody Starks) and the spatial configurations through which they define themselves and seek to impose definition upon Janie (notably, a rural and agrarian space on one hand and a somewhat urban and mercantile space on the other) provide as much social structure as the narrative requires. Furthermore, the narrative's frame—the conversation "in the present" between Janie and Pheoby—creates something new in that it, and not the tale, is Hurston's vehicle for presenting the communal and possibly archetypal aspects of Janie's quest and final posture. Presentation does not always provide substantiation, and the clanking of Hurston's narrative and rhetorical machinery calls attention to itself when Pheoby offers her sole remark in the final half of the frame: "Lawd! . . . Ah done growed ten feet higher from jus' listenin' tuh you, Janie. Ah ain't satisfied wid mah-self no mo.' Ah means tuh make Sam take me fishin' wid him after this. Nobody better not criticize yuh in mah hearin'." But these minor imperfections do not delimit the narrative's grand effort to demystify and site the somewhat ethereal concept of group- and self-consciousness, forwarded especially by *The Souls of Black Folk* and *Cane*. Clearly, Hurston is after a treatment of Janie and Pheoby that releases them from their immediate posture of storyteller and listener, and that propels them to one in which their sisterhood suggests a special kinship among womankind at large.

The one great flaw in *Their Eyes* involves not the framing dialogue, but Janie's tale itself. Through the frame Hurston creates the essential illusion that Janie has achieved her voice (along with everything else), and that she has even wrested from menfolk some control of the tribal posture of the storyteller. But the tale undercuts much of this, not because of its content—indeed, episodes such as the one in which Janie verbally abuses Jody in public abets Hurston's strategy—but because of its narration. Hurston's curious insistence on having Janie's tale—her personal history in and as a literary form—told by an omniscient third person, rather than by a first-person narrator, implies that Janie has not really won her voice and self after all—that her author (who is, quite likely, the omniscient narrating voice) cannot see her way clear to giving Janie her voice outright. Here, I think, Hurston is genuinely caught in the dilemma of how she might both govern and exploit the autobiographical impulses that partially direct her creation of Janie. On one hand, third-person narration of Janie's tale helps to build a space (or at least the illusion of a space) between author and character, for the author and her audience alike; on the other, when told in this fashion control of the tale remains, no matter how unintended, with the author alone.

Despite this problem, *Their Eyes* is a seminal narrative in Afro-American letters. It forwards the historical consciousness of the tradition's narrative forms, and helps to define those kinds of narratives which will also advance the literature in their turn. The narrative successes and failures of *Their Eyes* effectively prefigure several types of narratives; but, given the problems I have just discussed, one might say that the example of *Their Eyes* calls for a narrative in which the primary figure (like Janie) achieves a space beyond those defined by the tropes of ascent and immersion, but (*unlike* Janie) also achieves authorial control over both the frame and tale of his or her personal history. In short, *Their Eyes,* as a narrative strategy in a continuum of narrative strategies, directs us most immediately to Ralph Ellison's *Invisible Man.* Janie is quite possibly more of a blood relative to Ellison's narrator than either the "male chauvinist" or "feminist" readers of the tradition would care to contemplate.

As I have suggested in previous chapters, the Afro-American pregeneric myth of the quest for freedom and literacy has occasioned two basic types of narrative expressions, the narratives of ascent and immersion. The classic ascent narrative launches an "enslaved" and semi-literate figure on a ritualized journey to a symbolic North; that journey is charted through spatial expressions of social structure, invariably systems of signs that the questing figure must read in order to be both increasingly literate and increasingly free. The ascent narrative conventionally ends with the questing figure situated in the least oppressive social structure afforded by the world of the narrative, and free in the sense that he or she has gained sufficient literacy to assume the mantle of an articulate survivor. As the phrase "articulate survivor" suggests, the hero or heroine of an ascent narrative must be willing to forsake familial or communal postures in the narrative's most oppressive social structure for a new posture in the least oppressive environment—at best, one of solitude; at worst, one of alienation. This last feature of the ascent narrative unquestionably helps bring about the rise and development of an immersion narrative in the tradition, for the immersion narrative is fundamentally an expression of a ritualized journey into a symbolic South, in which the protagonist seeks those aspects of tribal literacy that ameliorate, if not obliterate, the conditions imposed by solitude. The conventional immersion narrative ends almost paradoxically, with the questing figure located in or near the narrative's most oppressive social structure but free in the sense that he has gained or regained sufficient tribal literacy to assume the mantle of an articulate kinsman. As the phrase "articulate kinsman" suggests, the hero or heroine of an immersion narrative must be willing to forsake highly individualized mobility in the narrative's least oppressive social structure for a posture of relative stasis in the most oppressive environment, a loss that is only occasionally assuaged by the newfound balms of group identity. (The argument is, of course, that these "shared epiphanies" were previously unavailable to the questing figure when he or she was adrift in a state of solitude.) When seen in this way, the primary features of the ascent and immersion narratives appear to call for an epiloging text that revoices the tradition's abiding tropes in such a way that answers to all of the following questions are attempted: Can a questing figure in a narrative occasioned by the pregeneric myth be both an articulate survivor *and* an articulate kinsman? Must all such quests in the narrative literature conclude as they began, in imposed configurations of social structure? And can the literary history of Afro-American narrative forms—which is, at root, the chronicle of a dialectic between ascent and immersion expressions—become, in and of itself, the basis for a narrative form?

The whole of *Invisible Man* is a grand attempt to answer these questions, but the burden of reply falls mainly upon the narrative's frame (its prologue and epilogue), rather than upon its tale. I do not wish to demean the tale, for it is a remarkable invention: it presents the spatial expressions of social structure as well as the nearly counterpointing rituals of ascent (to self-consciousness) and immersion (in group consciousness) which collectively contextualize and in some sense occasion the questing narrator's progress from muteness to speech, or formlessness to form. However, what is narratively new in *Invisible Man,* and what permits it to answer the above-cited questions, is not its depiction of a pilgrim's progress, but its brave assertion that there is a self and form to be discovered beyond the lockstep of linear movement within imposed definitions of reality. For this reason the inventive tale of the questing narrator's steady progression to voice and selfhood cannot stand alone as the *narrative* of Ellison's hero. The tale must be framed, and in that sense controlled, because progression as a protean literary form and progress as a protean cultural myth must be contextualized. *Invisible Man's* success as a fresh narrative strategy depends upon its ability to formalize in art the "fiction" of history expounded primarily in its frame. To the extent that *Invisible Man's* frame controls its tale, its hero may gloss his personal history, and art may impose upon event.

With all this in mind, we may proceed to examine certain aspects of *Invisible Man's* frame. I would like to begin with the hero's hole itself, which, in the context of the tradition, is clearly a revoicing of the private ritual ground to which Du Bois's persona retreats after his ritual of immersion in the Black Belt. Despite the fact that these ritual grounds are situated differently—the prefiguring space is a "high Pisgah," while the epiloging space is a "warm hole" below ground—there are many similarities between the two constructions. In the first place, both spaces are discovered or achieved after several literal and figurative rail journeys that clearly revoice the primary episode of flight on the "freedom train." I refer here on one hand to Du Bois's various symbolic rides in that social structure-in-motion called the Jim Crow car, rides which prompt his vision and hope of *communitas* in this world, and on the other hand to the Invisible Man's equally conspicuous subway rides which establish the particular rhythm of immersion and ascent that guides him finally to see the people of Harlem ("They'd been there all along, but . . . I'd missed them . . . I'd been asleep") and to consider hibernation as a viable if transient state of being. In either case, the elevated study or the subterranean hole, the private space is a construction wherein the best thoughts occasioned by these travels may collect and linger—wherein physical motion is interrupted, and body and voice are at rest, but the mind travels on.

Another point of similarity involves each space's distance from those spatial expressions of social structure (the Black Belt or Harlem) in which major acquisitions of tribal literacy are accomplished. In *The Souls* Du Bois's study is high up on Atlanta hill, not engulfed in the "dull red hideousness" of rural Georgia. In *Invisible Man* the hero's "warm hole" is not in "the jungle of Harlem," but in a "border area" that is, as the hero admits, a grand spatial and historical joke: it is of Harlem as far as the utility company's "master meter" is concerned, but out of Harlem according to most other conventional measurements of American reality, because it is a basement section of "a building rented strictly to whites" that was "shut off" (reconstructed?) and "forgotten during the nineteenth century" (Reconstruction?). In either case, vertical distance—placement upon a different plane—accentuates the more apparent horizontal displacement between tribal space and private space. These distances force each questing narrator to fashion a rhetoric that earnestly seeks to minimize the distances and to portray the narrators as group-conscious as well as self-conscious figures.

Here, I think, the points of congruence between Du Bois's study and Invisible Man's hole are most pronounced; yet here we can also begin to see how Ellison's construction assumes its own integrity. When the Invisible Man speaks in the epilogue of how his grandfather must have meant "the principle, that we were to affirm the principle on which the country was built and not the men, or at least not the men who did the violence" and also of how "we of all, we, most of all, had to affirm the principle . . . because we were older than they, in the sense of what it took to live in the world with others," he clearly restates in his own terms Du Bois's persona's claim that "we the darker ones come even now not altogether empty-handed: there are to-day no truer exponents of the pure human spirit of the Declaration of Independence than the American Negroes." Furthermore, both questing narrators seek to qualify or contextualize these assertions of race pride and responsibility by forwarding expressions of their abiding faith in the ideal of cultural pluralism. Certainly this is suggested when we recall the following passage from chapter I of *The Souls* (which is, for all intents and purposes, that narrative's prologue):

> Work, culture, liberty,—all these we need, not singly but together, not successively but together, each growing and aiding each, and all striving toward that vaster ideal that swims before the Negro people, the ideal of human brotherhood, gained through the unifying ideal of Race; The ideal of fostering and developing the traits and talents of the Negro, not in opposition to or contempt for other races, but rather in large conformity to the greater ideals of the American Republic . . . .

and place beside it these ringing, epiloging words from *Invisible Man:*

> Whence all this passion toward conformity anyway?—diversity is the word. Let man keep his many parts and you'll have no tyrant states. . . . America is woven of many strands; I would recognize them and let it so remain. It's "winner take nothing" that is the great truth of our country. Life is to be lived, not controlled; and humanity is won by continuing to play in face of certain defeat. Our fate is to become one, and yet many—This is not prophecy, but description.

Amid the similarities there lies one profound discrepancy: Ellison's refusal to sustain Du Bois's Herderian overlay of racial idealism. Ellison discerns a quite substantial distinction in meaning and image between the prospect of ideal races conforming to a national ideal, and that of intact races interweaving to become a national fabric. That distinction has much to do with how he subsequently fashions his questing narrator as a group-conscious and self-conscious human being.

In *The Souls,* Du Bois's hero's group consciousness is distinctly racial in character. Ensconced in his study after his immersion journey and transported by the bits of ancient song wafting up from below, he becomes a weary traveler in a tribal song—an embodied and embodying voice or, in terms indebted to Ellison, a tribally visible man. The creation of this voice and visibility is central to *The Souls*'s narrative strategy; it provides the rationale for Du Bois's refusal to formalize his first and last chapters as framing prologue and epilogue, even though they function largely this way in the narrative. Unlike Ellison, Du Bois is not after an expression of group consciousness that bursts beyond tribal boundaries. Therefore he need not situate his hero's private ritual ground outside the geography of his hero's tale any more than he already has. Here we must recall especially that Du Bois's final siting of his hero is occasioned in part by autobiographical impulses. Through generous reference to the "master" Sorrow Songs, Du Bois binds his narrative's resulting space and his narrator's resulting self to what has come before, and in that way seeks his own visibility in the events and images his narrative has recorded. The whole machinery of *The Souls* is geared for acts of unveiling (making *visible*) the soul of a race and of a man; it lacks the components for processing such subtleties as invisible articulate heroes residing outside History and Veil alike.

The final posture of Ellison's questing narrator may be clarified in the following terms. To begin with, the hero's hole is described in a formal frame removed from the tale. That frame is, in a sense, that hole, because Ellison is indeed after expressions of group consciousness and self-consciousness that respectively transcend tribal literacy and resist the infecting germs of heroic self-portraiture. The whole of the frame (or, if you will, the whole of the hole) proclaims that the narrative distinction to be drawn between tale and frame is a trope for other distinctions central to *Invisible Man,* including those between blindness and insight, sleepfulness and wakefulness, sickness and health, social structure and nonstructure, History and history, embodied voice and disembodied voice, and acts of speech and of writing. All this occasions a second and fresh rhetoric that is not found in the framing chapters of *The Souls,* but is prefigured instead by the "why do I write" passages in slave narratives, several examples of which were given earlier. The strategy behind Ellison's rhetoric is, however, quite different from that of the fugitive slaves.

Ellison is less interested in having his hero authenticate his tale (or rather, its content) and more interested in having that tale de-valorized in such a way that the principles of living (which are, at base, principles of writing or artfulness) delineated in the frame may finally take hold and control the way in which the narrative as a whole is read.

"So why do I write," the Invisible Man asks rhetorically, and again and again in the final pages of the epilogue his answers—brimming with references to release from lethargy, negation of "some of the anger and some of the bitterness," shaking off the old skin, springtime, and love—serve to minimize the distance between his private space and the "concrete, ornery, vile and sublimely wonderful" world in which, alas, the rest of us reside. Indeed, we sense that when he asks the question with which the narrative ends—"Who knows but that, on the lower frequencies, I speak for you?"—"for you" expresses that last distancing interval that remains before speech "to you." But finally it is writing or the experience of writing, and not speech, that shapes whatever group consciousness the Invisible Man will bring in tow upon his return. Writing has taught him much about himself—indeed, it has made him a highly self-aware invisible man. But it has also taught him that his personal history is but an arc of the parabola of human history, and that his personal tale is but a finite particle in the infinity of tale-telling. According to Ellison's vision, what group-orients the Invisible Man and ends his hibernation is his marvelously robust desire to take another swing around that arc of what other men call reality, to tell, shape, and/or "lie" his tale anew. In this way, then, he becomes both an articulate survivor and an articulate kinsman.

Before we follow the Invisible Man to a realm beyond hibernation, the whys and wherefores of his writing while underground should be examined further. What interests me specifically is the apparent cause-and-effect relationship between the explicit emptying of the briefcase at the end of the tale and the implicit filling of pages during the term of hibernation, a sequence that revoices a feature of slave narratives such as Douglass's 1845 *Narrative*. The Douglass narrative tells us that, in 1835, Douglass and a few of his fellow slaves concocted an escape plan that depended mainly upon each slave's possessing a "protection" or "pass," allegedly written by "Master" William Hamilton but actually composed by Douglass himself. Such a pass granted each man "full liberty" to travel to Baltimore and spend the Easter holidays—celebrating, one assumes, the ancient Resurrection of the One, and the more recent ascent of at least another one. Unfortunately, the plan is thwarted, and each slave has to save his skin by "denying everything" and destroying his "forged" protection. But through telling the tale Douglass manages to inform us once again of the great bond between freedom and literacy, and also of the great power that comes with an ability not only to read a culture's signs (in this case, a sign that is truly a written document) but also to write them and, in that supreme way, manipulate them. In short, the *Narrative*'s escape episode is a primary trope for acts of authorial control over text and context.

The lesson advanced by Douglass's escape or "protection" episode is one of many which Ellison's narrator is destined to learn the hard way; indeed, his remarkable innocence and gullibility regarding these matters provide a major comic strain in the narrative's tale. The perpetual sight of our valiant hero doggedly lugging his briefcase around New York, and even risking life and limb in order to retrieve it from a burning Harlem tenement, is funny enough; but the heart of the joke has less to do with the Invisible Man's attachment to his briefcase than with what he has consciously and subconsciously gathered inside it. Our hero's tale is substantially that of how he accumulates a motley array of cultural signs, mostly written "protections" or "passes" (diplomas, letters of recommendation, slips of paper bearing new names, etc.) that supposedly identify him and grant him "full liberty" in the "real" world beyond "home." Ellison's double-edged joke is that none of these "protections" are worth more than the paper they're written on (they are indeed "paper protections"), and that all of them ironically "keep a nigger-boy running," but not on a path that would be recognizable to Douglass or any other self-willed hero with any control over his fate.

This is not to say that the non-written signs are without importance. On the contrary, part of Ellison's point is that Tarp's leg iron, Mary Rambo's "grinning darky" bank, Tod Clifton's sambo doll, and the Rinehart-like dark glasses and "high hat" are all cultural signs of a tribal sort. Our questing narrator thinks he knows how to read them, but he only knows or reads in a very limited way. Collectively, these non-written signs represent the Invisible Man's illiteracy *vis-à-vis* his tribe as much as the written signs betoken his illiteracy *vis-à-vis* the non-tribal social structures besetting him; his unwitting act of gathering both types of signs in one bulging briefcase finally occasions the demystification of the one type by the other. Once the Invisible Man *sees* this—once he comprehends that seemingly mute objects such as the dark glasses, hat, and leg iron are the only "protections" he possesses, and that the written documents from Bledsoe, Jack, and the rest are the only signs that may be *usefully* destroyed (here, burned to light his way)—he is ready to begin his life and tale again, or rather to *prepare* to begin again. The demystification and nearly simultaneous use and destruction of the cultural signs gathered in the briefcase during the tale occasion his removal to a fresh space, the "warm hole" of the narrative's frame.

All this suggests that the Invisible Man is finally free in his framing hole, and that that freedom is expressed most conspicuously by his nearly empty briefcase. But this is not completely true—nor is it in keeping with the full measure of the lesson learned from an innocent but almost deadly trafficking in false "protections." Perhaps the most profound lesson our hero learns when the once-precious "protections" are demystified is that they are worthless, not because of what they do or do not say, but because they are authenticating documents over which he has absolutely no authorial control. (They impose on him and his tale much as the competing authenticating texts of white guarantors often impose upon a fugitive slave's tale.) Seen in this light, the Invisible Man's frenzied movement and speech (his "sleepwalking" and "sleeptalking") in the narrative's tale are tropes for his total lack of control over that history or tale, and his relative stasis in the narrative's frame (pointedly, his "wakefulness") is a trope for his brave effort to assume control of his history or tale (*and* of tale-telling) through artful acts of written composition. Thus, another aspect—perhaps *the* other aspect—of the Invisible Man's newfound freedom is that he may now pursue acts of written articulateness and literary form-making, filling the empty briefcase with what are in effect "protections" or "passes" from his *own* hand. To compose such "protections" is to assert a marvelous and heroic concept of self-willed mobility, an idea of mobility that is in keeping with the narrative's definition of hibernation: "A hibernation is a covert preparation for a more overt action." The covert filling of the satchel with the self-authored "protection" that constitutes the completed narrative (tale *and* frame) is Ellison's most convincing expression of his hero's inevitable return, partly because it revoices a primary trope inaugurated in the tradition by Frederick Douglass.

All in all, the frame in *Invisible Man* is a familiar construction in Afro-American narrative literature, primarily because it is the mechanism for authentication and authorial control in the narrative. At the beginning of the frame, the competing or imposing fictions that surface in the tale as items in the hero's briefcase are generally defined—"When they approach me they see only my surroundings, themselves, or figments of their imagination—indeed, everything and anything except me." By the end of the frame those fictive "certainties" have been subsumed by the hero's own self-authored "plan of living" or, as he also calls it, his "pattern to the chaos." Perhaps even more impressive and resilient, however, is the manner in which this trumping of fictions with fictions is occasioned and sustained by Ellison's remarkably explicit expression of one authenticating strategy overtaking and making a joke out of another. In the tale, the Invisible Man's briefcase is much more than a repository of cultural signs and false "protections"; it is, most ironically and humorously, *the* trope for the strategy of self-authentication the Invisible Man values during most of the tale. He carries it everywhere, never realizing that it possesses him far more than he possesses it. At the beginning of the tale, in the battle royal where he "earns" his briefcase and his first "protections" (the diploma and scholarship to Bledsoe's college), his speech full of echoes of Booker T. Washington's Atlanta Exposition Address is a signal not simply of initial rhetorical indebtedness to Washington, but (more profoundly) of an initial adherence to the Washingtonian strategy of narration and self-authentication as résumé. The briefcase substantiates this idea because it is, in effect, a résumé edited and amended by acts of sign-gathering during the course of the tale. In vivid contrast to Washington, however, the Invisible Man learns not only that he lacks a grand public speech to be authenticated by a tale of his life, but also that his accumulated résumé isn't his tale.

MAKING LIGHT OF THE LIGHT

Like *The Autobiography of an Ex-Coloured Man* and *Black Boy, Invisible Man* presents, as part of its narrative machinery, a series of portraits—on the wall as well as in the flesh—that may be loosely termed the narrative's portrait gallery. While it can be argued that any mobile or immobile character in any narrative is in some sense a portrait, the portraits which I'm about to discuss are special. They comprise a narrative strategy by which various models of voice and action are kept before the questing narrator, and by which the full range of human possibility in the differing social structures of the narrative may be defined and seen. In the chapter on *The Autobiography,* I described at some length the portrait gallery in the parlor of the Ex-Coloured Man's Club; it is important to recall that gallery here, because it is our best example of a symbolic construction in which all of the models (from Frederick Douglass to the minstrel who yearns to be a Shakespearean) are valorized as heroic examples that the narrator would do well to emulate. The whole point to the construction is that the Ex-Coloured Man could have learned from these "portraits," but didn't—because he could not really see them, let alone see through them. In *Black Boy,* virtually the opposite is true. Few if any portraits are displayed on the walls of the narrative's prison-like interiors; the major portraits are intentionally "in the flesh" and, with the possible exceptions of Ella (the schoolteacher who tells the story of Bluebeard), the editor of the Negro newspaper, and the Irishman who surreptitiously lends his library card to young Richard, they are all of men and women who are "warnings" rather than "examples." While the Ex-Coloured Man cannot fully see the heroic examples before him, and thus not only remains a non-hero but effectively relinquishes the narrative's space for heroic posturing to figures such as "Shiny," Wright's persona pursues a far different and aggressive course. In *Black Boy* the potential or assumed examples, especially the elder kinfolk, are systematically de-valorized and portrayed as "warnings"—partly so that a hellish landscape may be depicted and peopled, but mostly so that Wright's persona, as an emerging articulate survivor, may not only control but also fill the narrative's space for heroic posturing. In this way Wright's persona, unlike Johnson's Ex-Coloured Man, sees and aggressively *sees through* the major "portraits" in his tale. For this reason, to cite only one example, the persona meticulously buries his father alive in the red clay of Mississippi.

Invisible Man retains certain aspects of the portrait galleries found in both *The Autobiography* and *Black Boy.* The narrative offers portraits both on the wall and in the flesh, and the portrait motif is indeed central to Ellison's strategy of keeping both examples and warnings before the questing narrator. But more significant is how *Invisible Man* bursts beyond the strategies of portraiture and gallery construction that we find in Johnson's and Wright's prefiguring texts. At first glance, the portrait gallery in *Invisible Man* is much like that in *Black Boy,* in that it is not confined to a ritual space such as the Ex-Coloured Man's Club (or the outdoor revival in which the preacher, John Brown, and the master singer, Singing Johnson, are sketched) but is dispersed throughout the narrative. Furthermore, as in *Black Boy,* the portraits in *Invisible Man* are usually dismantled or demystified—that is, the figures are usually less than heroic. But this is also where the different treatment of this motif begins in each narrative. In *Black Boy,* one senses that Wright's portraits of would-be examples, such as the father and the persona's Uncle Tom, are *always* demystified; the figures thereby plummet from their assigned (if not always earned) heights to the depths of life as it is lived by partially animate warnings. But to judge from *Invisible Man,* Ellison appears perennially suspicious of such simple dichotomies, and in pursuit, therefore, of more complex and differentiated expressions. Hence we discover in his narrative that while Bledsoe, Norton, and the one-eyed Jack are indeed warnings, not examples, Trueblood, Brother Tarp, and most especially the advice-giving Grandfather are neither examples nor warnings, but enigmas of varying sorts. They occupy and enlarge a fresh narrative space.

While the demystification of these would-be examples is a prerequisite for the Invisible Man's blossoming as a truly literate figure, the thrust of the narrative is not to replace these portraits with that of the Invisible Man as a heroic example. Rather, it is to *identify* Bledsoe, Norton, and the rest as varying fictions of reality and history which must be deposed or, as we soon will see, defiled in order for the fiction that is the narrative to be imagined. The narrative and not the narrator, the "principle" and not the "men," and the frame far more than the tale collectively constitute the heroic example forwarded by Ellison's narrative and rhetorical strategies. To see this is to know a major way in which *Invisible Man* aggressively contradicts the abiding idea of the artist in *Black Boy,* and to know as well how it assumes its place in the Afro-American narrative tradition.

One final preliminary point is that the portrait motif in *Invisible Man* is joined by, and in some sense conjoined to, what I am going to call the narrative's museum motif. There are at least three great "museum collections" in the narrative, and these are important to the narrative's machinery as contexts or syntaxes, just as the portraits are important as relatively discrete expressions. What binds the portrait motif to the museum motif is not simply the fact that portraits frequently form an integral part of certain specific contexts or syntaxes, but that both motifs are reduced, in the narrative's frame, to being one and the same expression and sign—the collected and displayed light for which certain other people's measurements of reality cannot account. The narrator's warm hole is at once a portrait gallery of light and an exquisite museum collection of light; the light "confirms" his "reality" and "gives birth" to his "form," just as other, ostensibly more delineated, portraits and displayed objects confirm other realities and give birth to other forms—especially of a literary sort.

But perhaps, as the Invisible Man says of himself at the end of the beginning (which is the beginning of the end), I am moving too fast. The frame is not visible in its full splendor of invisibility unless we can see the proud visages and precious vestiges which it both visibly and invisibly frames. We must begin with *Invisible Man*'s tale—even though it is neither the narrative's beginning nor its end —and with the portrait of the grandfather who seems, as a highly visible invisibility, to begin and end it all.

The grandfather enters the tale at its beginning, in a speech— or, rather, *as* speech: " 'Live with your head in the lion's mouth. I want you to overcome 'em with yeses, undermine 'em with grins, agree 'em to death and destruction, let 'em swoller you till they vomit or bust wide open.' " This entrance is central to his place in the tale; he is a portrait-in-language that his grandson must learn to hear, read, and contextualize. But as the following passage from the end of the battle royal episode instructs, the grandfather is as much a portrait on the wall (of the mind, as well as of the space called "family" or "home") as he is one in language:

> When I reached home everyone was excited. Next day the neighbors came to congratulate me. I even felt safe from grandfather, whose deathbed curse usually spoiled my triumphs. I stood beneath his photograph with my brief case in hand and smiled triumphantly into his stolid black peasant's face. It was a face that fascinated me. The eyes seemed to follow everywhere I went.

Several things are afoot here, and one of them is certainly a radical revision of the "obituary" with which Wright's *Black Boy* persona buries his father alive by calling him a "stranger" and a "black peasant." In *Black Boy,* the implication is clearly that the father is a known quantity; that he is fixed or immobilized in a "culture's" time and space, and that his portrait has been completely and consummately read by his "civilized" questing kinsman. In *Invisible Man,* however, the grandfather is not quite so easily removed from the wall and (in that sense, among others) dismantled. As the phrase "the eyes seemed to follow everywhere I went" suggests, Ellison's narrator's grandfather is an unknown and mobile figure whose eyes are hardly "glazed" like those of the "dead" father in *Black Boy;* he will travel with and reappear before his youthful kinsman in word and image many times before the narrative's tale is finally complete. The grandfather, who provides the first portrait in the tale's portrait gallery, is neither a warning nor an example but a huge and looming question mark—an enigma. In this way his portrait prefigures those of other "peasants" in the narrative, such as Trueblood and Brother Tarp (Brother Veil? Brother Sail?), who are also enigmas, and the grandfather's portrait quite purposefully skews whatever preconceptions we might have regarding a simple system of dialectical or antipodal portraiture ("warning"/"example") in the narrative. The grandfather is, in short, a "Mr. In-Between," a Vergilian guide who occupies neither antipodal space not because he is supposedly dead (or thought "mad" by the intervening generation, the Invisible Man's parents), but because of the implicit distinction which the narrative draws between the spoken and written word and, hence, between guides and artists.

Another method of dismantling and possibly debunking an antipodal system of portraiture is simply to inaugurate a presentation in which examples, warnings, and the world they define are eventually and comically turned inside out. Ellison does essentially this with the portraits in the campus episodes and with the initially Edenic campus as a world within the world of the narrative. His activity differs from Wright's in *Black Boy,* mainly because Wright never allows a model to become an example before he shows it to be warning, or a space to assume paradisaical proportions before he demonstrates that it is a circle of hell. In the campus episodes, the portraits begin with the bronze statue of the college Founder. Ellison has a lot of fun with both his narrator and the conventions of heroic portraiture while describing this work of art:

> It's so long ago and far away that here in my invisibility I wonder if it happened at all. Then in my mind's eye I see the bronze statue of the college Founder, the cold Father symbol, his hands out-stretched in the breathtaking gesture of lifting a veil that flutters in hard, metallic folds above the face of a kneeling slave; and I am standing puzzled, unable to decide whether the veil is really being lifted, or lowered more firmly in place; whether I am witnessing a revelation or a more efficient blinding. And as I gaze, there is a rustle of wings and I see a flock of starlings flighting before me and, when I look again, the bronze face, whose empty eyes look upon a world I have never seen, runs with liquid chalk—creating another ambiguity to puzzle my groping mind: Why is a bird-soiled statue more commanding than one that is clean?

Of course, there is much serious activity here that advances the narrative's discussion of what is visible and invisible, seen and unseen. The second veil of a very organic tulle joins the first, of bronze, adding a necessary complexity to the abiding question of who is the prophet, who the sheep, and what indeed can that prophet see. Furthermore, it prefigures other tropes in the narrative, such as the Liberty Paint Factory's celebrated optic white paint. But basically this comic portrait of Founder and narrator achieves its humor not so much because a heroic example is draped in guano or because the youthful narrator attempts to make and unmake a philosophical puzzle out of that event. Rather, its humor arises from the more profound incongruities that displace the narrator as seer from the Founder who, according to one definition of history, is a Seer, but who, according to at least one other definition, is the seen.

This high comedy continues in the narrative when Homer A. Barbee, the noted blind minister, preaches on and adds further luster to the legend of the Founder's death. Indeed, the inanimate statue on the lawn and the highly animated tale or "lie" as sermon are parts of the same composite portrait of the Founder. Through a marvelous orchestration of images, reminding us of many other train rides in written and verbal art (recall, for example, Lincoln's cortege in Whitman's "When Lilacs Last in Dooryard Bloom'd"), Homer Barbee transports us on another ride, a solemn ride of sorrowful rest and joyous resurrection: " 'When the train reached the summit of the mountain, he [the Founder] was no longer with us. . . .' " But

there is a new and finally quite funny twist to all of this: Barbee and
Bledsoe, like two disciples become vaudevillians, are on board.
Were you there when they crucified my Lord? Yessir, as a matter of
fact I was! Me and Bledsoe! Right there!

Barbee's sermon is finally less a valorization of the Founder
than of A. Herbert Bledsoe. To put it another way, the text of his
sermon is less a strategy for authenticating the legend of the Founder
than one for authenticating the equally supreme fiction with which
Bledsoe wields power and proffers a particular construction of historical reality:

> "Oh, yes. Oh, yes," he [Barbee] said. "Oh, yes. That too is part
> of the glorious story. But think of it not as a death, but as a birth. A
> great seed has been planted. A seed which has continued to put forth
> its fruit in its season as surely as if the great creator had been resur-
> rected. For in a sense he was, if not in the flesh, in the spirit. And in
> a sense in the flesh too. For has not your present leader become his
> living agent, his physical presence? Look about you if you doubt it.
> My young friends, my dear young friends! How can I tell you what
> manner of man this is who leads you! How can I convey to you
> how well he has kept his pledge to the Founder, how conscientious
> has been his stewardship?"

With words like these Homer Barbee demonstrates how he and Herbert Bledsoe—the Preacher and the Principal—are indeed quite a
team, more than likely one of the most extraordinary comedy teams
in Afro-American narrative literature. Evidently they have made a
long black joke out of the long black song of the Founder's long
black train. Who follows in his train? The shadows do.

After the portrait of the Founder, the next arresting portrait in
the campus episodes is of Norton's daughter. Appropriately enough,
her image is not a photograph on the wall or a totem on the lawn,
but something of a cameo which her father reverently carries on his
person, as close to his waist as to his heart:

> Suddenly he fumbled in his vest pocket and thrust something
> over the back of the seat, surprising me.
> "Here, young man, you owe much of your good fortune in at-
> tending such a school to her."
> I looked upon the tinted miniature framed in engraved platinum.
> I almost dropped it. A young woman of delicate, dreamy features
> looked up at me. She was very beautiful, I thought at the time, so
> beautiful that I did not know whether I should express admiration

to the extent I felt it or merely act polite. And yet I seemed to re-member her, or someone like her, in the past. I know now that it was the flowing costume of soft, flimsy material that made for the effect; today, dressed in one of the smart, well-tailored, angular, sterile, streamlined, engine-turned, air-conditioned modern outfits you see in the women's magazines, she would appear as ordinary as an expensive piece of machine-tooled jewelry and just as lifeless. Then, however, I shared something of his enthusiasm.

Of course, the immediate business at hand here is a citing and sight-ing of Norton's erection of a pedestal for his "biblical maiden" of a daughter, which will soon crumple as he hears the sorrowful tale of Jim Trueblood. Perhaps, too, Ellison is up to some devilish tricks regarding what is unstated about Mr. Dalton and his virginal Mary in *Native Son*. Surely it is not stretching things to draw a parallel between Norton giving money for toys to the Truebloods and Dalton giving pingpong paddles to the "bloods" at the South Side Boys Club.

More to the point, however, regarding Ellison's demystification of this portrait, are the Invisible Man's remarks about Miss Norton's costume in the miniature, and what she would have looked like in contemporary "engine-turned" dress. In truth, at this point in the tale he hasn't met the likes of her; but he is about to meet her again and again—and phrases like "an expensive piece of machine-tooled jewelry" instruct us as to where and when. The portrait of Miss Norton in her father's vest pocket is but an abiding fiction of "mod-ern" women like Emma and other women in the Brotherhood epi-sodes—but especially of Emma, who, like a slick magician perform-ing an ancient trick, will pull the narrator's new name out of her otherwise empty but interesting bosom. Miss Norton, or rather her portrait, may return to New York in her father's pocket; but it is clear that, as that portrait is dismantled, it (and she) will not remain there. Indeed, one of the most remarkable images offered by the New York episodes is that of Norton's "daughters" entertaining the Brotherhood at the chic Chthonian, while Norton himself is lost in the subway.

But we're not yet ready to go to New York; we must return to the campus and to Bledsoe's office—which is a kind of annex to the college's museum of slavery, although no one there would dare call it that. Several aspects of this museum will be discussed shortly, but what interests me here are the "frame portrait photographs and relief plaques of presidents and industrialists, men of power." Evidently these portraits are redoubtable examples of heroic portraiture in which the "men of power" appear as heroic examples, or gods. In the process of attempting to describe their extraordinary presence in Bledsoe's *sanctum sanctorum,* the Invisible Man unwittingly stumbles upon much of the symbolic space's hidden significance when he writes that these men are "fixed like trophies or heraldic emblems upon the walls." He's right: the "men of power" *are* Bledsoe's "trophies"—he has bagged them (or, got them by their bags) in many senses of the term. The phrase "heraldic emblems" is also apt, because these men are messengers of given sovereignties, as well as of given fictions of historical reality. As such, they are harbingers of war, morticians to the dead, and custodians of national and genealogical signs. This fits them and, indeed, destines them for positions of stewardship to constructions such as Bledsoe's college; this is much of what the Invisible Man may finally see about them, once he is released from the pattern of their certainties and deep into the task of creating a competing fiction. In Bledsoe's office, however, wherein our hero is summarily expelled from "nigger heaven," the "men of power" are but a mute angelic choir (to Bledsoe's St. Peter) whose collective voices and visages seem to condemn him all the more with their silence.

In the Brotherhood episodes, Ellison continues to give his portraits a comic texture, but he also seems intent on enlarging the space for enigmatic models in which the grandfather has already been situated. Quite fittingly, these portraits appear on the walls of the Invisible Man's office within the Brotherhood's Harlem headquarters, constituting a significant portion of the narrative strategy by which that space is positioned (and thereby read) within a spatial dynamic that also embraces Bledsoe's "trophy room" and the framing warm hole. Especially in their conversation with one another, the portraits expose the hidden seams in the elaborate fiction that the Invisible Man jokingly calls, in retrospect, his "days of certainty" with the Brotherhood. The controversial "rainbow poster," for example, is described matter-of-factly—but not without a dollop of Ellisonian humor:

> It was a symbolic poster of a group of heroic figures: An American Indian couple, representing the dispossessed past; a blond brother (in overalls) and a leading Irish sister, representing the dispossessed present; and Brother Tod Clifton and a young white

couple (it had been felt unwise simply to show Clifton and the girl) surrounded by a group of children of mixed races, representing the future, a color photograph of bright skin texture and smooth contrast . . . [its] legend:

"After the Struggle: The Rainbow of America's Future"

The rhetoric of heroic example offered here is at once antithetical to that put forth by Bledsoe's display of the "men of power," and yet much the same as that rhetoric in that it is another imposed fiction of reality. However, at this point in the narrative the Invisible Man cannot see or read this rhetoric, any more than he can comprehend what certain Brotherhood members found objectionable about the poster. (Here, it is reasonable to assume that some brothers viewed the poster as being too "racial" and/or "nationalistic" in its statement and, therefore, insufficient as an expression of the international class struggle.) One guesses that the Invisible Man probably overheard some Harlemite in a bar telling a "lie" about Josephine Baker and her "rainbow tribe," and "ran" with the idea in his own newly ideological way. All such guesses aside, however, it is clear that the rainbow poster portrays not just a rhetoric our hero thinks he can see, but also a compromise he has made which he *can't* see.

The other portrait on the wall helps Ellison make much the same point. The first of several gifts the Invisible Man receives from Brother Tarp, it is of Frederick Douglass, and it is the first portrait of a truly heroic example to be hung in the narrative's gallery. But, unlike Johnson with his Ex-Coloured Man, Ellison is neither about the task of providing redoubtable examples for his confused protagonist nor about that of lamenting the sad fact that his narrator cannot see or see through Douglass. In the scene where the Douglass portrait is discussed, we receive instead another example of the Invisible Man's partial comprehension of a heroic rhetoric:

> . . . I liked my work during those days of certainty. I kept my eyes wide and my ears alert. The Brotherhood was a world within a world and I was determined to discover all its secrets and to advance as far as I could. I saw no limits, it was the one organization in the whole country in which I could reach the very top and I meant to get there. Even if it meant climbing a mountain of words. For now I had begun to believe, despite all the talk of science around me, that there was a magic in spoken words. Sometimes I sat watching the watery play of light upon Douglass' portrait, thinking how

magical it was that he had talked his way from slavery to a government ministry, and so swiftly. Perhaps, I thought, something of the
kind is happening to me. Douglass came north to escape and find
work in the shipyards; a big fellow in a sailor's suit who, like me,
had taken another name. What had his true name been? Whatever
it was, it was as *Douglass* that he became himself, defined himself.
And not as a boatwright as he'd expected, but as an orator. Perhaps
the sense of magic lay in the unexpected transformations. "You start
Saul, and end up Paul," my grandfather had often said. "When
you're a youngun, you Saul, but let life whup your head a bit and
you starts to trying to be Paul—though you still Sauls around on
the side."

Several things stand out in this remarkable piece of writing. One of
them is the presumably naive way in which the Invisible Man con-
vinces himself of the great truths subsumed within the fiction he is
living by means of creating an authenticating fiction for his own life
story. At the heart of this fiction is his questionable assertion that
Douglass defined himself as an orator—as a private-become-public
act of speech. Abetting this assertion are several revealing revisions
of Douglass's language in the 1845 *Narrative:* "from slavery to a
government ministry" is, for example, a remarkable revision or mis-
reading of Douglass's famous "from slavery to freedom." Of course,
he has the goal all wrong; but even more disastrously wrong than
the goal is the misconception of literacy and its uses that lies behind it.

In the Douglass *Narrative,* the phrase "from slavery to freedom," or more fully "the pathway from slavery to freedom," is
Douglass's most felicitous expression for acts of reading and writing.
He writes in chapter VI of what he learned when Mr. Auld forbade
Mrs. Auld to instruct him any further in "The A B C": "From that
moment, I understood the pathway from slavery to freedom. It was
just what I wanted, and I got it at a time when I the least expected
it. . . . Though conscious of the difficulty of learning without a
teacher, I set out with high hope, and a fixed purpose, at whatever
cost of trouble, *to learn how to read"* (italics added). This is the
abiding idea of literacy and its uses in the *Narrative* (and in the
Afro-American tradition). Given the events of the *Narrative,* it isn't
stretching things to say that, for Douglass, acts of literacy include
acts of reading the signs and events, or "patterns of certainties," that
comprise oppressive and imposing fictions of reality. Douglass didn't

"talk" his way to freedom; rather, he "read" his way and, as far as the *Narrative* is concerned (it being his personal history as and in a literary form), "wrote" his way.

In the Brotherhood episode wherein Douglass's portrait is hung, it is clear that the Invisible Man only partially comprehends the heroic example and rhetoric captured in that usually fierce visage, mainly because he is still wrapped up in the idea of composing a fiction in which he himself is a great speaker or act or sound. Somehow he senses—perhaps because Douglass's portrait forces him to hear unwelcome echoes of his grandfather's voice—that Douglass is as much an enigma to him as the grandfather, that both images will remain looming question-marks in his mind. Surely he will later sense that Douglass poses some very substantial questions about the fiction he is living, when he returns to Harlem to discover that Tod Clifton and Brother Tarp are missing and that Douglass's portrait has been torn down as well. In the meantime, however, during those days of certainty, the portraits on the walls of the narrator's bustling office only exhibit to him a full and sufficient expression of himself as a brother in the struggle—and on the make.

As I have suggested before, there is a museum as well as a portrait gallery in *Invisible Man;* that museum contains various collections that are contexts or syntaxes for certain portraits and, more to the point here, certain cultural artifacts or material objects. While a given portrait and artifact may function (and possibly resonate) in the narrative in much the same way, an essential distinction must be drawn between how the portraits as a group (the gallery) and the artifacts as a group (the museum) operate as narrative strategies, especially within the tale. While the portraits present the full array of examples, warnings, and enigmas before the questing narrator, the artifacts present the full array of prescribed or pre-formed patterns of mobility. Of course, the collected portraits and artifacts alike are, at base, systems of models; but in *Invisible Man* they are differing systems, in so far as the portraits are prototypes for the self and the artifacts are prototypes for the self-in-motion.

Returning to Bledsoe's office, which I have described before as an unofficial annex to the college's museum of slavery, we are led to discover, amid the heavy furniture, mementos of the Founder, and collective gaze of the "men of power," an artifact of which Bledsoe as both curator and custodian is very proud:

> He looked at me as though I had committed the worst crime imaginable. "Don't you know we can't tolerate such a thing? I gave you an opportunity to serve one of our best white friends, a man who could make your fortune. But in return you dragged the entire race into the slime!"
>
> Suddenly he reached for something beneath a pile of papers, an old leg shackle from slavery which he proudly called a "symbol of our progress."
>
> "You've got to be disciplined, boy." he said. "There's no ifs and ands about it."

I have quoted from the text at some length because we must see the leg shackle both as an object and as language. As Ellison makes so very clear, as an object it is *not* a charmingly rustic paperweight gracing Bledsoe's many papers, but something far more sinister and weapon-like that must be concealed—perhaps, as in this instance, by a cloak of words. As language, the leg shackle is less a silence or pause than a transitional phrase—a veritable link—between the two cited parts of Bledsoe's speech. For Bledsoe, the shackle is a charged rhetorical object in the present ("a 'symbol of our progress' "), principally because it is also a rhetorical expression of the past (the "slime" which is invariably the nearly excremental quicksand of slavery; recall here, in contrast, Du Bois's swamp) and a paradigm for a fiction that may be imposed selectively on the future—in this case, the narrator's future. The half-dozen or so letters of introduction (the "protections")—which Bledsoe is able to produce so mysteriously in thirty minutes' time, and which allow the Invisible Man no mobility whatsoever except, ironically, a bus ride to New York (undoubtedly on the Bloodhound or North Star line)—are prefigured before, in all of their nefarious qualities, by the "pile of papers" in collusion, as it were, with the leg shackle.

Another telling aspect of Bledsoe's shackle is that it is smooth and unsullied, perhaps still gleaming as if brand new—or not yet put to its purpose. But we do not learn this until Brother Tarp presents the narrator with a very different leg iron, in the same Brotherhood episode when he hangs the portrait of Frederick Douglass:

> He was unwrapping the object now and I watched his old man's hands.

"I'd like to pass it on to you, son. There," he said, handing it to me. "Funny thing to give somebody, but I think it's got a heap of signifying wrapped up in it and it might help you remember what we're really fighting against. I don't think of it in terms of but two words, *yes* and *no;* but it signifies a heap more. . . ."

I saw him place his hand on the desk. "Brother," he said, calling me "Brother" for the first time, "I want you to take it. I guess it's a kind of luck piece. Anyway, it's the one I filed to get away."

I took it in my hand, a thick dark, oily piece of filed steel that had been twisted open and forced partly back into place, on which I saw marks that might have been made by the blade of a hatchet. It was such a link as I had seen on Bledsoe's desk, only while that one had been smooth, Tarp's bore the marks of haste and violence, looking as though it had been attacked and conquered before it stubbornly yielded.

With these words the Invisible Man receives the first and only viable "protection" he is given in the tale. Shortly thereafter he fits the leg iron on his hand as if it were a pair of brass knuckles ("Finding no words to ask him more about it, I slipped the link over my knuckles and struck it sharply against the desk"), never dreaming that he will soon use it in this very manner in a pitched battle with Ras and his followers. Here we receive nothing less than a deft and momentous construction and ordering of the narrative as a whole. Tarp's shackle, in contrast to Bledsoe's, is worn, not just in the sense that it bears the marks of a violent attack and defeat, but also in that it has been literally worn—for nineteen years—by Brother Tarp. This suggests that Tarp is a very different kind of "curator" and, in some sense, *author* of the leg shackle and its accompanying fictions than is Bledsoe—recall here Tarp's earlier remark, " 'I'm tellin' it better'n I ever thought I could.' " As an author, Tarp has been both in and out of his tale, and has thereby gained the perspectives and techniques with which to *see* the tale and *tell* it well. He—like certain other "peasants" in the narrative, such as the grandfather, Trueblood, and Frederick Douglass—is something of an artist, while Bledsoe—like certain other "uplifted" types, including Brother Jack—is not so much an artist or tale-teller as a manipulator of them. In either case, Tarp's or Bledsoe's, the leg iron which each man possesses, displays, and in varying senses gives away is an abiding expression of a posture as a "man of power" in the narrative, especially as far as art-making is concerned.

Related is the substantial matter of how the two leg irons prompt another review of Bledsoe's and the Invisible Man's offices as contrasting symbolic spaces. I have already suggested how the portraits alone help to construct these spaces, but what is pertinent here is how they are further assembled by the beams of meaning that stretch between portrait and artifact. The heart of the matter, I believe, is that once the portraits and leg irons are bound before us, we see more clearly the profound distinction between a rhetoric of progress and one of liberation. In Bledsoe's office, the "men of power" are the smooth, closed shackle—and the shackle the men—not only because the men are, in various meanings of the term, a "closed circle," but also because the rhetoric of progress which they as trustees (or is it trusties?) oversee, and in that sense enclose far more than they author, is as fixed or static as their conception (and perception) of the present. Indeed, much as Bledsoe is characterized in another episode as a "headwaiter" and not a consummate chef (hence the continuity in his career, from his college days as the best "slop dispenser" up to the narrative present), the "men of power" must be seen as figures who "serve" power: they dispense its prevailing fictions, yet are shackled to those fictions. The unending circle of Bledsoe's leg iron is a remarkable manifestation of a particular and prevailing uplift myth in which "service" is not just equated with "progress," but is also its literary form.

In the Invisible Man's office, the portrait of Frederick Douglass is modally bound to the violently opened leg shackle partly because Douglass, like Tarp, set himself free, and partly because Douglass, like the filed-open shackle, is an expression of human possibility. The key, as it were, to this construction is the exquisitely rude aperture that "defiles" the otherwise completed (or closed) form of the leg iron. On one level, that space is an exit or entrance; on another, it is a void to be filled, not once and for all but continually. Douglass and the open shackle speak as one, not just of human possibility but also of artistic possibility. To fill the space is less to close the form than to shape the form; and, to be sure, there can never be only one form. After all, hadn't Douglass written at least three *tales* of his life? Hadn't he hung a mighty door in his shackle's space and shaped his form not once but three times? Douglass's breaking of the shackle, his artful movement out and back in and out of the shackle, and his forming and (in all senses of the term) *reforming* of the shackle is finally *the* trope before the questing narrator for a viable pattern of mobility and a viable system of authorial control. Once the Invisible Man takes Tarp's shackle with him down into the narrative's framing warm hole and learns to *read* it, as well as to *hear* his grandfather and to *return* Douglass's gaze, he is ready to hibernate and write. Once these portraits and artifacts are removed from what Ishmael Reed has called "Centers of Art Detention" and are displayed in that Center of Art Retention which Ellison calls the mind, he is ready to "birth his form."

It would appear, then, that Ellison is pursuing a narrative strategy in which aspects of the tale are turned inside-out in the frame, much as the narrator is transformed from an illiterate to a literate protagonist. But this is not the case. The means by which Ellison avoids such a closure—which would destroy his narrative— tell us much about the strategies by which he seeks to burst beyond the prototypical narratives of ascent and immersion provided by Frederick Douglass and W. E. B. Du Bois. Here I wish to suggest nothing less than that, on a level not altogether removed from the inner workings of *Invisible Man,* Bledsoe's smooth and closed shackle is a trope for inherited and, to a degree, imposed narrative forms in the tradition (of which Douglass's and Du Bois's forms are the dominant forms), and that Tarp's rudely opened shackle symbolizes both the release from these forms and the new form which is *Invisible Man.* Ellison appears only too aware that any step outside the shackles of what other men call reality necessitates an accompanying step outside what other men, including kinsmen, call literary form.

Douglass's 1845 *Narrative* is built upon a strategy and rhetoric of triumphant reversal: "how a man became a slave" becomes "how a slave became a man." Furthermore, the world of the narrative reverses somehow, in accord with the reversal of the persona's condition, even though the persona is still situated in an imposed social structure. *Invisible Man* breaks with this strategy most obviously by removing the transformed narrator from social structure, but also more subtly by not completing all aspects of the reversal in the first place. While the Invisible Man does indeed "reverse" from visible to invisible (or invisible to visible) as well as from illiterate to literate, and while the portraits and artifacts of the tale move from the surfaces of the tale's symbolic interiors to those of the narrator's mind, the darkness or dimness that once occupied his mind is *not* transposed to the surfaces of the new symbolic space (the hole). Instead, it quite simply and profoundly vanishes. What *are* on these surfaces are expressions, if you will, not of darkness but of light; there are 1,369 light bulbs, and apparently more to come. These lights "speak" not of a former somnolent dimness, but of a contemporary illuminated wakefulness. And in addition to not expressing the narrator's previous abiding "dim-wattedness," the many lights are not portraits and artifacts like those in the tale. They are not competing or guiding fictions, but expressions of something that is distinctly pre-fiction, pre-form, and pre-art. In the warm hole of hibernation (or so Ellison's new construction informs us), what is so "torturous" about writing is not that one must work in the presence of already formed artworks, but that this work must be accomplished under the scrutiny of a certain radiant and self-inflicted brilliance.

The "brilliance" interests me principally because it is a constructed brilliance and, as such, part of a strategy by which Ellison bursts beyond the narrative model provided by Du Bois. Of course, the model as a whole is *The Souls,* but the particular aspect of that model which Ellison must revoice and revise in order to achieve a new narrative expression is the obviously Romantic primary scene at the end of the narrative, where brilliance makes its visit to the self-conscious artist in the form of an enlightening "sunshine." By way of a reminder, let me mention further that in *The Souls* Du Bois's light must *enter* his persona's private space, and that it is above all a natural energy that binds him to whatever "Eternal Good" resides in this and other worlds. Furthermore, once these beams are entwined with those of the songs of his generations ("My children, my little children, are singing to the sunshine"), they bind him to his "tribe" as well, and, more specifically still, to his tribe's *genius loci.* Quite to the point, and in full accord with other Romantic aspects of the model, Du Bois remarks on how these magnificent energies are "free"; these remarks are as conspicuous as the absence of even a veiled suggestion that he, too, is free. This primary scene in *The Souls* indicates that a price must be paid for accomplishing immersion; it is the other side of the coin, as it were, to being self-consciously situated in an isolated space, where the windows are few and "high" and latticed with bars of light and song. The brilliance that enlightens Du Bois's persona as self and artist speaks as much of loss as of gain, and this brilliance and its accompanying idea of artistic compensation must be radically revoiced in order for the "shackle" of the immersion narrative form to be broken.

Ellison's deliberate positioning of the brilliance before his narrator *inside* the hole, all over the hole, and with many bulbs instead of a few high windows, is the beginning of such a revision and revoicing. Of course, there is more to his expression than this: the brilliance is a constructed brilliance in that it is manmade or "tinkermade," and it is an interior brilliance most particularly in that it is mind-made or "thinker-made." Indeed, as the Invisible Man informs us in the prologue, it is the self-work of a " 'thinker-tinker,' " an "inventor" with a "theory and a concept" who is almost anything but an embodiment of an "Eternal Good." This brilliance is "free" in a sense of the term very different from the one which Du Bois advances. In *The Souls,* the entwining beams of light and voice are free *only* in the sense that they are as visible, audible, and mobile as those who reside within the shadows of the Veil are invisible, inaudible, and immobile. This is clearly the sense of Du Bois's language when he writes:

> If somewhere in this whirl and chaos of things there dwells Eternal Good, pitiful yet masterful, then anon in His good time America shall rend the Veil and the prisoned shall go free. Free, Free as the sunshine trickling down the morning into these high windows of mine, free as yonder fresh young voices welling up to me from the caverns of brick and mortar below. . . .

However, as I've suggested, these energies are not free to the persona; he has paid for them in various ways, including the undertaking of a requisite pilgrimmage into more oppressive systems of social structure. For these reasons I think it might be said that the immersion narrative, like the narrative of ascent, is less about strategies for avoiding payment than about strategies for making payment that yield, in turn, a fresh posture within social structure which is somehow *worth* that payment—or *more than worth it.* Viewed in this way, ascent and immersion narratives are very much of a piece, and so it would appear that a strategy for bursting beyond the one is also a scheme for release from the other.

Ellison achieves such a strategy when he makes it clear that his narrator has found a way not only to stop paying for his life within what other men call reality, but also to avoid paying for his enlightenment once he has fallen outside those imposing fictions. The former discovery releases him as Du Bois and others are not released from various rhetorics of progress; the latter discovery allows him to gain as few others have gained a rhetoric of liberation. Above and beyond the hilarious joke of "socking it" to the power company with every socket installed (or of "screwing" them with every screw of a bulb) lies the very serious point that the self-initiated and self-constructed brilliance before the hibernating narrator does not, and in fact cannot, reverse the charge: it comes free and freely without a service payment, without a loss that the narrator must balance against his gain. In the narrative of hiberation—for so we must call it, because it is a new form in the tradition—what defines the new resulting posture and space for the questing narrator has nothing to do with whether he is situated in the most or least oppressive social structure of the narrative, and little to do with how much space lies between his hole and the "ornery" world above (after all, the Invisible Man can smell the stench of Spring), but everything to do with whether it is a context in which the imagination is its own self-generating energy. The new resulting posture and space beyond those of the ascent and immersion narratives are ones in which the narrator eventually gains complete authorial control of the text of the narrative, and of the imagination as a trope subsumed within that text. (For those who have said through the years that Ellison has "grabbed all the marbles," but who don't know by what sleight of hand he did it—this is how he did it.)

I have not forgotten that Du Bois's enlightening brilliance is an exquisite commingling of light *and* song—nor apparently has Ellison. Indeed, just as the Invisible Man wants more and more light, he also desires more and more machines with which to play Louis Armstrong's "What Did I Do to Be so Black and Blue." This music, like the light it accompanies, does not have to waft in some high window, but emanates instead from *within* the space; it is a "thinker-tinker" music, music that has been improvised upon. The Invisible Man touches on this matter when he writes:

> Sometimes now I listen to Louis while I have my favorite dessert of vanilla ice cream and sloe gin. I pour the red liquid over the white mound, watching it glisten and the vapor rising as Louis bends that military instrument into a beam of lyrical sound. Perhaps I like

Louis Armstrong because he's made poetry out of being invisible. . . . And my own grasp of invisibility aids me to understand his music. . . . Invisibility, let me explain, gives one a slightly different sense of time, you're never quite on the beat. Sometimes you're ahead and sometimes behind. Instead of the swift and imperceptible flowing of time, you are aware of its nodes, those points where time stands still or from which it leaps behind. And you slip into the breaks and look around. That's what you hear vaguely in Louis' music.

With these words Ellison clarifies an essential distinction between immersion and hibernation that is at root, in the terms afforded here, a distinction between embracing the music you hear and making the music you hear your own. The counterpointing image that immediately appears before us is one in which the good doctor is ensconced in his study, awaiting those entwined beams from above, while dear Louis is fashioning beams of a certain brilliance all his own. But of course the grand trope before us is the one with which we (and, in a certain sense, Ellison) began: Tarp's open leg shackle. Louis Armstrong's bending of a "military instrument into a beam of lyrical sound" is a magnificent and heroic revoicing of Tarp's defiling of the shackle. As these brilliant images conjoin and speak as one, we see as perhaps never before the extent to which each figure is a poet of invisibility, not because they make art out of chaos or out of nothingness, but because they make art out of art. As master craftsmen to whom the Invisible Man is apprenticed, their master lesson for him (and us) is that, while the artist must be able to burst beyond the old forms, he also must be able to make light of the light that fills the resulting hole—"slip into the breaks and look around." In *Invisible Man*, "making light of the light" is a rhetoric of liberation, a theory of comedy, and a narrative strategy rolled into one. Once Ellison's questing narrator becomes a hibernating narrator and finally comprehends all of this, he may truly say, "Light confirms my reality, gives birth to my form."

Bibliography

Aptheker, Herbert, ed. *The Correspondence of W. E. B. Du Bois. Volume I: Selections, 1877–1934.* Amherst: University of Massachusetts Press, 1973. I, 60–65.

Baldwin, James. *Notes of a Native Son.* Boston: Beacon, 1955.

Barthes, Roland. *Mythologies.* 1957; selected and translated by Annette Lavers, New York: Hill and Wang, 1972. Pp. 109–159.

Blassingame, John W., ed. *Slave Testimony: Two Centuries of Letters, Speeches, Interviews, and Autobiographies.* Baton Rouge: Louisiana State University Press, 1977. Pp. 639–655.

————. *The Slave Community: Plantation Life in the Ante-Bellum South.* New York: Oxford University Press, 1972. Pp. 227–238.

Bloom, Harold, *The Anxiety of Influence: A Theory of Poetry.* New York: Oxford University Press, 1973.

Brown, William Wells. *Clotel; or, The President's Daughter.* 1853; reprinted, New York: Collier-Macmillan, 1970.

Butterfield, Stephen. *Black Autobiography in America.* Amherst: University of Massachusetts Press, 1974.

Callahan, John F. "Chaos, Complexity and Possibility: The Historical Frequencies of Ralph Waldo Ellison." *Black American Literature Forum,* II (Winter, 1977), 130–138. Also in Michael S. Harper and Robert B. Stepto, eds. *Chant of Saints: A Gathering of Afro-Ameri-*

can Literature, Art, and Scholarship. Urbana: University of Illinois Press, 1979. Pp. 33–52.

Cooke, Michael G. "The Descent into the Underworld and Modern Black Fiction." Iowa Review, V (Fall, 1974), 72–90.

Davis, Charles T. "From Experience to Eloquence: Richard Wright's Black Boy as Art." In Michael S. Harper and Robert B. Stepto, eds. Chant of Saints: A Gathering of Afro-American Literature, Art, and Scholarship. Urbana: University of Illinois Press, 1979. Pp. 425–439.

Douglass, Frederick. Narrative of the Life of Frederick Douglass, an American Slave, Written by Himself. 1845; reprinted, Cambridge: Belknap Press of Harvard University Press, 1960.

Du Bois, W. E. B. The Conservation of Races. 1897; reprinted in Julius Lester, ed., The Seventh Son: The Thought and Writings of W. E. B. Du Bois. New York: Vintage, 1971. I, 176–187.

————. Dusk of Dawn: The Autobiography of a Race Concept. 1940; reprinted, New York: Schocken, 1968.

————. "The Evolution of Negro Leadership." Dial, XXXI (July 16, 1901), 53–55.

————. "The Freedmen's Bureau." Atlantic Monthly, LXXXVII (March, 1901), 345–365.

————. "The Negro as He Really Is." World's Work, II (June, 1901), 848–866.

————. "The Negro Schoolmaster in the New South." Atlantic Monthly, LXXXIII (January, 1899), 99–104.

————. "The Relation of the Negroes to the Whites in the South." Annals of the American Academy of Political and Social Science, XVIII (July, 1901), 121–140.

————. "The Religion of the American Negro." New World, IX (December, 1900), 614–625.

————. The Souls of Black Folk. Chicago: A. C. McClurg, 1903.

————. "Storm and Stress in the Black World." Dial, XXX (April 16, 1901), 262–264.

————. "Strivings of the Negro People." Atlantic Monthly, LXXX (1897), 194–198.

Ellison, Ralph. Invisible Man. New York: Random House, 1952.

————. Shadow and Act. New York: Random House, 1964.

Fabre, Michael. The Unfinished Quest of Richard Wright. New York: William Morrow, 1973.

Farrison, W. Edward. William Wells Brown: Author and Reformer. Chicago: University of Chicago Press, 1969.

Frye, Northrop. "The Critical Path: An Essay on the Social Context of Literary Criticism." Daedalus, XCIX (1970), 268–342.

Guillén, Claudio. Literature as System: Essays toward the Theory of Literary History. Princeton: Princeton University Press, 1971.

Harlan, Louis R. Booker T. Washington: The Making of a Black Leader, 1856–1901. New York: Oxford University Press, 1972.

————. ed. *The Booker T. Washington Papers. Volume I: The Autobiographical Writings*. Urbana: University of Illinois Press, 1972.

Harper, Michael S., and Stepto, Robert B. "Study and Experience: An Interview with Ralph Ellison." *Massachusetts Review,* XVIII (Fall 1977), 417–435. Also in Michael S. Harper and Robert B. Stepto, eds. *Chant of Saints: A Gathering of Afro-American Literature, Art, and Scholarship*. Urbana: University of Illinois Press, 1979. Pp. 451–469.

Hartman, Geoffrey. "Toward Literary History." In *Beyond Formalism: Literary Essays 1958–1970*. New Haven: Yale University Press, 1970. Pp. 356–386.

Hughes, Langston. "The Negro Writer and the Racial Mountain." *Nation,* CXXII (1926), 692–694.

Hurston, Zora Neale. *Their Eyes Were Watching God*. 1937; reprinted, Urbana: University of Illinois Press, 1978.

Johnson, James Weldon. *Along This Way*. New York: Viking, 1933.

————. *The Autobiography of an Ex-Coloured Man*. 1912; reprinted, New York: Hill and Wang, 1960.

Kent, George. *Blackness and the Adventure of Western Culture*. Chicago: Third World Press, 1972.

Levy, Eugene. *James Weldon Johnson: Black Leader, Black Voice*. Chicago: University of Chicago Press, 1973.

Northup, Solomon. *Twelve Years a Slave*. 1854; reprinted, New York: Dover, 1970.

Osofsky, Gilbert, ed. *Puttin' On Ole Massa: The Slave Narratives of Henry Bibb, William Wells Brown, and Solomon Northup*. New York: Harper, 1969.

Rampersad, Arnold, *The Art and Imagination of W. E. B. Du Bois*. Cambridge: Harvard University Press, 1976.

Reed, Ishmael. *Mumbo Jumbo*. New York: Doubleday, 1972.

Skerrett, Joseph T., Jr. "Take My Burden Up: Three Studies in Psychobiographical Criticism and Afro-American Fiction." Ph.D. dissertation, Yale University, 1975.

Smith, Sidonie. *Where I'm Bound: Patterns of Slavery and Freedom in Black American Autobiography*. Westport, Conn.: Greenwood Press, 1974.

Stepto, Robert B. " 'I Thought I Knew These People:' Richard Wright and the Afro-American Literary Tradition." *Massachusetts Review,* XVIII (Fall 1977), 525–541. Also in Michael S. Harper and Robert B. Stepto, eds. *Chant of Saints: A Gathering of Afro-American Literature, Art, and Scholarship*. Urbana: University of Illinois Press, 1979. Pp. 195–211.

————. "Teaching Afro-American Literature: Survey or Tradition; or, the Reconstruction of Instruction." In Dexter Fisher and Robert B. Stepto, eds. *Afro-American Literature: The Reconstruction of Instruction*. New York: Modern Language Association, 1979.

————. "Writing Afro-American Literary History: Crises in Conception." *Parnassus,* V (Spring–Summer, 1977), 235–242.

Stone, Albert E. "Identity and Art in Frederick Douglass's 'Narrative.' " *CLA Journal,* XVII (December, 1973), 192–213.

Thompson, Robert Farris. Personal communication. November 9, 1977.

————. "Siras Bowens of Sunbury, Georgia: A Tidewater Artist in the Afro-American Visual Tradition." *Massachusetts Review,* XVIII (Fall 1977), 490–500. Also in Michael S. Harper and Robert B. Stepto, eds., *Chant of Saints: A Gathering of Afro-American Literature, Art, and Scholarship.* Urbana: University of Illinois Press, 1979. Pp. 230–240.

Toomer, Jean. *Cane.* 1923; reprinted, New York: Harper, 1969.

Turner, Victor. *Dramas, Fields, and Metaphors: Symbolic Action in Human Society.* Ithaca: Cornell University Press, 1974.

Williams, Raymond. *Keywords: A Vocabulary of Culture and Society.* New York: Oxford University Press, 1976.

————. *The Country and the City.* New York: Oxford University Press, 1973.

Wright, Jay. *Dimensions of History.* Santa Cruz, Calif.: Kayak, 1976.

Wright, Richard. *Black Boy: A Record of Childhood and Youth.* New York: Harper, 1945.

————. "Blueprint for Negro Writing." *New Challenge,* II (Fall, 1937), 53–65.

————. *Native Son.* New York: Harper, 1940.

Yellin, Jean Fagan. *The Intricate Knot: Black Figures in American Literature, 1776–1863.* New York: New York University Press, 1972.

Index